The
GREAT
PUBLIC
GARDENS
of the
EASTERN
UNITED
STATES

By

DORIS M. STONE

Photography by Roger W. Stone

Pantheon Books

New York

The
GREAT
PUBLIC
GARDENS
of the
EASTERN
UNITED
STATES

LIBRARY OF CONGRESS CATALOGING IN PUBLICATION DATA

STONE, DORIS M., 1918–

THE GREAT PUBLIC GARDENS OF THE EASTERN UNITED STATES.

1. GARDENS—ATLANTIC STATES—GUIDE-BOOKS.

2. GARDENS—UNITED STATES—GUIDE-BOOKS.

I. TITLE.

SB466.U6S717   917.4'04927   81–18978

ISBN 0–394–70664–1 (PBK.)   AACR2

MANUFACTURED IN THE UNITED STATES OF AMERICA

FIRST EDITION

DRAWINGS BY BOBBI ANGELL

BOOK DESIGN BY ELISSA ICHIYASU

PHOTOGRAPHS ON PAGES 142, 144, 145, AND 188 BY VALERIE STONE

PHOTOGRAPH ON PAGE 144 COURTESY OF NATIONAL ARBORETUM

PHOTOGRAPH ON PAGE 173 COURTESY OF LONGWOOD GARDENS

PHOTOGRAPHS ON PAGES 195, 196, AND 197 COURTESY OF DUKE GARDENS

PHOTOGRAPHS ON PAGES 255 AND 257 COURTESY OF

MOHONK MOUNTAIN HOUSE GARDENS

To DICK, *with deep gratitude,*
who for the CAUSE *endured*
dishpan hands, housemaid's knee, and
other domestic hazards.

CONTENTS

LIST OF BOXES

PREFACE

STARTING IN MIAMI in late March 1980, we visited nineteen southern gardens, following spring as it unfolded northward. Finding ourselves ahead of the season in Washington, D.C., we stopped. After a period of reflection and assimilation, we visited the remaining gardens in the late spring and the summer. I have used the plural "we" because on this springtime jaunt my son, Roger, a professional bio-photographer, accompanied me. The photographs in this book are his, unless otherwise noted.

Many of the gardens described have important historic houses attached. No attention was paid to these except for a cursory inspection to get the feel for the historical influences under which the gardens were designed and created. I tried to capture the message of each garden, for each one makes its own statement, facilitating the reporter's task. The statement includes ambience, history, cultural values at the time of its creation, the kinds of people who were associated with it, and sometimes its evolution from something quite different.

Contrasts were vivid: the wild woodlands of the North Carolina Botanical Garden with the highly stylized Vizcaya, where plants are of secondary or even tertiary importance compared with water and stonework; the dignified Italianate waterworks of Longwood and the raucous, exuberant modern pastiche that is Florida's Cypress Gardens; the prim and prissy Dutch-English gardens of Williamsburg *vis-à-vis* the free-flowing beauty of Winterthur's woodlands; the water gardens of Charleston, whose charm and mystery suspend intellectual appraisal, juxtaposed to "cerebral" gardens like the Arnold Arboretum, where names and identification are paramount; the understated, intimate elegance of Dumbarton Oaks contrasted with the flamboyance and crass overstatement of Nemours.

Many of the gardens have strong links with their communities, forming a mutually beneficial relationship. This is important at Longwood, at Garden in the Woods, and at Brooklyn Botanic Garden, to name just three. An encouraging sign at a time when, as a society, we are obsessed with possessions, neglecting or downgrading aesthetic sustenance. Plants, with their quiet beauty, help to keep us sane in a mad, violent, materialistic world. And if we are not aware of this, we should be.

It surprised me to learn that on the east coast of the United States there is no public garden designed for the twentieth century as was New York's Central Park for the nineteenth. But on reflection, it should not be surprising. We have no landscape architect of the caliber of Frederick Law Olmsted, Central Park's designer, or of the contemporary Brazilian Roberto Burle Marx, who planned the gardens of the new capital, Brasilia. Working with tropicals, an entirely new medium for the landscape architect, Marx has constructed gardens that owe something to modern painting, creating patterns of color and texture in a manner that is, in some respects, not too far removed from the Victorian practice of carpet-bedding, though light-years away in others.

The only truly contemporary gardens that have developed in the eastern United States are those associated with shopping malls, urban plazas, and corporate headquarters, and the vest-pocket parks within cities. Innovative landscape designers in this country seem to function wholly within the private sector. Most of their creations are to be seen in California, where outdoor living is year-round, the ubiquitous swimming pool its focus.

Perhaps there are no public gardens for twentieth-century living because in the collective mind gardens have low priority in view of the many demands made on the public purse. Obsessed with maintenance problems, we prefer to settle for slabs of concrete—witness the World Trade Center Plaza in New York City, a vast expanse of windy nothingness.

To sum up: Although the late twentieth century intrudes little into the design of the gardens chosen here, they constitute a legacy of diverse beauty and tranquillity which, in today's stressful world, are indeed nourishment for the psyche.

D.M.S.

New York, August 1981

ACKNOWLEDGMENTS

T HE THIRTY-FOUR GARDENS described in this guide were not just the selections of the author. The opinions of six prominent horticulturists in different parts of the eastern seaboard were formally solicited, and informal advice was given by several more. The author, however, takes full responsibility for the final choices.

Thanks go to the owners, public-relations personnel, horticulturists, and directors of the gardens for the various kinds of help they provided; for their patience in answering follow-up telephone calls and letters; and more especially for the hospitality afforded to me and members of my family.

Special thanks go to Philip Pochoda, the editor at Pantheon Books—and a garden enthusiast—who had the idea for this book.

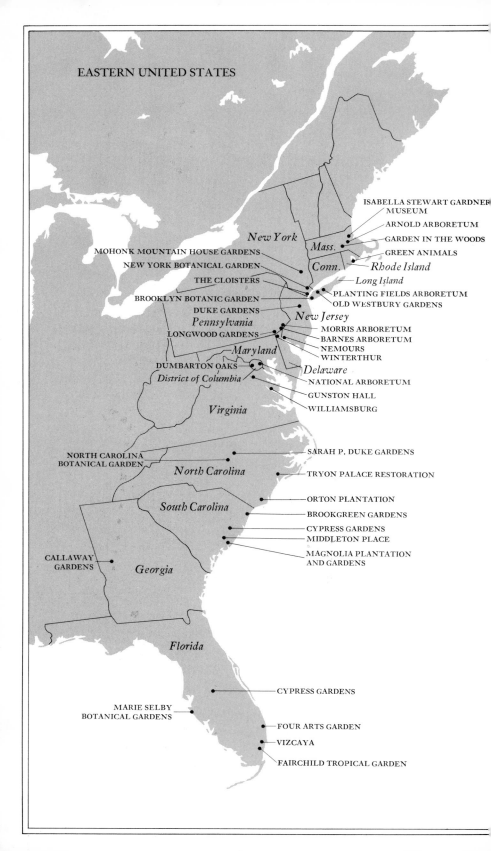

EASTERN UNITED STATES

ISABELLA STEWART GARDNER
MUSEUM
ARNOLD ARBORETUM
GARDEN IN THE WOODS
GREEN ANIMALS

New York

Mass.

Conn.

Rhode Island

MOHONK MOUNTAIN HOUSE GARDENS
NEW YORK BOTANICAL GARDEN
THE CLOISTERS
Long Island
PLANTING FIELDS ARBORETUM
OLD WESTBURY GARDENS
BROOKLYN BOTANIC GARDEN
DUKE GARDENS
Pennsylvania
New Jersey
MORRIS ARBORETUM
BARNES ARBORETUM
NEMOURS
WINTERTHUR
LONGWOOD GARDENS
Maryland
DUMBARTON OAKS
Delaware
District of Columbia
NATIONAL ARBORETUM
GUNSTON HALL
WILLIAMSBURG

Virginia

NORTH CAROLINA
BOTANICAL GARDEN
SARAH P. DUKE GARDENS
North Carolina
TRYON PALACE RESTORATION

South Carolina
ORTON PLANTATION
BROOKGREEN GARDENS
CYPRESS GARDENS
MIDDLETON PLACE
MAGNOLIA PLANTATION
AND GARDENS

CALLAWAY
GARDENS
Georgia

Florida

CYPRESS GARDENS

MARIE SELBY
BOTANICAL GARDENS

FOUR ARTS GARDEN

VIZCAYA

FAIRCHILD TROPICAL GARDEN

INTRODUCTION

H̲ow to use this book: This book is a guide to thirty-four public gardens of the eastern United States, each of which has been visited by the author at least once. The gardens are presented in terms of aesthetic appeal, landscape design, and history, while particular attention is paid to certain botanical and ethnobotanical aspects. Each garden is illustrated with photographs.

It is the author's assumption that many garden visitors want information above and beyond that provided by a mere guide. To satisfy this kind of curiosity a special format has been designed: the so-called boxes. Confining the specialized information within boxes, so that it does not intrude into the flow of the text, allows you to skip it or heed it according to your whim. The boxes are readily identifiable by their italic type and the ornamental rules that enclose them. A box occurs within the description of a garden to which it is particularly relevant. Since its topic may also be relevant to several other gardens, cross-referencing enables you to locate the information readily. Thus the box on "Camellias" is located within the description of Magnolia Plantation and Gardens. But camellias are also prominent features of Middleton Place, Callaway Gardens, and the United States Arboretum. Therefore, the sections on those three gardens include cross-references to this particular box. Forty-one other topics are similarly boxed and cross-referenced, ranging from "André Le Nôtre" to "The Renaissance Garden" to "Tropical Rain Forests." Most of the boxes are illustrated with line drawings.

For those who find themselves in any of the following horticulturally rich areas, mini-tours consisting of trips to several gardens in close proximity have been outlined: Florida (p. 291); Charleston, South Carolina (pp. 291–2); Brandywine valley, Delaware/Pennsylvania (p. 292); Washington, D.C. (p. 292); New York City (pp. 292–3); and Boston (p. 293). The mini-tours should make it convenient to plan easy trips to several outstanding gardens within these locales.

HOW TO LOOK AT A GARDEN: This question has been put to me frequently, yet I have no pet formula. How one looks at a garden depends entirely upon the individual—upon the interests and background one brings to the experience. To use an extreme example, the person with artistic inclinations sees a garden differently from one in whom scientific curiosity preponderates. Although a collection of plants does not constitute a garden (else a nursery would qualify), many visitors zero in on the plants, the arborist on the trees, the flower lover on the unusual blooms. Others, neither knowing nor caring about plants or landscape design, are sensitive to ambience. Is it restful? Are there surprises in store for the perambulating visitor? Is it a place of beauty where one can sit and dream, letting the world go by?

Each garden is first and foremost a microcosm, secluded from the everyday world, its fundamental aim to give pleasure to the senses. Sensations crowd in upon one: the murmuring sound of water and insects; colors, brilliant or muted; contrasting patches of light and shade; the play of sunlight on water; the feel of bark, of velvety petals, of leafy branches as one brushes against them, of raindrops on one's face, and of springy turf under one's feet. And in the subliminal background the mingling of perfumes —obtrusive or subtle—of lilac and lavender, or jasmine and tea olive, roses and mock orange, viburnum and linden, even the aroma of freshly mown grass, serves to heighten the experience so that one becomes more alert and receptive to everything else.

I am, of course, describing my own reactions to an unfamiliar garden. For me, the input from the senses is first savored and enjoyed. Intellectual appraisal and analysis follow—the design, the plants, the maintenance—all of which augment the initial sensory perceptions, just as a knowledge of music heightens and intensifies the pleasure derived in listening to a symphony.

Exploring a garden, however, is a unique and individual experience. We leave you to pursue your own special method, hoping that this guide will serve as a trusty friend while revealing unexpected pleasures.

The
GREAT
PUBLIC
GARDENS
of the
EASTERN
UNITED
STATES

FAIRCHILD TROPICAL GARDEN

Miami, Florida

UNIQUE FEATURES	• Outstanding collection of palms (over five hundred species), cycads, and tropical woody flowering plants, unparalleled in the continental United States. • Superb landscape design.

HISTORY: In 1935 the late Colonel Robert H. Montgomery bought the site for a public botanical garden to display the collections of the famous plant explorer David Fairchild. It was considered the warmest spot in mainland Florida. Opened in 1938, the garden was subsequently deeded to the Dade County Parks and Recreation Department. Today its eighty-three acres are maintained partly by the county and partly by gate receipts and membership dues. Administration is by a private board of trustees. Funding for the research staff, whose specialties are morphology and taxonomy, comes from federal grants.

- *Admission:* Entrance fee, which includes guide brochure with map.
- *Hours:* Open all year, 10:00 A.M.–5:00 P.M. daily. Closed Christmas Day.
- *Plants:* All labeled. They can be touched but not picked. Plant guides available in gift shop.
- *Physically handicapped:* Wheelchairs can maneuver on most paths, but not in Rare Plant House. Sight-impaired can touch specimens.
- *Address:* The Fairchild Tropical Garden, 10901 Old Cutler Road, Miami, Fla. 33156. Tel. (305) 667-1651.
- *Location and directions:* 7 miles south of downtown Miami. Take U.S. 1 south, then Lejeune Road south to Old Cutler Road. Drive south on Old Cutler Road. Garden is on left.

- *Parking:* Free, outside the grounds.
- *Gift shop.*
- *Snack bar.*
- *No picnicking.*

The Fairchild Tropical Garden is the only tropical garden in the continental United States. Yet it is not truly tropical. Occasionally winter can bring arctic chills—a challenge the horticulturists here must be prepared to meet. But for tropical plants displayed in a beautifully landscaped setting, the Fairchild Garden is indeed a paradise.

All seasons are good for a visit, but the best times are March for the flowering trees and October for the lush growth following summer rains. Bring sun protection and insect repellant; mosquitoes are never entirely absent from Miami. Plan a day's visit. Most visitors wish to see only the intensely cultivated twenty-five acres around the public buildings, leaving the distant hammocks and lakes to intrepid hikers and botanists. Retain the map provided; it will prove useful.

This is truly a garden; not only are the specimens well labeled, but the plantings are grouped to please the eye. W. L. Phillips, a pupil of the famous Frederick Law Olmsted, designer of New York City's Central Park, was commissioned to landscape the site. Florida's flat terrain is a challenge to any landscape architect, but Phillips succeeded in creating sweeping vistas, engulfing "forests," surprise views, all of which make a stroll through the garden an

The Overlook

Fishtail palm
(Caryota urens)

aesthetic as well as an educational experience. (This is not true of all botanical gardens.)

At the entrance is a tree common throughout the American tropics, the gumbo-limbo or West Indian birch, *Bursera simaruba*, easily identified by its rusty, paper-thin peeling bark. The nearby clump of blue-and-orange bird-of-paradise flowers, *Strelitzia reginae* of the banana family, with the palmetum beyond sets the stage for a tropical safari. Probably the best way to begin is to ride the tram; the driver is a trained guide. This gives a panoramic view of the magnificent design, while allowing one to decide where to linger subsequently.

THE MONTGOMERY PALMETUM

Fairchild is world-renowned for its Montgomery Palmetum, a collection of more than 500 palm species, collected mainly by David Fairchild from all over the globe (approximately 3,500 species of palm exist). The palmetum begins at the main gate.

PALMS: *Botanically palms are peculiar trees. Their structure is amazingly simple: a straight, unbranched stem or trunk terminates in a single growing point, from which arises a crown of huge evergreen leaves. If the growing point is eaten or damaged, the entire plant dies. The spiky rosette of leaves affords it some protection, as does height as the tree ages. (In contrast, the* branching oak has as many growing points as there are leaf buds, so that the destruction of one is of minor importance.)

Why are they called palms? The word comes from the Latin palma, meaning the palm of the hand. For the Romans this was logical: their most familiar palm, the native European Chamaerops humulis, had palm-shaped leaves. Actually, more palms have feather-shaped (pinnate) leaves—for example, the coconut and the royal palm. Palm leaves can be gigantic; in Corypha umbraculifera they measure sixteen to twenty feet across (each could shelter twenty people from the rain).

At times, pendent spikes of small yellow flowers (inflorescences) appear between the leaves. Usually male and female flowers occur on the same tree, though in the date palm the sexes are separate. The date is wind-pollinated (a fact the ancient Egyptians knew), but many palms are insect-pollinated. The fruits are one-seeded, each seed having only one seed leaf, or cotyledon. Palms are therefore classified as monocotyledons (monocots), a group that also includes grasses, orchids, lilies, and aroids.

The largest palm seed, which is actually a two-seeded fruit, is the double coconut, Lodoicea maldivica, of the Seychelles Islands, which may weigh thirty to forty pounds; the next in size is the coconut, Cocos nucifera. Air trapped within the fibers of the outer coat, called the coir, allows the coconut to float and remain viable in sea water for as long as six weeks, enabling these trees to establish themselves even on remote beaches all over the tropics.

Palms are restricted to the tropical and semitropical regions of the world. (One or two species exist as far north as Britain, but they are exceptional and small.) The economic importance of this family—Palmae, or Arecaceae—in the warm countries of the world cannot be overestimated. They supply all kinds of necessities: food (fruits, nuts, oil, sugar, sago); drink (coconut milk, wine); building materials; clothing; vegetable wax; as well as handsome ornamentals for gardens and streets. There is an old Arab saying to the effect that the date palm has as many uses as there are days in the year—a not too exaggerated statement.

It is not surprising that palms are the subject of worldwide botanical research. At present a virus disease, "lethal yellowing," attacks many species, including the coconut and the royal palm.

Hundreds of trees in Florida and the Caribbean have died. Combatting this disease is one aim of research. The Fairchild Garden has not been spared; however, its dead trees have been replaced with new, resistant cultivars.

Within the palm family there is great variety. Some have smooth trunks, like the elegant royal palm, *Roystonea regia*. Others, like the common Florida cabbage palm, *Sabal palmetto*, retain the bases of the dead leaves—"old boots"—so that the trunk is completely covered. A few lack old boots but have nasty prickles instead, possibly as a deterrent to climbing mammals. One species is remarkable for its black, shiny old boots: the *Borassus* palm of India, said to have not 365 uses but 600! There is a specimen south of the Rain Forest—it's impossible to miss. Other palms of note are the peach palm of Brazil, *Bactris gasipaes*, which yields tasty, starchy fruits, and the beautiful yellow latan, *Latania verschaffeltii*, an ornamental with stiff fan-shaped leaves.

The cycads constitute another important display at Fairchild, located primarily in the Cycad Circle. From the evolutionary point of view these are ancient plants, having predated the flowering plants by some fifty million years and coexisted with the dinosaurs. Today they are disappearing from the wild as their habitats—tropical and semitropical forests—are being destroyed. They are, however, valuable ornamentals, well represented in Florida gardens. One, *Zamia floridana*, is native and can be seen here.

Yellow latan palm

CYCADS: *Superficially, cycads resemble palms, but they are not palms; they are not even flowering plants. Cycads were the first seed plants to appear on earth, a tremendous leap forward in evolution. As a reproductive mechanism, a seed is infinitely more viable than a spore, the reproductive body of ferns, mosses, and algae. Because their sex organs are arranged in open cones and not within flower structures, cycads are classified as conifers, or gymnosperms (a Greek-derived word meaning "naked seeds").*

Like the flowering plants, cycads produce pollen but only in the male plants, the sexes being separate. (A cone from one of the larger, more virile species can produce one full cup of pollen!) A fact fascinating to botanists is that the male cell within the pollen can swim, just like the sperms of ferns and animals. This is further evidence that the cycads are indeed primitive seed plants. One theory maintains that of all the conifers these strange plants are the most likely forerunners of the flowering plants.

After the open palmetum the Moos Memorial Sunken Garden, with its cooling waterfall and lush tropical ferns, aroids, and epiphytes, is a welcome refuge. Live oaks, *Quercus virginiana* ("live" means evergreen), give shade to plants whose natural habitat is the forest floor. Among these are the bird's-nest fern, *Asplenium nidus*, and its flowering-plant look-alike, the aroid *Anthurium salviniae*. (For more on aroids, see p. 27.)

The epiphytes in the Moos Sunken Garden are ferns and bromeliads. The small resurrection fern, *Polypodium polypodioides*, common on live oaks, is so called because in dry weather it curls up as if dead, springing back to life when it rains. The bird's-nest fern, which here grows on the ground, is capable of an epiphytic life, its "nest" acting as a device to collect water and debris. (For more on epiphytes, see pp. 32–3.)

THE RARE PLANT HOUSE

This house is a shelter for truly tropical plants, too tender for the vagaries of the Miami winter. One is the breadfruit tree, *Artocarpus altilis*, a starchy staple of the tropics. Other inmates are more rare, requiring special care and protection. Two habitats are provided: a glassed-in section for the orchid collection and a house with a lath roof, affording shelter from sun and wind.

ORCHIDS: *For gorgeous floral display the orchids are unmatched among plants. It is not surprising that lives have been risked to procure rare specimens. Their vibrant colors and strange forms attract not only humans but all manner of insects, which in seeking nectar pollinate the flowers. In structure they are highly complex, being the epitome of floral evolution. Their anatomy is geared to the idiosyncrasies of their insect visitors. This can of course be self-defeating if the pollinator becomes extinct or the plant is transported to a new habitat. The Mexican vanilla orchid, which seems to have lost its pollinator, has to be hand-pollinated wherever it grows in order for the "beans" to develop.*

A most remarkable relationship has developed between some orchids and their pollinators. One flower mimics a female insect so well—even to smelling like one—that it provokes copulatory movements in the male insect which pollinate it. Such seductive behavior would have totally shocked the eighteenth-century botanists, who deplored the very existence of sex within the plant world. (Until that time, plants were thought to be asexual.)

If palm seeds are the biggest, orchid seeds are the smallest—so small that they appear as particles of dust. (The black flecks in some brands of ice cream are vanilla orchid seeds.) Because of their size orchid seeds can be carried great distances by wind. And since many of them are epiphytic, this is the way they reach their habitats high in the treetops. Having an almost nonexistent food store, most of the seeds would soon die were it not that each acquires a fungal partner very soon after germination. The fungus inside the seedling's roots absorbs organic food from the environment, allowing the seed to grow. This mutually beneficial relationship between a fungus and the roots of a flowering plant is called mycorrhiza (see also p. 176).

In Greek the word orchid *(really* orchis*) means "testicle," the name having been conferred on the family because the bulbs of terrestrial members look like human testicles. (For information on epiphytic orchids, see p. 34.)*

The lath house has a "gardenesque" appearance. Water lilies float in the pool. Tree ferns that look like palms (but note their fiddleheads) tower over herbaceous tropicals such as lobster-claws (*Heliconia* spp. of the banana family), *Alpinia* spp. (members of the ginger family), and the familiar begonias. Bromeliads are everywhere, growing on the walls and in beds. Along the south wall at the time of our visit, *Guzmania lingulata cardinalis*, with its red leaf rosettes, made an eye-catching border. Bromeliads are prized both for their flowers and for their decorative leaf rosettes.

In March and April look for the flowers of the jade vine, *Strongylodon macrobotrys*, high up on the wall opposite the entrance. A member of the pea family with flowers of an astonishing turquoise-green, it is a rampant climber in the Philippine forests, though rare in Florida. A little to the left is another striking plant, the sealing-wax palm, *Cyrtostachys lakka*, with brilliant red leaf sheaths; older plants are even more stunning.

At this spot a pause at the snack bar under the American sapodilla tree, *Manilkara zapota*, may be welcome. The brown sapodilla fruit is delicious—and may be sampled—while the sap or latex, called chicle, is used in the manufacture of chewing gum.

THE RAIN FOREST

Obviously, in such a small area and with a path leading through it, conditions in a real tropical rain forest cannot be approximated, even though the sprinklers are specially designed to deliver water onto the canopy. However, plant life here is layered as in all tropical forests: a canopy of *Cecropia*,* which have large palmate leaves with gray undersurfaces, and live oaks; an understory of palms and other short trees; and a ground flora of cycads, tall herbaceous gingers, philodendrons, and spathiphyllums. The non-woody climbers here are the aroids *Monstera* and *Philodendron*.

From the Rain Forest, wend your way past Glade Lake to the Garden Club of America Amphitheater, with its attractive pool, and cross the natural bridge between Glade Lake and Royal Palm Lake. Around Pandanus Lake look for curious palmlike trees supported by stout strut roots and bearing tufts of sword-shaped leaves. These are the screw pines, *Pandanus* spp., neither pines nor palms but monocots related to the palms and aroids. Female trees produce an edible fruit of no culinary distinction.

* The sole food of that strange South American beast the sloth.

TROPICAL RAIN FORESTS: *The rain forests of the tropics have no seasons; they are hot and moist 365 days of the year. In the South American forests rain falls two days out of every three. Clearly, this is the most favorable environment on earth for plant growth, yielding the greatest variety of plant life in terms of forms and species. It is not that plants grow faster than they do in northern summers, but that they continue at the same pace the year round. Hence the veritable tangle of vegetation we call jungle.*

As in all forests, plant life in the rain forest is layered. Tall trees form the canopy; shorter trees make up the understory; and shrubs constitute the ground flora. The shorter the plant, the less light it receives. To compensate, the leaves of plants inhabiting the forest floor are often huge. Large leaves can be a hazard; wind can tear them and much water can be lost by transpiration. But in the interior of the forest these dangers are negligible.

To northern eyes perhaps the most exotic inhabitants are the epiphytes. One tree may harbor as many as one hundred individual plants. (Epiphytes are virtually nonexistent in northern forests, not because of the cold, but because of the dryness of the winter air.) Vines too are much more common, making these forests almost impenetrable. Most are woody and of great length and are called lianas or "monkey ladders." Climbing is an economical way of reaching the light without the heavy expenditure of materials on a bulky trunk.

Tropical rain forests such as those of Brazil are vital to the ecology of the planet: they control the water cycle, give off tons of oxygen, and provide habitats for a great diversity of plant and animal life, some 50 percent of which are still not known to science. They are self-supporting and self-reproducing communities that have been in continuous existence for millions of years. Yet man has already begun to destroy them at an incredible pace, replacing them with beef ranches or tree plantations. According to one reliable authority, fifty acres disappear under the bulldozer every minute. Results will be catastrophic in the long run. Apart from many other considerations, plant species that might one day have proved useful to mankind are vanishing forever. Biological knowledge, it seems, cannot prevail over greed.

THE FLOWERING PLANT SECTION

Collected here are tropical and semitropical trees, shrubs, and vines that produce, not insignificant blooms like the palms, grasses, and aroids, but "proper" flowers, advertising their pollen or nectar to any interested animal. All are dicotyledons (dicots), which means that each of their seeds has two seed leaves. Most are arranged in their plant families. Labeling is good; not only is the name provided but also additional tidbits of information.

Tropical trees characteristically have thin bark (drying up is usually no threat), buttressed trunks, and subsidiary trunks developed from down-growing aerial roots; the huge banyan tree, *Ficus benghalensis*, illustrates this well. Flowers and fruits can appear at any time of the year because animals are always active to pollinate and to disperse seeds. The trees here are not tropical rain-forest types: we are safe in assuming this because most of them lose their leaves in the winter season. The deciduous habit is an adaptation to drought. The natural habitats of these trees are warm regions having a wet and a dry season. But unlike the deciduous trees of the temperate zones, they do not enter a dormant state during the dry season. This is their time of flowering; the lack of leaves makes the flowers more conspicuous.

Red and orange flowers predominate, for the eyes of nectar-eating birds, the chief pollinators in the tropics, are specially sensitive to these colors. Good examples here are members of the pea family (Leguminosae or Fabaceae): *Erythrina variegata orientalis*, *Saraca indica*, and the mountain rose, *Brownea grandiceps*.

Another tropical family well represented are the Bombacaceae, the shaving-brush trees, spectacular with their red, pink, and white flowers of massed stamens—the "bristles." Nearby is the floss-silk tree, *Chorisia speciosa*, readily identified by the stubby prickles on its trunk. Its beautiful pink or white blossoms of autumn and early winter are replaced in March by "cotton balls," actually fruits expelling plumed seeds. These balls are used for stuffing cushions.

A rare and strange tree is the baobab, *Adansonia digitata*, native to the African savannah. It is seldom seen in Florida, but there are two specimens here. In its native habitat the trunk sometimes attains such a girth that it can be hollowed out to make a room—a small one, of course. Like another bizarre tree you will see here, the sausage tree, *Kigelia pinnata*, it is bat-pollinated. In both instances the flowers, catering to their special clientele, are evil-smelling.

Obviously there are too many trees here to mention individually. But because of Fairchild's good labeling policy and its bookstore, information is readily available. Its library is open only to members.

Unusual tropical fruits that actually mature in this garden may be of interest to south Florida residents. The American sapodilla has already been inspected, and perhaps tasted, beside the snack bar. Another delicious fruit is the star fruit (star-shaped in cross-section), or carambola, *Averrhoa carambola*, a member of the oxalis family. The mammee apple, *Mammea americana*, tasting of apricots, is made into a liqueur in the Caribbean.

Running along the fence parallel with Old Cutler Road is the Semple Vine Pergola, showing exotic, flamboyant vines that can be grown in the Miami area. The most impressive display is that of the *Bougainvillea* spp. on the northeast corner. The colored parts of this gorgeous vine are bracts, not petals. (A bract is a leaf that is usually associated with a flower—a spathe is a bract.) Three colored bracts surround three tiny white flowers. The plant was named for Louis de Bougainville, a French navigator of the eighteenth century, who found it in Rio de Janeiro. *Solandra maxima*, the cup-of-gold, has flowers eight to ten inches long. Cascades of mauve flowers are produced in March and April by the bluebird vine, *Petrea volubilis*. (It was named for Lord Petre, who introduced the camellia into England in the eighteenth cen-

Edge of Rain Forest

tury.) Actually, only the petals are purple; the grayish-mauve sepals persist after the petals drop, prolonging the vine's decorative period. The deep-blue pea flower, *Clitoria ternatea*, from which a blue dye is made, would be a worthwhile addition to any garden. The yellow *Allamanda cathartica*, and the passion flower, *Passiflora* sp., are familiar. Early missionaries in tropical America saw the Crucifixion symbolized in the floral parts of the latter, hence its common name. Another marvel is the white herald's-trumpet, the Indian *Beaumontia grandiflora*—not to be confused with the poisonous angel's-trumpet of the *Datura* genus.

At the end of this pergola is the Arid Rock Garden, a small and rather unimpressive collection of desert plants from Africa and America. Obviously, Fairchild cannot do everything with distinction. Wisely, it has concentrated on those groups which, among botanical gardens, only it can grow, and grow well. Other gardens have larger and more comprehensive collections of desert plants, the New York Botanical Garden being one.

Before you leave, a final viewing of Phillips's ingenious landscape design from two vantage points is recommended: from the Overlook, and from the west end of the Bailey Palm Glade. Besides plants, no matter how beautiful and elegant, a garden needs vistas—expected or unexpected—to make it whole. Fairchild has both.

The Piedmont azalea
(Rhododendron canescens),
a native species

The Reflection Pool,
Middleton Place

Orton Plantation

The garden seen
from the mansion,
Vizcaya

Goddess with
bougainvillea, Vizcaya

Epiphytic orchid
(Dendrobium nobile) with
aerial roots,
Fairchild Tropical Garden

Bluebird vine
(Petrea volubilis),
Fairchild Tropical Garden

Greenhouse display,
Callaway Gardens

Lake Eloise,
Cypress Gardens,
Florida

*The Spanish Facade,
Four Arts Garden*

*Parterre at
Gunston Hall*

Butterfly orchid
(*Oncidium cultivar*),
Fairchild
Tropical Garden

"Living Cliff,"
Selby Botanical
Gardens

Anemone coronaria

Governor's Palace and garden, Williamsburg

Prentis House garden, Williamsburg

Magnolia Gardens

Indica azalea
and Spanish moss

VIZCAYA

Miami, Florida

UNIQUE FEATURE	· The best representation of a Renaissance Italian garden in the United States.

HISTORY: During the years 1912–1916, James Deering, vice-president of International Harvester Company, built Vizcaya as his winter home. In 1952 his heirs sold it to Dade County for $1 million, and the art objects were deeded to the county as a gift. Today, there being no endowment funds, the museum and gardens are dependent upon gate receipts, the subscriptions and donations of the membership (the Vizcayans), and some state and private grants.

- *Admission:* Entrance fee. Extra fee for museum includes map and guide brochure.
- *Hours:* Open all year, 10:00 A.M.–5:00 P.M. daily. Closed Christmas Day. Ticket window closes 4:30 P.M.
- *Plants:* Not labeled.
- *Physically handicapped:* Gardens not accessible to wheelchairs.
- *Address:* Vizcaya, 3251 South Miami Avenue, Miami, Fla. 33129. Tel. (305) 854-6559 (the Vizcayans).
- *Location and directions:* Drive south on U.S. 1 to South Miami Avenue, a short distance south of junction of U.S. 95 and Rickenbacker Causeway. The avenue leaves U.S. 1 on the left at a very acute angle.
- *Parking:* Free, outside the gates.
- *Gift shop.*
- *Snack bar.*
- *No picnicking.*

To find a Renaissance palazzo surrounded by an authentically designed garden is something of a surprise in urban Miami. Most visitors are attracted to the mansion with its sumptuous furnishings and give no more than a cursory look at the garden. But anyone at all interested in the history and evolution of garden design cannot fail to be fascinated by this faithful reproduction of garden art of the sixteenth century, executed in a subtropical setting.

To appreciate this unique garden, some background is necessary. Before a visit it may be helpful to read the following section.

THE RENAISSANCE GARDEN: *In medieval times gardens were small, walled in against marauders, and intended primarily for growing utilitarian herbs, vegetables, and fruit. There might be a small "pleasance" garden as well, but this too would be cramped and diminutive. The Renaissance changed all of that.*

Writings of the ancients were rediscovered by scholars of the fourteenth century, and as a result, nearly every intellectual activity was affected. In Italy, garden design was one. The descriptions of Pliny the Younger's Roman garden, the horticultural writings of Theophrastus and of Xenophon, all had their effect. Architects of the day turned their hand to garden design; huge outdoor "rooms" were built, extending from the house and down the hillside. Trimmed and pruned trees (topiary) in the Pliny manner provided a background for classical statuary and exuberant fountains. Obviously, this did not happen all at once. It could not take place until there was a modicum of peace in the countryside, encouraging the rich—mainly popes and cardinals—to spend money on lavish living quarters.

In these new gardens flowers were unimportant. The soil and climate of Italy are not especially favorable to lush plant growth, though coniferous trees thrive. Consequently, the new design emphasized stone, water, and greenery. In this the Renaissance gardens were similar to those of Japan; they were intended for all seasons. Dense greenery provided shade in summer and protection from chilly winds in winter.

Fortunately for us, a few of these masterpieces, among them the Villa d'Este and the Villa Lante, have persisted. For unlike a painting, the "canvas" of the soil can easily be reworked to produce something more up-to-date.

*In transplanting Italianate design to France, embellishments were added in the form of parterres (*parterres de broderie*). The word* parterre *literally means "on the ground." Shrubs were planted in intricate patterns and clipped to form miniature hedges, the spaces between filled with contrasting colored gravel or flowers, or sometimes turf. To appreciate the complex design, one had to view the garden from a height—a hill, or a window of the house. Usually, it was laid out so that it could be seen to best advantage from an upper entertaining room. To enjoy such gardens it was not necessary to walk in them—a development well suited to the ample girth and portly stature of the patrons.*

The house at Vizcaya should be viewed first to get some idea of the scale of James Deering's enterprise. Furthermore, the only way to get a map of the gardens, which you will need, is to tour the house. The best view of the gardens is from the breakfast room on the second floor, and this is as it should be. Only from here—or from a helicopter—can one appreciate the elaborate design.

With its parterres, Vizcaya cannot be called a classical Italianate Renaissance garden. The flat terrain makes this impossible. The vista ends with the casino, a small, elegant summerhouse built on an artificial hill, the mound. The terraces of an Italian hillside are suggested by the double staircase leading to the mound, with its central cascading step-fountain. The two parallel *allées* of clipped live oak, *Quercus virginiana*,* separated by the moated island lead the eye to the casino. The mound in its turn serves as a viewing platform, not only for the parterres but for the villa and the seascape. (As an element in garden design the mound persisted well into the eighteenth century; one can be seen in the gardens of the Governor's Palace at Williamsburg.)

Vizcaya may not be in a pristine state of maintenance—that is almost impossible in these days. Unfortunately, the greatest visual and sensual delight of this subtropical garden, its fountains, were

---

* Any plant with the specific name of *virginiana* or *virginica* is native, not necessarily to the present state of Virginia, but to the considerably larger territory of the eastern United States that constituted the original colony of Virginia.

Central courtyard of the palazzo

not working to near capacity at the time of writing (1980). The sixty-year-old plumbing system needs extensive repair and replacements. The modern decorative stonework, executed in oolite limestone, is badly eroded. The porous nature of this rock was not known until permanent damage had been done by humidity and water seepage.

On the positive side, Vizcaya is the best reproduction of a true Renaissance garden in the United States. Fifoli Garden in Woodside, California, has a Renaissance section, but Vizcaya surpasses it because of its compactness, its association with an authentically designed villa, and its superb location on the water.

Vizcaya viewed from the mound

It is in this light that the garden should be viewed and evaluated. Horticulturists will naturally be intrigued by the clever substitution of Florida plants for their Mediterranean counterparts. Boxwood, *Buxus sempervirens*, used in French and Italian parterres, will not stand up to the Florida sun. An Australian jasmine, *Jasminum volubile*, has proved a most successful substitute. The topiary trees are neither boxwood, yew, nor cypress but an Australian tree, *Casuarina equisetifolia*, often planted along beaches in Florida and called Australian pine, though it is not a pine nor even related to the pines. Another topiary tree is made from *Eugenia myrtifolia*, a subtropical. The shade trees of the mound are the native live oak. Begonias fill the parterres, and the blue leadwort vine, *Plumbago capensis*, decorates some of the urns. It should be reiterated that a Renaissance garden is *not* a flower garden. Those who come to Vizcaya to see lush tropical flora will be disappointed. The Italians of that period grew cutting flowers in a separate garden, often in the secret garden (see below). Since Renaissance gardens were designed as outdoor entertaining rooms, the festive dress of both men and women provided the brilliant color the gardens themselves lacked.

Apart from the modern stonework already mentioned, the sculpture, urns, and other garden ornaments are mainly Italian antiques of the seventeenth and eighteenth centuries. The mythological figures gracing the east and west statuary walks are a good indication of the type of stone embellishments considered appropriate to garden design in those days.

The only antique fountain is the beautiful Bassani di Sutri Fountain in the rose garden to the east of the mound. This fountain formerly supplied water to the town of that name near Rome, and Deering purchased it on the condition that he replace it with a town water supply. (Clearly, money was no object!) The water stairway and the central moat were inspired by features in the Villa Farnese and the Villa Lante.

The two grottos at either side of the water staircase are typical of those which afforded a cool retreat from the burning Italian sun. Here the ceilings are decorated with a variety of local sea shells. This was typical of the Renaissance grottos; it helped to reinforce the cool, damp feeling. (Incidentally, grottos in English gardens are miserable places, proving that garden design cannot always be successfully imported or exported.)

To guarantee outdoor privacy for the family, most Renaissance gardens had a room-sized walled garden close to the house, the

The secret garden

giardino segreto, or secret garden. Here favorite flowers might be grown, children might play and adults partake of refreshments, away from the prying eyes of visitors. (Clearly, in Renaissance times the great gardens were open to the public.) At Vizcaya the secret garden is to be found east of the south terrace. The clipped shrubs are *Eugenia myrtifolia*. Creeping fig, *Ficus pumila*, covers the walls. The border outlining the wall beds is mondo grass, *Ophiopogon japonicus*—not really a grass but a member of the lily family that periodically produces blue flowers. This is a very formal garden, the only colorful note introduced by begonias and leadwort. One cannot imagine people relaxing in such a place, nor children playing; it hardly seems a replica of its historical ancestor, the *giardino segreto*.

Close by is a small theater garden where outdoor plays and masques could be performed—though this was more a feature of eighteenth-century than of fifteenth-century gardens.

South of the theater garden is the maze, another tiny garden "room." It is being restored at present with a planting of coco plum, *Chrysobalanus icaco*, a native shrub with edible fruits. Hedge mazes of this type were common from the fifteenth through the eighteenth centuries. It was then believed that they had existed in the Roman gardens of antiquity, though there is little evidence to support this.

The casino, another private retreat, was a common feature of these great gardens. Usually it was located as far as possible from

The theater garden

the bustle of villa life, as it is here. It was the place where the master could read or write or entertain a few intimates. The Vizcaya casino, besides being the focal point of the whole garden, was used for serving tea. In Deering's day the land across the canal to the south was mangrove jungle. There were no neighbors to disturb the peace (not true today). Elegant is the word for this small building; it deserves more than a cursory look.

Returning to the east façade of the villa, one is beguiled by the panorama, as well as by the tiny harbor with its lateral canals and its breakwater "folly"—a stone barge. Immovable stone barges as decorations have fascinated garden designers for centuries. The wonderful island garden of Isola Bella in Lake Maggiore in Italy, constructed in the seventeenth century, was meant to be shaped like a boat; it has its "decks"—terraces—but the prow was never completed. In Peking in the late nineteenth century the Dowager Empress Tz'u Hsi took tea on a marble barge constructed in a fresh-water lake in the Summer Palace. There is no evidence that James Deering used his barge for entertaining. While stilling the choppy waters around the yacht basin, it injected a note of fantasy into the opulent world of Vizcaya.

The best time to visit Vizcaya is from November to April: it was built as a winter home. During the dog days of July and August, Deering and his guests were up north. Vizcaya came back to life at Thanksgiving. But by the end of March, all but the servants had gone.

FOUR ARTS GARDEN

Palm Beach, Florida

UNIQUE FEATURES	• An amazing variety of tropical and semitropical plants compressed into a small area, approximately one acre.
	• A demonstration of twelve themes that could be used in small private gardens in south Florida.

HISTORY: In 1936 the Society of the Four Arts of Palm Beach was formed for the promotion of painting, music, literature, and drama. Later a garden, consisting of seven demonstration models, was constructed by the members of the Four Arts. The intention was to show new homeowners the kinds of gardens that could be constructed in the Palm Beach area. Today no one would suspect its origin, its original model gardens—whose number has since increased to twelve—having been unified into a little horticultural gem. It is cared for by the members of the Palm Beach Garden Club who are also members of the society; one person is responsible for each garden. Future plans include a sculpture garden to be associated with the art gallery.

- *Admission:* Free.
- *Hours:* Open all year, Monday to Friday 10:00 A.M.–5:00 P.M. Saturday, November 1 through May 1, 10:00 A.M.–5:00 P.M. Sunday, January 1 through April 15, 2:30 P.M.–5:00 P.M.
- *Physically handicapped:* Gardens accessible to wheelchairs.
- *Plants:* Not labeled. Guidebook and information available in library.
- *Address:* The Four Arts Garden, Four Arts Plaza, Royal Palm Way, Palm Beach, Fla. 33480. Tel. (305) 655-7226 (the art gallery); (305) 655-2766 (the library).
- *Location and directions:* From Florida Turnpike and Interstate 95: take exit 40, drive east on Okeechobee Boulevard, cross

Lake Worth on Royal Park Bridge (center bridge) to Royal Palm Way. Four Arts Garden is on the left.

· *Parking:* Free, on north side of the buildings.
· *No gift shop.*
· *No snack bar or restaurant.*
· *No picnicking.*

To see the Four Arts Garden involves a minimum of walking. First, locate the library on the eastern side of Four Arts Plaza, across the street from the parking lot. Adjacent to the library's south wall is the main gate. The suggested route is as follows:

Walk straight ahead to the Urn Garden, turning left to view the Rose and Herb gardens, also the Patio behind the library. Return. Halfway back to the main gate, turn left; the Chinese Garden is now on your left and the Moonlight Garden, so called because it originally contained only white flowers, is on your right. Now continue in a clockwise direction until you return to these two gardens. In the course of the route you will encounter the Jungle Garden, the Spanish Façade, and the Tropical, Madonna, Fountain, and Rock gardens, in that order.

The informality of Four Arts is charming, but for the visitor with questions it can be frustrating. The library, however, is a fund of information. Open to all without charge, it keeps the same hours as the garden. Here you can buy a booklet containing a map, a walking guide, and an accurate botanical listing of the

The Urn Garden

plants. For the serious plantsman the list of south Florida plants alone is worth the modest price.

The Four Arts Garden is recommended for those who wish to see and study tropical and subtropical plants yet cannot spend their time and energy exploring the comparatively huge Fairchild Garden in Miami.

Because of their contrasting features, four of the demonstration gardens are singled out below for closer inspection.

THE CHINESE GARDEN: Created as a memorial garden, this is the *pièce de résistance* of the whole Four Arts. "Happiness and harmony" is the meaning of the Chinese character above the gate, which leads to an exquisite outdoor room, entirely walled except for the "moongate." Every attempt has been made to create an authentic garden, though subtropicals have had to replace traditional Chinese plants. For instance, the willow, symbolizing grace, is replaced by the southern weeping yew, *Podocarpus gracilior*. Intrinsic to all Chinese religions is the worship of nature. Thus the Chinese approach to a garden is fundamentally different from that of the West—as the wall poem here suggests. Renaissance man sought to tame nature, to make nature his handmaiden. But to the Chinese way of thinking, man is just an evanescent eruption on an enduring landscape.

Everything here is symbolic: the carefully chosen rocks, signifying distant mountains; the pool, representing life-sustaining

The Chinese Garden

The Chinese Garden,
detail

rivers and lakes; the winding paths, which defeat evil—"evil walks in a straight line"; the plants, depicting human virtues.

Restraint is the keynote. Nothing is cluttered. The form and symmetry of each tree are evident: the two species of *Podocarpus*, *P. gracilior* and *P. macrophyllus*, the black olive, *Bucida buceras*, the false aralia, *Dizygotheca elegantissima*, and the traditional bamboo, *Bambusa glaucescens*, signifying the gentlemanly virtues of hardiness and resilience.

Unlike the Japanese, the Chinese considered flowers an indispensable part of a garden, so here are a profusion of flowering herbs and shrubs. Noteworthy are the unusual blue-and-white bird-of-paradise, *Strelitzia nicolai*, and the red lobster-claw, *Heliconia caribaea* (both of the banana family), the yellow walking iris, *Neomarica longifolia*, and the pomegranate, *Punica granatum*. Instead of the lotus, the night-blooming tropical white water lily, *Nyphaea odorata*, grows in the pool.

The statues that contribute to the mood of this garden are all antiques, the Foo dogs being of the tenth century.

THE JUNGLE GARDEN: That water is an indispensable element in good garden design, gardeners of both East and West agree. Here the focus is an irregularly shaped pool filled with fish and white water lilies. A peninsula promotes greater intimacy with the water and its inhabitants. Encircling palms create a jungle effect. The ornamental Senegal date palm, *Phoenix reclinata*, together with the areca palm, *Chrysalidocarpus* sp., and the lady palm, *Rhapis excelsa*, adorn the far bank, shading the ferns and begonias along the water's edge. The Fiji palm, *Veitchia joannis*, and more lady palms mark the fork in the path. Two cycads, *Zamia floridana* (a native species) and *Z. pumila*, round out the jungle scene. Gracing the peninsula are the heart-shaped leaves of the purple taro, *Xanthosoma violaceum*, and the beautiful lily-of-the-Nile, *Agapanthus africanus*, under a small green-ebony tree, *Jacaranda mimosifolia*.

THE SPANISH FAÇADE: This small patio in front of a "house" was planted to reinforce the Mediterranean motif. The central wishing well is covered with creeping fig, *Ficus pumila*; there is a bench of colorful Portuguese tiles; and two Italian cypresses, *Cupressus sempervirens*, emerging from terra-cotta urns guard the doorway. Planters of red geraniums add color, and in spring the glorious bluebird vine, *Petrea volubilis*, decorates the doorway with its pendent blossoms. The hedge is clipped chalcas, *Murraya paniculata*, and the patio border consists of mondo grass, *Ophiopogon japonicus*. Two clipped "standard" *Hibiscus rosa-sinensis* cultivars punctuate the entrance.

THE FOUNTAIN OR FORMAL GARDEN: Again the focal point is water. A fountain plays in an octagonal pool of multicolored water lilies set in the middle of a lawn. (This is the only demonstration garden that features a lawn, presumably because in Florida lawns pose problems owing to the dry winter season.) Surrounding the

The Fountain Garden

lawn is a brick walk with connections to other gardens. The walk is circumscribed in turn by a closely clipped hedge of weeping fig, *Ficus benjamina*—to northerners an unexpected use of this common house plant. Behind the hedge are a variety of shrubs and trees: palms, cycads, crotons (*Codiaeum variegatum*), and a sweet orange (*Citrus sinensis*). The tallest tree, a kassod, *Cassia siamea*, is a "Town of Palm Beach Specimen Tree." In front of it is the edible-fruited carambola, *Averrhoa carambola*. Climbing up the trees are various big-leaf aroids.

Aroids: *The anthuriums, elephant-ears, philodendrons, caladiums, dumb canes, spathiphyllums, and monsteras are members of a large tropical monocot family, the Araceae, collectively known as the aroids. Unlike those of other monocot families, their leaves do not have parallel veining. A typical "flower" is that of the common house plant* Spathiphyllum patinii, *with its white leaflike structure, the spathe, loosely surrounding a central column, the spadix, which bears many tiny flowers. The plants are usually grown for the beauty of their leaves rather than for their flowers. An exception is the flamingo flower,* Anthurium scherzerianum, *with its brilliant red bract or spathe. Taro and yautia are two aroids that provide food. While* Monstera deliciosa *has a sweet edible fruit, it is hardly a staple. All aroids are moisture-loving, even the few oddities that live in the temperate zones, like the skunk cabbage,* Symplocarpus foetidus, *and jack-in-the-pulpit,* Arisaema *spp.*

From the north end of this garden an impressive vista has been created, looking towards the decorative gate and beyond to the distant palms of Royal Palm Way. The visitor should drive down this avenue; it is perhaps the most impressive in all of Florida. Here the difference between the royal palms of West Palm Beach and of Palm Beach is very noticeable. Those in West Palm are suffering from the fatal "lethal yellowing" virus disease, whereas those of Palm Beach are healthy because its garden club has led an active inoculation campaign. Scars from inoculation holes can be seen on the trunks of the trees in Royal Palm Way approximately three feet from the ground.

MARIE SELBY
BOTANICAL GARDENS

Sarasota, Florida

UNIQUE
FEATURES

- The only botanical garden in the United States specializing in the preservation, study, care, and enjoyment of epiphytes ("air plants").
- The world's largest collection of gesneriads (African violets and their relatives).

HISTORY: Marie Selby, who died in 1971, bequeathed her seven-acre estate, along with an endowment, for "a botanical garden . . . for enjoyment by the general public." In 1972 her next-door neighbors, in sympathy with the will, sold their four-acre lot, including the Christy Payne house, to the Selby Foundation. Today the Selby Botanical Gardens encompasses almost the entire peninsula between Sarasota Bay and Hudson Bayou. Since the original endowment proved insufficient for a botanical garden actively engaged in research, additional support continues to be sought from grants, donations, and community events. A staff was assembled in 1973, and in 1976 the gardens were opened to the public. At present (1980) plans for a new science building are in the making.

- *Admission:* Entrance fee.
- *Hours:* Open all year, 10:00 A.M.–5:00 P.M. daily. Closed Christmas Day.
- *Plants:* Well labeled.
- *Physically handicapped:* Selby house, display greenhouse, and most paths accessible to wheelchairs.
- *Address:* The Marie Selby Botanical Gardens, 800 South Palm Avenue, Sarasota, Fla. 33577. Tel. (813) 366-5730.
- *Location and directions:* In downtown Sarasota. Driving north on U.S. 41, South Palm Avenue is the next left turn after traffic

light at intersection with Orange Avenue. Driving south on U.S. 41, South Palm Avenue is the next major right turn after traffic light at intersection with Keys Causeway.

· *Parking:* Free, outside the gates.
· *Shops:* Gift shop, plant shop, book shop.
· *Snack bar.*
· *No picnicking.*

There was a need in south Florida for a garden where animals did not overshadow the plants. The Busch Gardens in Tampa and the Jungle Gardens in Sarasota have fine ornamentals, but these are completely upstaged by the birds and beasts roaming the grounds. For plant lovers, the more pressing need was for an institution where plants could be observed, enjoyed, identified, and studied.

This neophyte botanical garden, situated in downtown Sarasota, answers that need. Within a block of U.S. 41, it is secluded; just short of eleven acres, it is small; it is devoted to one type of plant and therefore specialized. But it occupies a marvelous location—a peninsula with Sarasota Bay on one side and Hudson Bayou on the other. U.S. 41 and its continuous parade of commercialism could be light-years away. From one path a tiny beach is accessible.

Designing a garden devoted to epiphytes, or "air plants," is a challenge. Though insignificant, these plants are numerous and important inhabitants of the tropical rain forests (see p. 11).

Foliar design

Fittonia argyroneura

Unlike an aboretum, where specimen trees can simply be planted in orderly fashion, a collection of epiphytes needs careful "staging" if the whole is to add up to a garden.

Selby has solved the problem by compromise. It has left undisturbed the marvelous trees planted by the late owners: the great Chinese banyans, *Ficus retusa*, with their fantastic tangle of secondary trunks; the bamboo "forest," *Bambusa vulgaris*, with underplantings of *Zebrina pendula* (the common house plant); the various choice ornamentals such as *Pandanus* spp., the tree-of-gold (*Tabebuia argentea*) with its yellow flowers gleaming from leafless branches, the tree ferns, and various species of palm, leaning at the water's edge.

Chinese banyan under-planted with Zebrina pendula

Bamboo "forest"

But modifications had to be made. Paved walks were constructed, following the peninsula's contours while skirting the huge trees and allowing views of the surrounding waterways. Expanses of lawn highlight and contrast with grouped plantings around the buildings. A new redwood boardwalk leads past the Selby mansion to a tree-shaded terrace where visitors may enjoy refreshments. Nearby, a half-acre of greenhouses accommodate the valuable collections from South America, added to each year by the gardens' plant explorers. Recently, this area has been extended outdoors by a roofed-over trellis walk where sculpture and other art objects as well as plants are exhibited. Close by are a waterfall and a lily pool.

Lily pool

A grove of about fifteen live oaks behind the Selby house is the main stage for the outdoor exhibit of epiphytes. Each tree is draped with hanging baskets and with perching bromeliads, ferns, and orchids, while from below, aroids with their clinging roots clamber towards the light. The curious epiphytic fern aptly called the staghorn, *Platycerium* spp., is prominently displayed. It has two kinds of leaves: the green stag's horns that photosynthesize and the brown leaves that, pressed flat against the tree, form pockets in which water and organic debris collect. The fern's roots, growing into these pockets, absorb water and mineral salts derived from organic decay. The rest of the collection is mainly bromeliads: *Tillandsia* spp. (*T. cyanea*'s blue inflorescence forms part of Selby's logo), *Billbergia* spp., *Vriesea* spp.—all familiar to house-plant buffs.

The air plants on view in this oak grove would probably be encountered on trees along a highway or a riverbank rather than deep in a steamy forest. These are the tough ones and also the commoner species. The rare and delicate ones are in the greenhouses.

EPIPHYTES: *Characteristic of moist tropical regions, epiphytes do not belong to any one plant group. All are green, obtaining light for photosynthesis by perching on trees or occasionally rocks (the word is from the Greek* epi, "upon," *and* phyton, "plant"*). Because they make their own food, they are not parasites like the mistletoe. Their water comes from rain or humid air; their mineral salts, from dust or organic debris that collects in their woody roosts.*

Spanish moss, Tillandsia usneoides, *is the most familiar epiphyte to southerners. A flowering plant, it can exist even on telephone wires. It can kill trees by cutting off the light supply to their leaves, though storms help to keep it in check. Spanish moss is an unusual member of the pineapple family, Bromeliaceae. Most bromeliads have rosettes of leaves which function as water-collecting tanks, special hairs on the inner leaf surfaces acting as absorptive organs. In the wild these small pools are often homes for tadpoles, frogs, mosquito larvae, and other aquatic animals. (The capacity of a tank can amount to one gallon of water!) Debris falling into them decays, releasing mineral salts necessary for the plant's nourishment. The gray color of most bromeliad leaves, especially noticeable in Spanish moss, is due to wax, which effectively reduces transpiration—one of many adaptations they have evolved for coping with the desert-like conditions of the treetops. (For a description of epiphytic orchids, see p. 34.)*

Across from the oaks is another collection of bromeliads, planted in the ground to afford a close-up view of their structure. One of the problems of field botanists in a tropical rain forest is that they are, willy-nilly, terrestrial, so that they cannot even see what they are supposed to be studying. The solution is the construction of platforms or treehouses in the canopy. In extreme cases trees have to be felled in order to identify both the trees and their epiphytic lodgers. The study of tropical rain forests is by no means a passive occupation. The variety of species within such a forest is so great that a botanist may have to walk a mile to see two trees of the same species.

The display greenhouse and its trellised walk are beautifully maintained. A living cliff of epiphytes against a mossy background constitutes one entire wall. Here a vivid and varied mixture of flowering orchids, bromeliads, aroids, and gesneriads can be examined. In the foreground and nearby grow bird-of-paradise (*Strelitiza reginae*), tree ferns, cycads, *Alpinia* spp., and aroids.

Selby is reputed to have the largest collection of gesneriads in the world. This was achieved partly by donation and partly by the assiduous efforts of its plant explorers. The gardens have been responsible for introducing many new species into the trade.

G ESNERIADS: *Epiphytes occur in many tropical families. Quite a few come from the African violet family, Gesneriaceae, named for Conrad Gesner, a sixteenth-century Swiss naturalist. Three genera (37 percent of the species in this family) are epiphytic:* Columnea *and* Episcia *from the New World and* Aeschynanthus *from Asia. Representatives from all three can be seen here. Because of their habit of growth they do well in hanging baskets.* Columnea, *sometimes called the flying-goldfish plant because of the color and shape of its flowers, is probably the most familiar.*

Gesneriads are very desirable ornamentals because of their gorgeous flowers, their florifer-

ousness, and their ease of propagation. *The African violet,* Saintpaulia ionantha, *now exists in a plethora of cultivars—singles and doubles of every color except yellow and scarlet—and is the most popular house plant in the world. Discovered in Tanganyika in the 1890s, it is not a violet nor even remotely related to violets. The gloxinia,* Sinningia speciosa, *and the Cape primrose,* Streptocarpus *spp., are two other popular types; the miniature* Sinningia pusilla, *which fits into a pot the diameter of a quarter, is a favorite in small terrariums.*

Selby's orchid collection is also extensive—again thanks to the explorers. Because of its expertise in these fields, this botanical garden is now the headquarters of both the Orchid and the Bromeliad Identification Centers.

EPIPHYTIC ORCHIDS: *The epiphytic orchids—some of which are to be seen here, mostly in the display greenhouse—have roots of two kinds: those which act as anchors, and those which, surrounded by a special spongy tissue called the velamen, absorb rain or dew as they dangle in the moist air. Often green, the aerial roots photosynthesize, whereas the leaves are reduced in size and number or may be entirely lacking. At least two genera of epiphytic orchids are leafless, their green roots functioning as food factories. During drought the velamen fills with air, effectively reducing water loss from the inner living tissues. Some species shed their leaves at this time, leaving structures called pseudobulbs, which store food and water to tide them over until rain falls.*

It might seem that science has all the answers regarding life in the treetops, but this is not so. Knowledge of the ecology and physiology of epiphytes is still surprisingly incomplete. For the scientific staff here at Selby, much work lies ahead. The director, Dr. Calaway H. Dodson, himself a plant explorer, writes: "Estimates of the number of undiscovered organisms in the tropical forests show that a million species may never be known by man." Of the epiphytes, Dr. Dodson thinks it unlikely that more than 30 to 50 percent of the so-far undiscovered species can be saved, so fast is the pace of destruction (see p. 11). It is some comfort, though small, that concerned botanists are doing all they can.

Greenhouse—"living cliff"

Before leaving the gardens, visit the elegant Christy Payne house (now called the Museum of Botany and the Arts) to inspect a display of botanically inspired art. Next-door a class may be in session—an opportunity to see what Selby's educational program has to offer.

Note: The dependence of epiphytes on high air humidity is well demonstrated by the distribution of Spanish moss. As you drive through the South, notice that it occurs only near large bodies of water such as the sea, the lakes, the rivers. Temperature seems not to be the determining factor.

CYPRESS GARDENS

Winter Haven, Florida

UNIQUE FEATURES	· For the plant lover, lush tropical vegetation: magnificent specimens of exotic trees and shrubs, especially in the Original Gardens. · For the tourist, aqua shows, and much else besides.

HISTORY: In 1932, Richard Pope and his wife, Julie, bought 14 acres of swamp beside Lake Eloise. Four years later it emerged as a landscaped garden full of exotics from all over the world. Because of the ancient cypress trees (*Taxodium distichum*) hugging the shores of the lake, it was called Florida Cypress Gardens. Today it encompasses 228 acres, but is much more than just gardens. A major tourist attraction, rivaling Walt Disney World, it is world-famous for its aqua shows.

· *Admission:* Entrance fee, which includes map.
· *Hours:* Open all year, 8:00 A.M. till sundown daily.
· *Plants:* Labeled in some areas. Booklet for identifying plants is on sale at entrance.
· *Physically handicapped:* Free wheelchairs and strollers available at main entrance. No steps in garden, but some bridges in Original Gardens are steep.
· *Address:* Cypress Gardens, Post Office Box 1, Cypress Gardens, Fla. 33880. Tel. (813) 324-2111.
· *Location and directions:* In central Florida, 4 miles southeast of Winter Haven on Florida 540. A half-hour drive from Walt Disney World.
· *Parking:* Free, outside grounds.
· *Shops:* Gift shops, shopping mall.
· *Restaurant.* Also snack bars, cafeterias.
· *Motel:* Quality Inn, Cypress Gardens.
· *Picnicking permitted.*

For a serious plant lover to find himself or herself surrounded by a mob of noisy kids, tired moms and dads, and crinolined southern belles seems odd at first. Is *this* a garden? It is, perhaps—in the Italian Renaissance and seventeenth-century French sense, in which a garden became a garden only when full of colorfully dressed people bent on pleasure. Of course, Louis XIV's conception of a pleasure garden was something different from Dick Pope's. But Versailles, Vaux-le-Vicomte, the Villa Lante with its "joke fountains," were all intended to be places where people could observe natural beauty (and each other), eat, drink, and enjoy themselves exuberantly. Raucous laughter rather than polite titters must have accompanied the "water jokes" common in those old gardens. The evidence suggests that the pleasure gardens of the sixteenth and seventeenth centuries were more like Cypress Gardens today, rather than the quiet retreats envisioned by harried modern man.

But what has Cypress to offer the dedicated garden lover, fresh from Fairchild or Selby, who momentarily recoils as she or he passes through the turnstile? Let's answer the question in this way: undaunted, consult the map, make a bee-line for the boat station, and take a half-hour electric-boat ride (for a fee). Even on a hot, busy day in Easter week there is no waiting, so efficiently does everything run at Cypress. These rides have been running since 1938, using the original swamp-drainage canals as waterways. (Bridges are low, so in times of heavy rain the boats may not operate.) This trip will give you an overview of the most spectacular vegetation in all of Florida. Never mind if you cannot understand the guide; the gardens speak for themselves. Past the ancient cypresses in Lake Eloise, you navigate the canals of the Original Gardens into the famous Big Lagoon, where a pretty, crinolined girl waves to you from the bank with queenly languor.

Returning to land, explore the same area on foot. (The best time to do this in peace and quiet is during the aqua shows, which occur every two hours.) Fifty years of growth have produced the luxuriant and gorgeous trees and shrubs you see. Yes, there are forty-eight gardeners and horticulturists lurking in the background—evidence to the contrary elsewhere. And yes, there are huge "mechanized" greenhouses producing masses of bedding-out material (Cypress always has to be ready for frost damage). Plant selections are made here. This year (1980) a new croton

The Big Lagoon

cultivar, *Codiaeum variegatum*, is being introduced to the trade. But when the history of the gardens is taken into account, this is not surprising. For forty years Richard Pope, besides planning miniature zoos, ante-bellum streets, and spectacular water shows, has traveled the world in search of new plants for his garden. This gets obscured by the hyperbole now so evident at Cypress.

Within the Original Gardens the bougainvilleas, *Bougainvillea glabra* and *B. spectabilis*, are stupendous; so are the flame vine, *Pyrostegia ignea*, and the masses of azaleas, mainly the Indica series (see p. 58), which start blooming in December. It seems almost as if the plants are rearing up amid all this hoopla and demanding attention. Never has the author seen anything like the purple-flowered princess tree, *Tibouchina urvilliana* (also called glory-bush), for sheer size (thirty to forty feet) and floriferousness. Among this lush growth, it is difficult to single out individual species, but noteworthy are the banana "trees," *Musa* spp. —not really trees but giant herbs since they die down to ground level after flowering; the crotons with their ornamental leaves; the luxuriant climbing aroid *Monstera deliciosa*, sometimes called the Swiss-cheese plant because of the natural holes in its leaves, thought to drain off water (possibly a protection against fungi); the bird-of-paradise flowers, *Strelitzia reginae*, as well as *Hibiscus* cultivars and gardenias, *Gardenia veitchii*. Don't miss the giant banyan tree, *Ficus benghalensis*, with its dark forest of secondary trunks formed from downward-growing aerial roots (it is marked on the map). It is two hundred feet in diameter, and has been

Patio of Saint Fiacre

designated a "Specimen Tree of the State." In summer, look for the Brazilian giant water-platter, *Victoria amazonica*, in the Big Lagoon below the gazebo. Its leaves sometimes attain a diameter of six feet. (For more on the water-platter, see p. 172.)

Visit the charming patio featuring Saint Fiacre, the seventh-century saint of gardens. The tree ferns here are particularly fine specimens. Often mistaken for palms, these gigantic ferns, which may reach heights of up to eighty feet, are restricted to frost-free areas. (For more information on ferns, see pp. 227–8.)

In your wanderings, by all means visit the Oriental Garden, but please do not think it authentic, nor that it remotely resembles the garden at Kamakura in Japan. Admire the landscaping and the marvelous vegetation; some beautiful cycads grow here (see p. 8). But if you want authenticity, visit the Brooklyn Botanic Garden's Japanese gardens.

Leaving the Original Gardens, proceed to the Rose Garden. (Quickly pass by "Gardens of the World"; for those with discriminating tastes there is no point in lingering here.) Cypress has the only All-American Rose Selection Garden in Florida. It is small, but it displays twenty-three award-winning roses covering the years 1941 to the present. Here you can see the fragrant, deep-crimson 'Mr. Lincoln,' award winner of 1955; the orange-red 'Tropicana,' a color breakthrough of 1963; the multicolored 'Double Delight,' winner in 1977, with its delicious fragrance; as well as the old favorite 'Peace' of 1953—a beautiful yellow, but lacking the fragrance demanded in the new roses. All of these are hybrid

The Dutch Garden

teas, but grandifloras and floribundas are well represented. (For more on roses, see pp. 182–4.)

The rose garden flowers nearly all year long, peak bloom occurring from Thanksgiving through March. For a very short period in early spring, it is flowerless because of the annual pruning (our visit coincided with this). Roses must be pruned regularly to keep the bushes well shaped and to promote blooming. If you think Florida is too hot for roses, this garden will reassure you.

The Trial Rose Garden is not open to the public. It is one of twenty-five gardens in the United States which for two years test

Lake Eloise and cypresses

newly developed roses to determine whether they should be recommended, first, for sale to the public, and second, for yearly awards by the All-American Rose Selection Corporation. All the award-winning roses in the public garden were selected by this method.

The final port of call for the garden or nature lover at Cypress is a stroll along Cypress Point Pier, a rustic boardwalk through a natural stand of swamp or bald cypress, *Taxodium distichum*, on the shores of Lake Eloise and way beyond the recently opened "Southern Crossroads" and the "Living Forest." Strolling or sitting, you can observe the fish and wildlife as well as the centuries-old trees with their peculiar "knees." One specimen in the Original Gardens is estimated to be sixteen hundred years old (for more on these trees, see pp. 71–2). Here a little of Florida as it was before civilization discovered it can be relished and enjoyed. It is a quiet place to cleanse the mind of some of the man-made monstrosities witnessed in today's excursion. (Did a giant cement caterpillar leer at you from behind a bush?)

Cypress Gardens may feel that it has to compete with nearby Walt Disney World—a possible reason for those new ventures that may seem mildly unfortunate. Still, Cypress attendance figures and clientele testify to its popularity. On a family outing, children as well as adults are entitled to their particular modes of entertainment. And in today's world, gardens desperately need money. Only by attracting people of all ages and walks of life can money be made. Many garden owners apologize for their petting zoos, pony rides, and other non-garden diversions—to put it euphemistically—but who can criticize? It seems an economic necessity for survival in the world of the 1980s. And perhaps their kind of outdoor entertainment is indeed the modern version of the pleasure gardens of the Renaissance.

CALLAWAY GARDENS

❧

Pine Mountain, Georgia

UNIQUE FEATURES	• An extensive hardwood forest, within which are labeled trails featuring popular ornamentals and wild flowers.
	• One of the most extensive collections of native and exotic hybrid azaleas in the South.

HISTORY: In the 1930s textile industrialist Cason J. Callaway, Sr., acquired 2,500 acres of land impoverished and eroded by agricultural mismanagement. Twenty years later, the soil reconditioned, the land reforested, lakes excavated, golf and tennis facilities as well as a lakeside beach constructed, the resort, Callaway Gardens, came into being. Named the Ida Cason Callaway Gardens after his mother, it was opened to the public in 1953, when the founder turned the entire enterprise over to the Callaway Foundation to be maintained as a public facility for the enjoyment of natural beauty, for recreation, and for education.

The foundation is a nonprofit charitable organization whose primary purpose is to maintain the gardens. Its subsidiary, Garden Services, Inc., which runs the hotel, restaurant, and shops, is a regular business enterprise. But all profits, after taxes, are funneled back into the foundation.

- *Admission:* Entrance fee (waived if you stay at Callaway Inn or Cottages).
- *Hours:* Open daily all year. May 1 through Labor Day, 7:00 A.M.–7:00 P.M. Labor Day through October 31, 7:00 A.M.–6:00 P.M. November 1 through April 30, 7:00 A.M.–5:00 P.M.
- *Plants:* Labeled.
- *Physically handicapped:* Can be driven in cars along scenic routes, but trails and greenhouse unsuitable for wheelchairs.

Garden areas around greenhouse and Mr. Cason's Vegetable Garden accessible.

- *Address:* Callaway Gardens, Pine Mountain, Ga. 31822. For restaurant and hotel reservations write Department X56 at this address, or call toll free (800) 282-8181 in Georgia, (800) 241-0910 outside Georgia.
- *Location and directions:* On U.S. 27 at Pine Mountain in west Georgia, 75 miles south of Atlanta, 70 miles north of Plains, and 35 miles north of Columbus.
- *Parking:* Free, throughout gardens.
- *Shops:* Information center for books; gift shop at Callaway Inn; Country Store in Pine Mountain.
- *Restaurants:* Five formal and informal restaurants.
- *Hotel:* Callaway Inn and Cottages.
- *Picnicking:* Permitted in recreation area.

Callaway Gardens consists of small gardens within a vast land-scaped woodland, interrupted by thirteen lakes that offer striking panoramas. In restoring the hardwood forest once native to the area, Cason Callaway and his horticultural team augmented it with choice plants of native and exotic origin. Some of the non-indigenous plants added in abundance were azaleas, hollies, magnolias, flowering quince, and wild flowers. The lakes attract ducks, geese, and coots. One is stocked with fish; to prevent destruction of the vegetation at the water's edge, all fishing is from boats. Gardens, in the sense that the word is used in this guide, constitute a very small percentage of the acreage. Spring bulbs, summer annuals, and fall chrysanthemums are planted seasonally around the greenhouse area. In addition there is Mr. Cason's Vegetable Garden, seven and one-half acres devoted to the growth of both common and unusual fruits, vegetables, and herbs. The produce is not for sale but may be sampled in season at the garden's restaurants or taken away as preserves or pickles —a nice homey touch that summer visitors in particular enjoy.

Do visit the information center before entering the gardens: the beautiful orientation film is worth the time spent. Also retain the map. To see the gardens thoroughly, a week is needed. (You may, of course, decide to be selective, in which case two days should be sufficient.) A car is really a necessity. For those staying at the inn, transportation to a special spot can be arranged, but there is no substitute for the freedom to stop and go at will. The more athletic can rent a bicycle. The gardens can be seen with a minimum of walking since driving and cycling are permitted along the thirteen miles of paved roadway. But unless the trails are explored on foot, much of the flavor of the place, much of what Cason Callaway had in mind when he developed this parkland, will be missed. He expected his guests to walk the trails and savor the natural beauty, thereby returning refreshed to city and suburban life.

THE AZALEA TRAIL

Callaway is one of the famous azalea gardens in the South. In April and to some extent in May, the azalea fan can spend hours examining all the wonderful cultivars, all labeled and concentrated on the Azalea Trail. Massed plantings of some six hundred hybrids set the woods aglow in springtime. In other gardens the setting may be more aesthetic, but Callaway is especially appreciated by the serious student who needs to compare and take notes. Looking at the profusion of color and form, one is awestruck by the amazing feats the plant breeder can accomplish by applying the laws of heredity—discovered a little over a hundred years ago—followed by careful selection and testing.

Four series of hybrids prosper at Callaway, all of them derived from the Asiatic evergreen azaleas: the Glenn Dale and Back Acre series, developed by B. Y. Morrison, former director of the National Arboretum, and the Satsuki and Kurume series from

Azaleas in spring

Japan. The Kurumes were brought to the United States in 1915 by plant explorer Ernest H. "Chinese" Wilson. In 1972 Callaway, through the efforts of Fred C. Galle, a noted authority on azaleas, was so fortunate as to secure one of these original collections.

The hybrids seen in the North—the Ghents, the Mollis and Exbury series—are not represented here. They were bred in Europe from native American deciduous azaleas and prefer a cooler climate. Likewise, the Indica azaleas admired in the Charleston gardens and on the Gulf coast are also absent; they are not suited to Callaway's more rigorous winters. (For more on evergreen hybrid azaleas, see pp. 146–7.)

Since azaleas are so much a part of the spring scene at Callaway, a little general botanical information on these prized ornamentals seems appropriate here.

AZALEAS: *Azaleas are dicotyledons belonging to the heath family,* Ericaceae, *to which also belong heathers, mountain laurel, trailing arbutus, and andromeda (*Pieris spp.*). They are classified in the genus* Rhododendron *(meaning "rose tree" in Greek). Around 1900 only about three hundred species were known, but since then phenomenal feats of plant exploration in Asia, especially in Tibet and the Himalayas, have brought the number up to approximately one thousand. Most are Asiatic, some North American; four are European; and almost without exception they belong in the Northern Hemisphere.*

Differentiating between an azalea and the gardener's "rhododendron" is not easy. Usually, azaleas have five stamens and are deciduous. But there are azaleas with ten stamens, and many are evergreen, though their leaves are not nearly so tough or so long-lived as those of the rhododendron. Still, most people can tell an azalea from a rhododendron when they see one, even if they cannot defend their diagnosis. Even Linnaeus, the great father of botany, fell into this trap in his great classification scheme by forming two genera: Azalea *and* Rhododendron. *After his death his successors solved the knotty problem by lumping them all into one genus,* Rhododendron, *leaving the hair-splitters to sort things out. And this is exactly what we shall do. (For details on the evergreens popularly called rhododendrons, see pp. 249–50.)*

From April to August the native azaleas blossom along the drives and in the woodlands. Blooming starts in early April with the yellow Florida azalea, *Rhododendron austrinum*, and the Piedmont azalea, *Rh. canescens*, and ends in late July and August with the white sweet azalea, *Rh. arborescens*, and the red plumleaf azalea, *Rh. prunifolium*, indigenous to only a small region of southwest Georgia. Cason Callaway received an award for saving the plumleaf from extinction. He found it on his newly acquired property. Now, thanks to him and his horticulturists, it is no longer rare.

NATIVE AZALEAS: *Depending on which taxonomist you consult, there are sixteen or seventeen species of wild azalea in North America, all but one occurring in the eastern states (Callaway prides itself on growing fifteen of them). These azaleas are deciduous. Often called "bush honeysuckles," they are quite unrelated to the true honeysuckles of the* Lonicera *genus. Perhaps it is their protuberant styles and stamens that give them a honeysuckle look.*

All native azaleas make good garden plants. They are hardier than the hybrids, and being deciduous, often have attractive fall foliage. Northern gardeners should understand, however, that some species may not be hardy in their home states. Buying indigenous azaleas is not always easy, as nurserymen have little demand for them. Your best bet is to collect seed, or even to dig them up when their territory is threatened by bulldozers.

Hybrid rhododendrons may be seen at Callaway in April along a trail in the Meadowlark Area. For display they cannot compete with those of gardens farther north. These plants thrive in colder climates, their ancestors having come from the Himalayan and Appalachian mountains. Summer heat affects them adversely.

THE MEADOWLARK AREA

Not everyone is seduced by azaleas. This area has trails devoted to other ornamentals and particularly those dramatic evergreens the hollies, *Ilex* spp. Five trails are devoted to approximately 450 cultivars of holly of mixed parentage—American, English, and Asiatic. Interplantings, many deciduous, break up the monotony.

Camellia sasanqua, blooming in late fall, and daffodils in spring will be encountered on these trails, as well as an assortment of shrubs including the sacred bamboo, *Nandina domestica* (not a real bamboo, but a favorite all over the South), *Cotoneaster* spp., firethorn, *Pyracantha* sp., and tea olive, *Osmanthus fortunei.* Another trail is devoted to *Magnolia* spp. and flowering quince, *Chaenomeles* spp., and yet another to wild flowers. Allow about fifteen minutes to follow each trail. An afternoon can be whiled away in this living museum, even in late autumn or winter. And as in a museum, every specimen is labeled.

The wild-flower trail is no more than two-thirds of a mile long, yet in this short distance the author encountered the beautiful atamasco lily (*Zephyranthes atamasco*), *Trillium* spp., shooting-star (*Dodecatheon meadia*), the halberd-leaved yellow violet (*Viola hastata*), the aquatic golden-club (*Orontium aquaticum*, an aroid), and many other April-flowering species.

THE CALLAWAY WOODLANDS

In the sense that a garden is a place, usually out of doors, made by man for his pleasure, the woodlands at Callaway constitute a garden. A man took a raped landscape and turned it into a thing of beauty for the enjoyment of others. Left to itself in the 1930s, it would have turned into a dustbowl or, over a period of several hundred years, have become deciduous forest, by the natural process called succession.

End of a trail
(*Meadowlark Area*)

The Callaway woodlands are oak-dominated. In ecological language, this means that of all the plants, the oaks exert the most influence on the lives of the other inhabitants—plant and animal —of the community. Oaks common in the Callaway woods are:

· The white oak, *Quercus alba*
· The red oak, *Q. rubra maxima*
· The chestnut oak, *Q. montana*
· The water oak, *Q. nigra*
· The willow oak, *Q. phellos*

Interspersed among the oaks are a few conifers left from the degraded landscape of the thirties: red cedar, *Juniperus virginiana*; loblolly pine, *Pinus taeda*; shortleaf pine, *P. echinata*; and longleaf pine, *P. palustris*. Beech, *Fagus grandifolia*, and hickories will be found occasionally—the pignut hickory, *Carya glabra*, and the sweet pignut, *C. ovalis*. In moister places, the tulip tree, *Liriodendron tulipifera*, the black gum, *Nyssa sylvatica*, and the red maple, *Acer rubrum*, are evident. Two of the southern magnolias, the umbrella tree, *Magnolia tripetala*, and the sweet bay, *M. virginiana*, may be seen, their white flowers appearing after the leaves have unfolded.

Among the shrubs the red buckeye, *Aesculus pavia*, and the oak-leaf hydrangea, *Hydrangea quercifolia*, are very obvious in early April, even to passing motorists. Other shrubs common in these woods are the witch hazel, *Hamamelis virginiana*, flowering in the fall as the leaves drop; plums, *Prunus angustifolia* and *P. umbellata*; and the bayberry, *Myrica cerifera*, whose berries yield the wax that scents bayberry candles. And last but not least, the fifteen species of wild azalea.

TEMPERATE-ZONE FORESTS: *The deciduous forests of the temperate zones have essentially the same physical structure as the tropical rain forests: they too are layered. The ground flora must make do with the amount of light that filters through the layers of trees and shrubs above. But there is a big difference: the trees of the temperate zones bear leaves for only half of the year, and this is also true of many of the shrubs. Consequently, early spring provides the ground flora an opportunity to photosynthesize actively, if the plants can break their dormancy long enough before the trees. Winter in the temperate zones is a quiescent or dormant time for all plants except the evergreens, which continue to photosynthesize slowly at the lower temperatures. Ever-*

greens might include red cedar, certain pines, mountain laurel, holly, and a few ground-level plants like pipsissewa, Chimaphila maculata—though the ground flora may have their activities curtailed by snow.

Consequently, a deciduous wood in spring is a wonderful place to see wild flowers. Not only have the leaves developed early because of food stored the previous year in underground storage organs, but the flowers too have opened, taking advantage of the good light to advertise their wares to hungry insects. Trees whose flowers are inconspicuous and wind-pollinated, such as oak, ash, and hickory, may also be in bloom, but their leaf buds are still tightly closed, so that adequate light reaches the forest floor. By the time the tree canopy expands, the dogtooth violet, Erythronium americanum, for example, has flowered and fruited and its leaves are turning yellow after several weeks of productive photosynthesis. Evolution has favored those woodland herbs that could start growth as early as possible in the spring. They were the species that could make the most food for the next year, while setting the most seed (a skunk cabbage in full flower on February 10, 1969, was found by the author just north of New York City). They represent a wonderful adaptation to life in a community of taller plants in a cold climate. By contrast, the ground flora of a tropical forest exists in low light, but the high temperature and constant moisture favor active photosynthesis the year round.

Using a wild flower book (see Bibliography), you can readily identify the ground flora—if it is in flower. If not, you may find it rather difficult. All this may give the collector of names—the serious botanist—sufficient material to feel the day has not been wasted.

THE GREENHOUSE AREA

A stop here is worthwhile. The flamboyance and exuberance of the floral display provide a counterpoint to the muted beauty of the woods (unless it is the azalea season). The greenhouse is designed for those who want to see big, beautiful flowers tastefully arranged in a confined area. In 1980 its director received the Royal Horticultural Society's award for distinguished work in the field of horticulture. Having viewed a recent Easter display, I find this hardly surprising. A medley of hydrangeas, cinerarias, foxgloves, antirrhinums, calceolarias, daisies, and forget-me-nots

was capped by a *tour de force*—a triumphal arch of salmon-pink ivy geraniums, *Pelargonium peltatum* 'King of Balcomb', rising from a bed of geraniums and hydrangeas. For flower-hungry people, this is a mecca, a celebration of things floral. Holidays are the best and the worst of times to come—best because of the wonderful shows, worst because of the crowds. If you must come at holiday time, be there when the doors open. It's worth it, even if you get watered with the plants. Before you leave this area, don't forget the formal gardens outside—plants bedded out in the best tradition.

Callaway as a resort is not inexpensive.* This may not have been the founder's intention, but the costs at the inn, the cottages, and the restaurant are high for this section of Georgia. One can avoid them by staying in adjacent communities, a strategy also to be recommended at peak holiday times, when congestion in the inn and the restaurants can be frustrating. The gardens themselves are so large that huge crowds can be comfortably accommodated.

For the gardener and nature lover, spring and fall are probably the best times for a visit. Springtime has been described, but fall in woodland country cannot fail to be enchanting. The leaf colors, the late-blooming flowers, the cooler temperature (making hiking again pleasurable), can all rival spring's attractions. But for families seeking active recreation and entertainment,

* In summer the rates do include the recreational program.

*Easter show in
greenhouse*

summer is best. Even if the woods are not as attractive, the cultivated gardens, especially Mr. Cason's Vegetable Garden, are in
top form. May, however, is the recommended month. Spring
bloom is everywhere, but the northern visitors have gone, allowing Callaway Gardens to return to the tranquillity its founder
envisaged.

MAGNOLIA PLANTATION
AND GARDENS

Charleston, South Carolina

UNIQUE FEATURES	• In spring, a glorious display of Indica azaleas and camellias in a superlative water-garden setting. • A plantation garden in continuous cultivation for over three hundred years, held by one family despite revolution, war, and an earthquake (1886).

HISTORY: From 1676 to the Civil War, Magnolia-on-the-Ashley was a rice plantation. Like all such plantations, it had a garden for the family's enjoyment, which still exists today in somewhat altered form. Until 1836, when the Reverend John Grimke-Drayton inherited the estate, the garden was formal, following the French manner. But soon after, it was redesigned along naturalistic lines, using some of the newly discovered plants from the Orient. The Civil War marked the end of the plantation's rice cultivation, as it did for so many southern plantations, their markets having disappeared and their labor force—slaves—being depleted. Facing ruin, the Drayton family fortune was salvaged by the discovery of rich phosphate deposits on the property.

Slowly, Dr. Drayton was able to restore the garden to its pre-war state. In the late 1860s, by popular demand, "Dr. Drayton's Garden" was opened to the public every spring, visitors making the trip by paddle steamer up the river from Charleston. By 1900 Baedecker's guide was recommending Magnolia Gardens, along with Niagara and the Grand Canyon, as one of the three major attractions in America.

No longer just a spring garden, Magnolia Gardens is currently owned and managed by a great-great-grandson of Dr. Drayton as a nonprofit organization. All profits are reinvested in the gardens. Today it encompasses five hundred acres, the famous gardens and planted lawns occupying fifty of these; the remaining acreage is a wildlife refuge with lakes for canoeing and trails for hiking and bicycling. Other attractions are mini-horses and a petting zoo.

- *Admission:* Entrance fee (increases during peak spring season, usually March 15–April 15). Tour of plantation house extra.
- *Hours:* Open all year, 8:00 A.M.–6:00 P.M. daily.
- *Tours:* Frequent guided tours of plantation house.
- *Plants:* Most are labeled.
- *Physically handicapped:* Paths accessible to wheelchairs. House not accessible.
- *Address:* Magnolia Plantation and Gardens, Route 4, Charleston, S.C. 29407. Tel. (803) 571-1266.
- *Location and directions:* 10 miles south of Charleston on South Carolina 61; 1 hour from Interstate 95. From Interstate 95 (going south) take Interstate 26 south to U.S. 78. In Summerville take South Carolina 165 to junction with South Carolina 61. Drive south on 61. Gardens are on left, 4 miles south of Middleton Place. From Interstate 95 (going north) take U.S. Alternate 17 to junction with South Carolina 61, then proceed as above.
- *Parking:* Free, outside gardens.
- *Shops:* Gift shop, retail nursery.
- *Restaurants:* Snack Shop; Plantation Kitchen Restaurant (spring only).
- *Picnicking:* Outside the gardens, in wildlife refuge and lawn areas.

Using the map, follow the walking tour. The formality of that garden of long ago has completely disappeared. Enchantment intensifies as you explore the prescribed path, not knowing what to expect amidst this drapery of vegetation. Harold Nicolson,* who cared little for the formal in garden design, once said that gardens need surprises. Magnolia Gardens is full of them: the sudden glimpse of a reflected bridge in a velvet-dark pool; a long vista framing the tranquil river; an unobtrusive statue appearing in the shrubbery.

This is a water garden. Its lakes, darkened by the tannic acid exuded from the roots of the native bald cypress, *Taxodium*

---

* Harold Nicolson and his wife, Victoria Sackville-West, created the now famous gardens at Sissinghurst Castle in Kent, England.

*The velvet waters—
cypress "knees" in
foreground*

distichum, are eerie mirrors for trees and sky. The Japanese emphasize the importance of watery reflections in contributing to
a garden's changing beauty, a viewpoint that is admirably demonstrated at Magnolia. Above the dark waters tall live oaks, *Quercus
virginiana,* festooned with gray Spanish moss, *Tillandsia usneoides,*
form a backdrop for the clouds of floral color beneath. And if
the azaleas are blooming, a paradise virtually unfolds with every
step.

Graceful bridges span the somber waters. Straight avenues
with distant views of the Ashley River invite exploration. At the
river's edge one experiences the nineteenth-century visitor's first

The Ashley River

glimpse of Magnolia Plantation—when roads were poor, the river was the lifeline. Other paths curve away from the river, around the lakes, and through the dense shrubbery, which parts every so often to reveal a small lawn graced by a pedestaled statue. No statuary adorned Dr. Drayton's garden, but the present owner feels that, discreetly used, it heightens interest.

The Reverend John Grimke-Drayton planned an informal naturalistic garden and what we see here is basically his conception. Having traveled extensively as a young man, he realized that the natural vegetation and topography of the Low Country of South Carolina were in themselves spectacular. He could envision the oaks, the Spanish moss, the cypresses, and the reflecting pools setting off the vibrant colors of the new plants from the Orient, namely, the Indica azaleas and the Japanese camellias. Like many famous English gardens, Magnolia has fostered the natural vegetation, using exotics for color and embellishment—a style that has persisted into this century. The Savill Gardens in Great Windsor Park is an English example, while Winterthur is one nearer home (see pp. 155–63).

Magnolia as it is today has evolved from the garden created by Dr. Drayton. Gone is the great avenue of magnolias that gave the garden its name, though many handsome specimens are dotted around the grounds.

THE SOUTHERN MAGNOLIA: *Native to the southern states,* Magnolia grandiflora *is one of the most prized of ornamentals. When it was introduced into Europe in 1721, people came from far and wide to see it. Its attractions are glossy evergreen foliage and large, creamy-white summer blooms followed by autumnal "cones" of red seeds. Horticulturally, it is so different from the deciduous oriental magnolias grown in the North that it appears a totally unrelated species. The orientals in their leafless early-spring state go into a great spasm of bloom, remaining nondescript for the rest of the year.*

Incidentally, Pierre Magnol, for whom these plants were named, was a seventeenth-century professor of botany at Montpellier who first had the idea of classifying plants into families. For this valuable contribution to taxonomy, Linnaeus honored him in 1753 by creating a genus in his name.

Spanish moss on live oak tree

Subsequent owners of Magnolia Gardens have searched extensively for more exotics to make this a year-round garden, not just a glory of camellias and azaleas in the spring. This might at first thought seem easy, but the climate of Charleston is fickle—freezes down to 14 degrees Fahrenheit have been known. Still, visitors can be sure of experiencing horticultural interest and beauty at all times of the year.

Prominent in the fall are the sasanqua camellias, *Camellia sasanqua*, from Japan, blooming from September through January, while the cool nights cause the roses to regain their spring floriferousness. The winter landscape is accentuated by the red-berried *Nandina domestica*, various hollies, *Ilex* spp., and the firethorn, *Pyracantha* sp., accompanied by early-flowering bulbs like *Crocus* spp. and the paper-white narcissus, *Narcissus papyraceus*.

Starting in early October and extending through mid-April, the sculptured blossoms of hundreds of *Camellia japonica* cultivars appear. Some are the original shrubs—really trees—imported in 1840; others are seedlings and cultivars selected from them and named at Magnolia. There is even a horticultural maze constructed with camellias.

CAMELLIAS: *Linnaeus named camellias for the Jesuit pharmacist and botanist Georg J. Kamel (1661–1706). A thousand years before their discovery by Europeans, these flowers were revered and cultivated by the Chinese. While medieval gardeners in Europe were preoccupied with raising useful plants such as herbs, the mandarins were busy producing new varieties of garden flowers, among them camellias.*

Native to the Orient, camellias belong to the tea family, Theaceae. The tea plant itself, Camellia sinensis, *believed to have originated in China and possibly also in Burma, has the most insignificant flowers in the entire genus. What it lacks in beauty, it has made up for in the solace and consolation it has provided to generations of tea drinkers. What would have become of the British or the Japanese without their tea-drinking rituals? (The tea plant can be seen at Magnolia in the small herb garden in front of the plantation house.)*

No members of this family occur naturally in Europe. The southern United States, however, has three native genera: Stewartia, Gordonia, *and* Franklinia *(for more on* Franklinia, *see pp. 285–6). The family has the same discontinuous distribution as the magnolia family, Magnoliaceae, a fact some authorities explain in terms of the different physical geography of the three continents of Asia, Europe, and North America (see pp. 284–5).*

Camellia japonica, *native to Korea and Japan, is the commonest species developed in China, Japan, Europe, and North America; hundreds of cultivars exist.* C. sasanqua, *previously mentioned, and* C. reticulata, *which is spring-blooming and less hardy, also have many cultivars. All three have been crossed with each other and with less common species to yield many hybrids, whose names range from the romantic 'Black Lace' to the down-to-earth 'Spanked Baby'—a bright pink.*

Camellias are prized not only for their elegant, "perfect" flowers but for their dark, glossy evergreen foliage. The petals are white, crimson, or various shades of pink, striped or unstriped, single or double. Blossoms that shed their petals are usually valued over those that die an unsightly death on the bush. All garden camellias are surprisingly scentless. But this may change; a goal of the current camellia-breeding program at Glenn Dale, Maryland, is fragrance—a not impossible dream, since some obscure and "mousy" members of the genus are fragrant. (Some may recall that Alexandre Dumas's "Dame aux Camélias," who disliked scented flowers, always carried a bouquet of camellias.)

In 1739 Lord Petre (of Petrea volubilis *fame) introduced the common camellia into England. In 1798 it reached the green-*

houses of America. In 1840 it was introduced out-of-doors for the first time, in South Carolina gardens.

North of Philadelphia, camellias are not hardy out-of-doors. In the latitudes of New York and New England, they belong in cool greenhouses.

Masses of flowering fruit trees, cherry, apple, and pear—belonging to the genera *Prunus, Malus,* and *Pyrus* respectively—together with jonquils and violets, punctuate the spring. In late March the dwarf Kurume azaleas bloom, followed closely by the towering "Indian"* or Indica azaleas. So floriferous are the Indicas in their prime that not a single leaf is visible, even though the bushes are evergreen. By mid-April the display that has made Magnolia famous for over a century reaches its peak. (In Kew Gardens in England, a sign beside the Indica azaleas reads: "Azaleas in their highest glory are to be found in Magnolia Gardens, near Charleston, South Carolina, U.S.A.") One of the most gorgeous and most numerous of the cultivars is 'George Lindley Taber,' its white petals suffused with violet, each flower having a magenta blotch.

INDICA AZALEAS: *The southern "Indian" azaleas were originally bred in Belgium as house plants. The Reverend John Grimke-Drayton was the first to introduce them to the United States (1840). Their hardiness demonstrated out-of-doors in Charleston,* *they quickly spread to gardens all over the Southeast. Derived most probably from interbreeding two Japanese species,* Rhododendron mucronatum *and* Rh. indicum, *and one Chinese,* Rh. simsii, *they exhibit a wide range of color with large single or double blooms.*

At Magnolia the Indicas are followed by the Satsuki hybrids (see p. 146), which appear in May and June along with other late-blooming varieties of the Glenn Dale, Exbury, and Pericat series.

In early April, as the azalea bloom reaches a crescendo, climbers like the mauve wisteria, *Wisteria sinensis,* the yellow banksia rose, *Rosa banksiae,* and the white Cherokee rose, *R. laevigata*—all Chinese in origin—appear in the branches of the oaks and

---

* In the nineteenth century, "Indian" was synonymous with "Asiatic."

End of a vista

cypresses, or adorn the pergolas. The graceful indigenous atamasco lily, *Zephyranthes atamasco*, dots the ground, its white
petals touched with crimson. The bulbs of this lily were eaten by
the Indians, who also gave it its name—*atamasco* means "turning
red."

Magnolia has some huge specimen trees and shrubs. Among
them is what is reputed to be the world's largest tea olive,
Osmanthus fragrans, a shrub in the olive family with fragrant
white flowers used in China to perfume tea. The pervasive odor
of the tea olives is very evident at azalea time. Another species
that has reached a record size here is the broadleaf Japanese holly,
Ilex latifolia, looking somewhat like a cherry laurel with its large,
unprickly leaves.

Summer, beginning in May, is not the riot of bloom of March
and April. But many semitropical evergreens, such as oleanders
(*Nerium oleander*), pomegranate (*Punica granatum*), and *Bougainvillea* sp., now take over. Simultaneously, a score of rose beds
come to life, blooming until December. Slightly later come the
hydrangea varieties and the conspicuous crepe myrtle, *Lagerstroemia indica*. This Chinese tree, introduced into America in
1747, is valued throughout the South for its colorful flowers—
red, pink, mauve, or white—and long period of bloom. Its petals
are crinkly like crepe paper: hence its name. Green-and-white
caladiums, *Caladium bicolor* (a member of the aroid family),
planted profusely along the paths and clustered at the bases of
statues, infuse a cool note into the tropical heat of July and

August. And in the vicinity of Charleston it would be remiss not to mention the delightfully perfumed gardenia, *Gardenia jasminoides*, blooming here in summer and fall. Linnaeus named it after one of Charleston's eminent scholars of the mid-eighteenth century, Dr. Alexander Garden, a botanist and physician (in times past these two professions often went hand in hand).

Magnolia's nursery of over one hundred acres, besides raising woody plants, prepares great numbers of bedding-out annuals, which augment the summer-blooming perennials.

Obviously, the best time to visit these gardens is in spring. But what really makes Magnolia Plantation worth a visit at any season is not just its enduring natural beauty but the historic atmosphere it evokes. The authentic plantation house, the former slave street, the family tomb by the river, the monument to the Low Country explorer of the seventeenth century, all combine to transport the imagination back to epoch-making times in the life of this great republic.

Note: Discerning gardeners who have also visited Callaway Gardens (pp. 42–51) may wonder why the natural vegetation of the two gardens is so different, considering that both lie in the same latitude. Callaway, being inland and a thousand feet higher, has colder winters and drier air; therefore its natural vegetation is more like that of inland North Carolina (the Piedmont, see pp. 95, 99). Charleston's climate is moderated by its low elevation and proximity to the sea. It can support a semitropical vegetation, including epiphytes like Spanish moss, in spite of occasional severe winters.

MIDDLETON PLACE

Charleston, South Carolina

UNIQUE FEATURES	· The earliest landscaped garden constructed in America (1755). · A demonstration of the self-sufficiency of a huge rice plantation of the ante-bellum period.

HISTORY: In 1741 Henry Middleton acquired, through marriage, the plantation on the Ashley River subsequently known as Middleton Place. By 1755 he had constructed the famous gardens and built two flanking wings to the original house. An important landowner supporting some eight hundred slaves, he became a delegate to the First Continental Congress and later its president. This position passed to his son Arthur, who, after fighting in the Revolutionary War, signed the Declaration of Independence.

The family survived the Revolution, but the Civil War caused a decline in its fortunes. Arthur's grandson Williams Middleton, having signed the Ordinance of Secession, actively supported the Confederate cause. When Union troops reached Charleston, Middleton Place was an obvious target. The main house and the north wing were gutted; only the south wing was reclaimable. The earthquake of 1886 leveled the gutted buildings, though it left the repaired south wing unharmed.

The Middleton family continued to own the estate but lived in greatly reduced circumstances; the gardens were neglected and the plantation more or less abandoned. As at Magnolia, rice cultivation was no longer possible; in five years the market had disappeared and most of the slaves had left.

In 1916 a direct descendant of Henry Middleton, J. J. Pringle Smith, and his wife began to restore the south wing to something resembling its former elegance. At the same time they reclaimed the gardens from the wild and opened them to the public. Some of its former grandeur returned to Middleton Place.

In 1970 the Smiths' grandson, Charles H. P. Duell, opened the newly reconstructed Stableyards, an outdoor working museum, to the public. And in 1975 the house, with furnishings, silver, and paintings collected from family members all over the United States and in England, was opened as a museum. Today Middleton Place is administered by the Middleton Place Foundation, a non-profit organization.

- *Admission:* Entrance fee, which includes self-guided tour. Extra fee for plantation house tour.
- *Hours:* Open all year. Gardens and Stableyards: daily 9:00 A.M.–5:00 P.M. House: Tuesday to Sunday 10:00 A.M.–4:30 P.M.
- *Tours:* Guided tours of plantation house (restored wing only). Ask for program of special events.
- *Plants:* Not labeled, for the most part.
- *Physically handicapped:* Wheelchairs available. An alternate garden route can be suggested if inquiries are made at gate. House not accessible to wheelchairs.
- *Address:* Middleton Place, Route 4, Charleston, S.C. 29407. Tel. (803) 556-6020.
- *Location and directions:* 14 miles northwest of Charleston on South Carolina 61; 20 minutes from Interstate 26; 1 hour from Interstate 95.
- *Parking:* Free, inside gates.
- *Gift shop.*
- *Restaurant:* Open Tuesday to Sunday 12:00 noon–3:00 P.M., February through November. Closed Mondays.
- *No picnicking.*

If Magnolia Gardens has a beauty that is indigenous to the Low Country, Middleton Place has the studied splendor of an eighteenth-century garden. Whereas Magnolia has soft, feminine charm, Middleton has masculine elegance. Each is beautiful; only four miles apart, they provide fascinating contrasts, and one should not fail to see both. Gardens are sometimes created to impress, and Middleton is in this category. Unlike the Reverend Dr. Drayton, who was told by his physician to "dig in his garden," Henry Middleton was a servant of the state and, in typical eighteenth-century style, created a garden befitting his secular place in society. This in no way disparages Middleton and Middleton Place, any more than it does Versailles, Vaux-le-Vicomte,

Hampton Court, and a score of other gardens, all designed to impress their contemporaries.

Again, this is a water garden. Its grace and beauty stem from the juxtaposition of the reflecting pool, the lakes, the flooded rice fields, and the distant river. Like those of all rice plantations, Middleton's front door faced the river, where guests arrived by boat. The design of the gardens was adapted accordingly. The central axis is the walkway leading from the river to the front door of the original house, now in ruins. Partway, the axis traverses a grassy bridge, which forms the body of a butterfly, the flanking lakes its outstretched wings. From the butterfly lakes a terraced greensward leads up to the house. The essence of the "grand design" popularized by André Le Nôtre, the seventeenth-century French landscape architect, was that the central axis, as viewed from the house, should lead the eye into infinity. Here at Middleton this is indeed true: the vista ends in the misty woods on the far bank of the Ashley River. Le Nôtre would also have approved the absence of flowers in this landscaped area. (For more on Le Nôtre and his "grand design," see pp. 150–1.)

The formal gardens northwest of the house would have been part of a garden of this type: the rectangular Reflection Pool with its regal swans; the octagonal sunken garden for lawn bowls; the Sundial Garden, strictly geometric; the so-called secret garden for family games and secluded conversation; and the camellia *allées*, now tunnels rather than *allées*, their paths strewn with fallen petals in late spring. As far as possible, the plants growing

The Wood Nymph

here are those of the eighteenth century—boxwood (*Buxus sempervirens*), crepe myrtle (*Lagerstroemia indica*), *Camellia japonica*, and species roses.

These period gardens are not remarkable as gardens go. What is remarkable is the scale of Henry Middleton's entire enterprise. At a time when other important gardens in the colonies were small and executed compactly in the seventeenth-century Dutch-English manner, as at the Governor's Palace in Williamsburg (pp. 108–13) and Tryon Palace in New Bern (pp. 84–92), the Le Nôtrean geometric landscape taking shape on the banks of the Ashley River was positively avant-garde. After all, a mere forty-one years had elapsed since Le Nôtre's death. The colonies tended, for obvious reasons, to lag far behind European fashions, but this particular instance was an exception. The geometric precision of Henry Middleton's plan is illustrated in the self-guided tour brochure. That it took one hundred slaves ten years to complete this ambitious project is hardly surprising—imagine the tons of earth that had to be moved to make the rippled terraces above the butterfly lakes. (Today these terraces often serve as seating for theatrical events.)

The architecture of the house was in keeping with the garden. The newly reconstructed south wing is clearly European in style, even if the foundation planting of palms and yuccas is not. It must have been a charming contrast to the Greek Revival plantation houses so popular in ante-bellum days (see Orton Planta-

The great Middleton Oak

The Reflection Pool

tion, pp. 78–83). To acquaint you with the family history and the mood of the period, a tour of the house is a must.

In spring and fall visit the New Camellia Garden, admiring the wood-nymph statue on your return. One would expect a Le Nôtrean garden to have more statuary, but this is the only piece that survived the Civil War. Prior to the arrival of the Union troops Williams Middleton buried her in the garden. (She is now Middleton's logo.)

Seek out the famous Middleton Oak on the bank of the flooded rice fields. It is believed to be the oldest live oak (*Quercus virginiana*) in the United States. Unfortunately, because it is

Rice Pond with Rice Mill

hollow, the methods used to determine the annual ring count of living trees will not work, so that its age is a matter of guesswork. (Some claim it to be one thousand years.) Like all the oaks of the Low Country, it is draped in Spanish moss. A new fact learned at Middleton: the epiphytic "moss" can be hazardous to trees during ice storms, infrequent though they are in the Low Country. Weighed down by the ice-encased moss, branches can break. Trees as old as this one are at greatest risk. Prevention involves periodically denuding the tree of its "widow's weeds."

Two other historic trees are the huge *Camellia japonica*, which still flower every year, located above the terraces and flanking the central axis. Legend has it that they are the survivors of several cuttings given to the Middletons by André Michaux, a French botanist who visited the colonies in the late eighteenth century in search of new plants. The American Camellia Society, however, very much doubts this.

During this century naturalistic additions were made to Middleton. The Rice Pond to the south with its banks of Indica azaleas, planted in the 1930s, is reminiscent of nearby Magnolia, though the black and white swans and the occasional strutting peacock inject a little formality into the scene. To the north the environs of the Azalea Pool and the Cypress Lake are also landscaped in a naturalistic style.

Middleton Plantation was a self-supporting community of many hundreds of people, based on the revenue derived from rice and, to a lesser degree, from cotton and indigo. To learn a little more about the operation of such a community, visit the Old Rice Mill and the Stableyards behind the house, which in the old days must have been a hive of activity. Climatic conditions would have permitted two crops of rice per year in the Low Country, but only one was attempted owing to the heavy infestation of the swamps in summer with the malaria-carrying mosquito—difficult to believe in now.

Like Magnolia Gardens, Middleton Place has bloom nearly all the year, but for these water gardens the real floral drama unfolds in spring. History buffs will of course enjoy the plantation at any time, as will students of garden design and architecture. No season can downplay Middleton's splendid landscape.

Note: For more information on the Middleton plants—camellias, azaleas, magnolias, tea olives, and crepe myrtles—see the section on Magnolia Plantation and Gardens (pp. 52–60). The bald cypress, *Taxodium distichum*, though not mentioned above, is important in Middleton's naturalistic sections. (For more on the bald cypress, see pp. 71–2.)

CYPRESS GARDENS

❧

Oakley, South Carolina

UNIQUE FEATURE	• A water garden that can be thoroughly explored by boat.

HISTORY: Cypress Gardens was originally part of a huge rice plantation on the Cooper River called Dean Hall. During the eighteenth century the plantation reached the height of its prosperity, a thriving community of more than five hundred persons. It was named after a Scotsman, Sir John Nesbitt Dean, the original owner. The lake, which today constitutes most of this garden of 250 acres, was a natural reservoir used to flood the rice fields when the river was brackish (salt being lethal to the crop). With the Civil War rice cultivation ceased and the land reverted to its natural state of watery cypress forest. Before the settlement of the plantation, during the Revolutionary War, and after the Civil War, the region was a perfect hideout for fugitives and guerrilla fighters.

In 1927 the idea that this native forest could be converted into a unique kind of garden occurred to B. R. Kittridge, then owner of Dean Hall. He set out to make the lake navigable to small boats and to plant the banks with masses of ornamentals and bulbs. Two hundred men working for several years turned the somber, watery forest into a charming and highly unusual garden. In 1963 his son, B. R. Kittridge, Jr., donated Cypress Gardens to the city of Charleston. It is now owned and operated by the Department of Leisure Services in Charleston.

• *Admission:* Entrance fee, which includes walking map. Boat ride, including operator, is extra.
• *Hours:* Open February 15 through April 30, 8:00 A.M. till dusk daily.

68

- *Plants:* Not labeled.
- *Physically handicapped:* Paths not suitable for wheelchairs, but gardens accessible by boat if persons are able to embark and disembark.
- *Address:* For information, write to Department of Leisure Services, Hampton Park, Charleston, S.C. 29403.
- *Location and directions:* In Oakley, South Carolina, 24 miles north of Charleston. From Charleston: take Interstate 26 north; exit at U.S. 52/Moncks Corner. Follow U.S. 52 past Goose Creek. Turn right at Cypress Gardens sign. From Magnolia Gardens and Middleton Place: follow U.S. 61 north; turn right into U.S. 17A and follow to intersection with U.S. 52. Take a right on U.S. 52 and enter gardens on right.
- *Parking:* Free, outside the gardens.
- *No gift shop.* Souvenirs available at kiosk.
- *Snacks:* Available at kiosk.
- *Picnicking permitted.*

Having visited the other Charleston gardens, you may be tempted to omit Cypress because it seems out of the way. Don't. Only a half-hour's drive from Middleton Place, it is an entirely different garden experience. Naturalistic in style, it capitalizes on the myriads of ancient, lichen-encrusted cypresses that emerge from the seemingly never-ending dark lake. Against this backdrop, the camellias, the azaleas, the flowering vines, gleam more vividly, being close enough to the water to be reflected in all their glory.

Watery reflections

In February, color springs from the three hundred cultivars of *Camellia japonica* (see pp. 56–7), from the drifts of daffodils and jonquils, *Narcissus* spp., as well as from the snowy star magnolias, *Magnolia stellata*. In March and April the massed Indica and Kurume azaleas (see pp. 58, 45), the purple pendent wisteria, *Wisteria sinensis*, the white Cherokee rose, *Rosa laevigata*, and the native Carolina jessamine, *Gelsemium sempervirens*, all make their brilliant contributions. The jessamine, often called jasmine because it is a fragrant vine, bears no relationship to the genus *Jasminum*. And to mix up things even further, its generic name comes from the Italian *gelsemino*, meaning "jasmine."

Fragrance has not been overlooked in this garden. From February on, the essential oils of the little *Daphne odora* from the Orient, the tea olive, *Osmanthus fragrans*, and the native jessamine perfume the air. And all around in the hollows wild flowers abound: our little friend the atamasco lily, *Zephyranthes atamasco* (see p. 59), the jack-in-the-pulpit, *Arisaema* sp., as well as the Spanish bluebell, *Endymion hispanicus*. Two climbers that may not be familiar to northern gardeners are common here: the orange cross vine, *Bignonia capreolata* (so called because a transverse section of the stem reveals a cross), and supplejack, *Berchemia scandens*. Like wisteria, these vines have ropelike stems reaching up into the treetops. That this is a habitat favorable to plant growth is demonstrated by an American holly, *Ilex opaca*, easily fifty to sixty feet tall. Occasional stands of bamboo interrupt the azaleas.

If time permits, take the walk as well as the boat ride. From the boat you perceive the over-all effect, but the walk allows closer examination of the plants, especially the wild flowers; also a chance to watch and listen to birds. Many different birds make Cypress their home. The shorter walk, indicated on the map, is made so by a series of Chinese-style bridges, which carry you over to the opposite bank. Its length is such that one assumes the complete walking tour must encompass a fair distance.

During the two-and-a-half months when the garden is open to the public, there is no best time for a visit; all times are good. April is different because the trees are becoming green—the bald cypresses are losing their baldness. Oddly enough, there is little Spanish moss. Perhaps it is cleared away when the garden is closed. Certainly, it would obstruct the boater's view of the cypress groves, the *raison d'être* of the ride.

S WAMP OR BALD CYPRESS: *The swamp cypress,* Taxodium distichum, *so much at home here, is native to the Atlantic and Gulf coasts of the southeastern United States. It is the tallest native tree in the East, attaining heights of 100 to 150 feet. A gymnosperm, it belongs to the same family as the dawn redwood,* Metasequoia glyptostroboides, *with which it has many features in common (see pp. 287–8), the Californian big tree,* Sequoiadendron giganteum, *and the coast redwood,* Sequoia sempervirens. *Like the larch and the dawn redwood, it is unusual among conifers in being deciduous, its foliage turning a ruddy brown in the fall.*

Like its Californian relatives, it can attain a great age; many of the trees here are probably one thousand years old. The bald cypress has a typically fluted or buttressed base. Large roots called "sinkers" penetrate deep into the mud, often sending up into the air conelike appendages called "knees." Many books glibly state that these are breathing devices, supplying air to the living roots in these badly aerated swamps. Anatomical studies of the "knees," however, do not confirm this. A more plausible explanation is that they are just parts of an elaborate buttress-root system, a necessary adaptation of tall trees growing in unstable mud.

Bald cypress do not need swamps. They grow quite happily in regular soil. Healthy specimens can be seen at Longwood (an entire avenue of them), the Brooklyn Botanic Garden, and the Arnold Arboretum. In that kind of habitat they never develop knees, a fact which might, be said to support either theory. It is surprising that, though native to the South, they can survive the hard northern winters. Perhaps their deciduous habit makes this possible. In summer they bear small green cones about one inch in diameter, proving that they are indeed conifers.

Here at Cypress Gardens the bald cypresses grow in a swamp for only part of the year, as the lake is drained in summer to protect the hardwood trees: the oaks, *Quercus* spp., the red maples, *Acer rubrum*, and the sweet gum, *Liquidambar styraciflua*, which would die if subjected to flooding all year round. It is also reported that young cypress seedlings need the extra air that damp, as opposed to water-logged, soil provides.

Compared with Magnolia and Middleton, Cypress has an air of having seen better days. Some of the boats are "unseaworthy," gradually subsiding into the clutches of the dismal swamp. One assumes that the budget for this garden is minute. Gate receipts cannot amount to much, since it is open for so short a period each year. And presumably, little or no endowment came with the Kittridge gift. Its poverty-stricken air in no way detracts from its beauty nor from one's enjoyment of it. Still, it is fervently to be hoped that Cypress does not go the way of so many city-operated parks and gardens. It is unique, and must not be allowed to disappear into oblivion.

Cypress "knees"

BROOKGREEN GARDENS

Murrells Inlet, South Carolina

UNIQUE FEATURE	· An outdoor museum of American sculpture displayed in a garden.

HISTORY: The original plantation, devoted to indigo and rice, dates from the early 1700s. Its most prosperous period as a rice plantation was from the late eighteenth century to the Civil War. Of the original plantation house only the kitchen has survived.

In 1930 Mr. and Mrs. Archer M. Huntington bought the property from a hunting club, along with several adjoining plantations. Besides acquiring a winter home, the Huntingtons had two other purposes in mind: to create a garden to exhibit Mrs. Huntington's sculpture (she was already famous), and to generate a greater appreciation of the fauna and flora of South Carolina.

In 1931 Archer Huntington gave the deeds for the land, plus an endowment to support its development, to Brookgreen Gardens (a nonprofit organization concerned with preservation of southeastern flora and fauna) for the purpose of exhibiting the plants and animals of the region, together with appropriate objects of art. In 1932 the gardens were opened to the public. The construction of U.S. 17 in 1935 assured greater attendance by vacationers. Today the entire complex of garden, museum, wildlife park, and sanctuary constitute a public trust, administered by a board of trustees.

- *Admission:* Entrance fee, which includes map. Extra fee for Sculpture Garden.
- *Hours:* Open all year, 9:30 A.M.–4:45 P.M. daily. Closed Christmas Day.
- *Tours:* Acoustiguide tape tour of Sculpture Garden available from visitors' pavilion.

- *Plants:* Labeled.
- *Physically handicapped:* Wheelchairs and strollers available at visitors' pavilion. Sculpture Garden and Wildlife Sanctuary accessible.
- *Address:* Brookgreen Gardens—a Society for Southeastern Flora and Fauna, Murrell's Inlet, S.C. 29576. Tel. (803) 237-4218.
- *Location and directions:* On west side of U.S. 17, 18 miles south of Myrtle Beach and 18 miles north of Georgetown.
- *Parking:* Free.
- *Gift shop.*
- *No snack bar or restaurant.*
- *Picnicking:* Permitted in picnic area.

Amid the commercialism of U.S. 17 in and around Myrtle Beach, Brookgreen Gardens is a haven of peace and tranquillity. If one is unaware of the garden's history, it seems an eclectic combination—a wildlife refuge and a zoo surrounding a sculpture garden. Judging from the numbers of spring visitors, however, Brookgreen is attractive to all members of the family. Garden lovers and the artistic-minded enjoy the formal Sculpture Garden designed by Anna Hyatt Huntington, while children of all ages are delighted by the otters, the alligators, the deer, and the Cypress Bird Sanctuary. A native-plant walk introduces naturalists to South Carolina flora.

The best way to orient yourself is to go first to the modern visitors' pavilion, which houses the gift shop, a small museum, and rest rooms. Then walk past the Diana pool (the statue is an excellent example of Mrs. Huntington's work) to the entrance of the Sculpture Garden. This garden, whose center marks the site of the old plantation house, is surrounded by a low openwork brick wall, sprayed with cement to mute the original red to a neutral gray. The most impressive natural feature is an avenue of live oaks, *Quercus virginiana*, believed to have been planted as an approach to the house in the eighteenth century. Note the epiphytic Spanish moss, *Tillandsia usneoides*, and the resurrection fern, *Polypodium polypodioides*, lodging on the trees (for more on epiphytes, see pp. 32–3). The ground cover is a thick carpet of English ivy, *Hedera helix*. From here the garden opens up to display various works of art, some executed by Anna Hyatt Huntington (1875–1973), some by other American sculptors,

Avenue of live oaks

the original concept of a "one-man show" having been modified. Today Brookgreen claims to have the best collection of nineteenth- and twentieth-century sculpture of the realistic school, the subjects being animals—not excluding people. In this garden, wind will not whistle through the holes of abstract creations of the Henry Moore/Barbara Hepworth school, nor will one see geometric art in the Noguchi style.

Be sure to see the Museum of Small Sculpture. This is an unroofed structure, beautifully designed for its purpose. Children will enjoy it because the art objects are small enough to be almost pettable.

Even if one does not have an interest in statuary, one must concede that it has played a major role in garden design for thousands of years. To the Romans a garden without statues would have been unthinkable. The Renaissance brought sculpture back into the garden. But in an outdoor museum, there is no compulsion to examine the art forms; the plant lover is free to concentrate on the living components. And one must admit that the pools surrounding many of the figures are in themselves attractive. (They also serve the very practical purpose of deterring vandals.)

Considering the original purpose, it is not surprising to find so many native species in this garden and the surrounding arboretum. The saw palmetto, *Serenoa repens*, embellishes the statuary of one small garden. Hedges are constructed of yaupon, *Ilex vomitoria* (see p. 86), a small-leaved evergreen holly indigenous to the South. Another holly, the native dahoon, *I. cassine*, is used as evergreen shrubbery. Dogwoods, *Cornus florida*, adorn another garden, and native deciduous azaleas—seven species in all (see p. 46)—are dotted about to add touches of color in early spring. In the arboretum an *allée* of southern magnolia, *Magnolia grandiflora* (see p. 55), has been planted in honor of the first director, Frank Tarbox, Jr. A shrub of the heath family, *Elliottia racemosa*, now very rare in the wild, is to be found here, well labeled.

Landscaping the formal areas with purely native plants was found to be too restricting, so in recent years exotic species have

Museum of Small Sculpture

gradually been added. Now exotic evergreen azaleas as well as oriental magnolias provide dazzling displays in spring. Other spring-flowering exotics make the gardens attractive to a wider audience, hungry at this time for the sight of growing and blossoming things rather than for the eternal verities of art. One unusual shrub featured here and previously unknown to the author is the Brazilian pineapple guava, *Feijoa sellowiana*. Its fruits are said to taste like the common guava, *Psidium guajava*.

A drive to the Wildlife Sanctuary is recommended. The walk-in aviary called the Cypress Bird Sanctuary enables visitors to see close at hand the larger Carolina birds, herons, ibises, and anhingas, within their watery cypress-forest habitat. (A board-walk makes wheelchair travel easy.) Beyond the aviary is the Deer Savannah, reminiscent of an English deer park. In both places binoculars may be useful. At this time (1980), some of the animals are still incarcerated in old-fashioned cages. This, however, is a temporary measure. Plans are afoot to create a modern "habitat" type of display.

Brookgreen Gardens are different and original and for that reason should not be missed.

ORTON PLANTATION

❦

Winnabow, North Carolina

UNIQUE FEATURES	• A "scroll" garden—a modified parterre—in a magnificent lagoon setting.
	• A house and garden that complement each other in creating an ante-bellum mood.

HISTORY: A former rice plantation, dating from the time of the early settlers around Cape Fear, Orton has seen violence in the form of hostile Indians, pirates, and the battles of two wars. Eventually, rice cultivation had to be abandoned, but for some time lumber was a valuable asset.

Since 1904 the property has been occupied by three generations of the Sprunt family, who developed the gardens as they appear today. Mrs. James Sprunt (Miss Luola) was the original gardener. It is to her memory that the small chapel near the garden entrance was erected in 1915 by her husband. Her grandson, Kenneth Sprunt, co-owns and manages the gardens today, operating them on a "break-even" basis.

- *Admission:* Entrance fee, which includes guide brochure.
- *Hours:* Open daily all year. Mid-March through Labor Day, 8:00 A.M.–6:00 P.M. Day after Labor Day to mid-March, 8:00 A.M.–5:00 P.M. Closed Christmas Day.
- *Plants:* Labeling incomplete.
- *Physically handicapped:* About 85 percent of garden can be toured by wheelchair.
- *Address:* Orton Plantation Gardens, Winnabow, N.C. 28479. Tel. (919) 371-6851.
- *Location and directions:* About 25–30 minutes' drive from U.S. 17. From Wilmington: take North Carolina 133 south. From the south: take North Carolina 211 east to Southport, then drive north on North Carolina 133. Watch for Orton signs.

- *Parking:* Free, outside the gardens.
- *No gift shop.*
- *No snack bar.*
- *Picnicking:* Permitted in picnic area nearby.

Having visited the other Carolina water gardens, you may feel that you can skip Orton. Resist the temptation. Though it is small, its charm lies in its originality. And you can see it all in one to one-and-a-half hours. On arrival, you feel as if you were at the end of nowhere, such is the effect produced by the landscape of flooded rice fields, river lagoons, and distant woods.

Styles within the garden vary, so that one can distinguish discrete smaller gardens. The most memorable, and to the author the most unusual, is the Scroll Garden. A short peninsula, jutting out into a lagoon and at a lower level than the rest of the garden, has been developed in a formal style. It is not French parterre (see p. 17), but it resembles parterre in that its evergreen hedgelets are planted in the form of curves and arabesques. Unlike those in authentic parterre, the hedgelets do not surround beds; they merely describe dark green scrolls in definite patterns upon a bright green lawn. Every so often the evergreen English yew, *Taxus baccata,* is allowed to grow upward to a short, stocky column, which looks almost as if it should be sculpted into topiary. But it is not—a wise decision: the natural effect is better. Beds of colorful pansies, *Viola* spp., contrast with the two shades

Former rice fields; Spanish moss

The Scroll Garden

of green, and in spring the banks are aglow with evergreen azaleas. Distant palms, *Sabal palmetto*, live oaks, *Quercus virginiana*, and cypresses, *Taxodium distichum*, mark the edge of the lagoon. Here the palmettos are at the limit of their hardiness. But the other palms you see, the jelly palms—*Butia capitata*, natives of Brazil—are fairly hardy at this latitude. They are called jelly palms because a delicious jelly can be made from their fruits.

The Scroll Garden is closed to the public. The brilliant lawn, so important to the over-all effect, would not withstand trampling, and walks have not been incorporated into the design. Like a parterre garden, it is best viewed from above. Viewing platforms have been provided in the form of two small piers that jut out towards the lagoon. Since the Scroll Garden is one flight of steps down from the main garden, it can of course be surveyed from here. Its lateral fences, like those of the piers, are of white wood and executed in the pseudo-Chinese design so typical of the eighteenth century and called chinoiserie. (This can be seen also in benches in Williamsburg and at Gunston Hall.) If you visit Gunston Hall, compare the garden overlooking the Potomac there with this one; there are amazing similarities. The proximity of the water gives Orton the scenic advantage, while the elegance of eighteenth-century garden art is Gunston Hall's asset.

The body of the garden is a combination of formal and naturalistic styles. Avenues of camellias, *Camellia japonica*, are at their best in February, making a visit at that time rewarding for winter-weary travelers. (For more on camellias, see pp. 56–58.) Even in April the cultivar 'Pink Perfection' was freshly flowering. (Orton is sufficiently far north of Charleston to have a later spring, so that in a garden tour, plants missed there can be seen here and vice versa.) Masses of Indica and Kurume azaleas (see pp. 58, 45) make this an azalea garden in April.

Small gardens lie hidden behind shrubbery. Focal points may be beds of flowering annuals—pansies, impatiens, geraniums; a statue surrounded by a lily pool; a decorative urn emerging from a handsome ground cover, usually with a convenient bench nearby. Bridges span the narrow necks of lakes, and here the style is purely naturalistic, even Victorian. The quaint zigzag bridge built to confuse evil spirits, who the Chinese believe walk in straight lines, is a kind of Victorian folly. Decked with wild clematis, *Clematis virginiana*, it is fanciful and unexpected. So is the tree house covered with banksia roses, *Rosa banksiae*.

Some noteworthy plants are to be found here. In spring the many banana shrubs, *Michelia fuscata*—so called because their deep-beige flowers emit a heavy bananalike perfume—claim one's attention. An evergreen, the banana shrub is a member of the magnolia family, Magnoliaceae. In fact, it looks a little like the southern magnolia except that its flowers are not nearly so beautiful and occur on the sides of the branches, not at their tips. Like the banksia rose, the banana shrub was discovered in China by Sir Joseph Banks between 1780 and 1817.

PRIMITIVE FLOWERING PLANTS: *The Magnoliaceae are believed to be the most primitive of flowering plants. In other words, they were one of the first of this kind of plant to appear on earth about 135 million years ago. Genera of Magnoliaceae, such as* Magnolia *and* Liriodendron *(tulip trees), show a larger number of primitive characteristics than do genera of other families. Whether a characteristic is primitive is based on fossil discoveries. If it appears in fossils in the oldest rock formations, it is deemed to be primitive. For example, fossil flowers in the oldest rocks are regular and saucer-shaped and have many separate petals or*

petal-like parts. Michelia, Magnolia, *and* Liriodendron *all have flowers of this type. In these rocks no fossils of irregular flowers such as orchids, snapdragons, or mints occur; consequently, these are all believed to have appeared on earth much later. Cycads (see p. 8) are now thought to be the ancestors of these early flowering plants.*

Other plants of note here are the pearlbush, *Exochorda racemosa*, from China, bearing white flowers in the spring; and the tung-oil tree, *Aleurites fordii*, which used to be widely cultivated in the South because an oil extracted from its fruits was used in paints and varnishes; now it is just an attractive ornamental hardy as far north as Virginia.

The Zigzag Bridge

The mansion

Summer brings bloom to the crepe myrtles, *Lagerstroemia indica*, and the hydrangeas, *Hydrangea* spp. Vacationers at nearby Myrtle Beach may find a visit to Orton (as well as to Brookgreen Gardens at Murrells Inlet, South Carolina) a change of pace from golf and sand. The Scroll Garden is one for all seasons, and so is the view.

It goes without saying that the handsome Greek Revival mansion, so evocative of the ante-bellum period, lends charm to the entire garden. It provides the focal point. Like all water-plantation houses, it faces the river, so that the strolling visitor can admire its classical façade from many angles.

TRYON PALACE
RESTORATION

೭ಎ

New Bern, North Carolina

UNIQUE FEATURES	• A beautiful demonstration of a transitional stage in garden design from the seventeenth-century Dutch-English school to the natural-landscape school of the eighteenth century.
	• Impeccable upkeep in a garden that is both under-staffed and open to the public.

HISTORY: The original Tryon Palace was built in 1767–1770 as the residence of the governor of the royal colony of North Carolina. Until the outbreak of the Revolutionary War it served in this capacity. Subsequently, it was the state capitol until 1794. Accidentally burned down in 1798—except for the west wing— it eventually became the site of small residences.

In 1952–1959 the Tryon Palace Commission reconstructed the palace and its gardens on the original site with funds provided by a bequest from Mrs. James Edwin Latham of Greensboro. The plans of the original architect, John Hawks, were still available for the palace (though not for the grounds). These plans, together with artifacts from a dig at the site and an inventory left by William Tryon, the royal governor, made possible an authentic restoration of the residence. The gardens, however, are the result of speculation based on investigations of comparable estates existing in England at the time.

The Latham bequest was used to restore and furnish three other New Bern houses of historical importance, either already situated beside the palace or moved to its vicinity.

Continuing financial support comes from the endowment left by Mrs. Latham and from the state of North Carolina. The state, for example, pays the salaries of all the employees.

- *Admission:* Entrance fee is all-inclusive, but individual parts of complex can be visited for a lower fee. Tickets must be purchased from reception center, corner of George and Pollack streets.
- *Hours:* Open all year. Tuesday to Saturday 9:30 A.M.–4:00 P.M. Sunday 1:30 P.M.–4:00 P.M. National holiday Mondays 9:30 A.M.–4:00 P.M. Closed all other Mondays, Thanksgiving Day, December 24–26, and January 1.
- *Plants:* Unlabeled for the most part.
- *Physically handicapped:* Wheelchairs available. Part of house and gardens accessible; Latham Garden can be viewed. If advance notice given, side door will be open so pebbled walk can be avoided.
- *Address:* Tryon Palace Restoration Complex, 613 Pollack Street, New Bern, N.C. 28560.
- *Location and directions:* In heart of historic New Bern, one block from U.S. 17, North Carolina 55, and U.S. 70. From Orton Plantation, drive north on U.S. 17 (2 to 2½ hours).
- *Parking:* Free, outside the grounds.
- *Shops:* Gift shop inside reception center. Garden shop sells plants, soft drinks.
- *No snack bar or restaurant.*
- *No picnicking.*

One to two hours should suffice to view the palace gardens and those of the neighboring historic houses. Even if the history of garden design is of no interest to you, the flowers and all the other plants are so well cared for that it is a delight to wander among them. Except in winter, the Maude M. Latham Memorial Garden is always bursting with color. If you do enjoy garden art, this reconstruction will prove fascinating. It is as if the original garden designer had been unable to go all out on the new landscape cult, which was at its height in England of the 1770s. His "wildernesses" and the spacious lawn are gestures in that direction, but the small intimate gardens near the palace are strictly seventeenth century—the *hortus inclusus* concept with its strict formality. It makes for an interesting combination. Perhaps John Hawks, who designed the original gardens, was indeed conservative and did in fact plan a garden like this. We shall never know. It is a delight in contrasts, and especially so if you have already been to Williamsburg. In that reconstruction, where greater documentation of the gardens existed, any gesture towards the natural-landscape school of design is minimal: the canal of the Governor's Palace and the Everard pond.

Starting at the reception center, first tour the palace. Then, using your walking guide and map, enter the Poultry Yard. Pause by the well and look at the vista through the garden to the far-distant statue. This is good garden planning. Now for the Green Garden. What a feat of pruning, shearing, and clipping! Clearly, the gardeners are kept extremely busy. The green miniature hedges of yaupon, *Ilex vomitoria*, are shaped into interlocking scrolls, which, like all Renaissance garden art, can best be appreciated from the upper floor of the palace. Note the symmetry, the four identical triangular beds (alternating with the scrolls), each with its edging of lavender cotton, *Santolina chamaecyparissus*, enclosing a bed of periwinkle, *Vinca* sp. Dead center is a statue, "Boy with Grapes." At the four corners are topiary shrubs of cherry laurel, *Prunus laurocerasus*, and a neatly sculptured hedge forms the walls. Altogether charming—an extreme example of the formal garden, where no plant is allowed to grow in its own sweet way. Living things are treated and molded like inanimate materials. But this was the fashion for a couple of hundred years during the gardeners' (or rather their patrons') love affair with *parterre de broderie*.

YAUPON: *Native to the southeastern United States, yaupon,* Ilex vomitoria, *is a good substitute for the European box,* Buxus sempervirens. *Although it can grow to a height of twenty-five feet, it can stand being clipped back to one to two feet. The early colonists observed the Indians using this holly to make a black ceremonial drink. Copying them, the colonists dried the leaves to make a milder brew reminiscent of China tea. The scientific name suggests dire results from ingesting this plant, but vomiting occurs only after prolonged consumption of cassine tea, as the drink was often called. In South America another holly,* I. paraguensis, *is used to make the popular tea called* maté. *Hollies, some of them containing caffeine, are used in other parts of the world for tea making. The ilexes, however, are quite unrelated to the real tea or coffee plants.*

The Maude M. Latham
Memorial Garden

The Maude M. Latham Memorial Garden is dedicated to the philanthropist who made the entire restoration possible. The white Greek pavilion on a dais a little above the garden protects the memorial tablet. Against the opposite wall and facing the pavilion are Italian statues representing the four seasons. The foreground for these is a row of small box bushes underplanted with blue creeping phlox, *Phlox divaricata*. The parterres, extremely elaborate, seem to swirl around the central hexagonal fountain pool. Each is edged in meticulously clipped yaupon. Small round topiary bushes of cherry laurel grow out of diamond-shaped beds edged with white candytuft, *Iberis sempervirens*, and brick. Paths of brick enable one to walk between the parterres. As in the Green Garden, scrolls of pure yaupon form part of the design. Flowers growing in the parterres are chosen for their brilliant colors: tulips and pansies in spring, annuals in summer, and chrysanthemums in fall. This garden was meant to be a showstopper, and it is. But it is unfortunate—especially for a photographer—that there is no viewing platform; one cannot take in the pattern from ground level. Such a garden was meant to be appreciated from above and from afar—a two-story gazebo at one corner might have helped. The garden is walled, the two gates carefully placed to allow vistas to catch the eye. This is an amazing *tour de force*. Yet one wonders if any historic garden ever really looked like this. It is the presence of so many big, colorful flowers that seems out of character.

Hawks's Allée is hardly an *allée* but rather a rectangular grassy

Pleached allée of yaupon

lawn surrounded by high walls of American holly, *Ilex opaca*. Five antique Italian statues are focal points—four on the west and one on the south wall, to make the endpoint of the vista from the well in the Poultry Yard. It is fitting that these statues which grace Hawks's Allée should have come from the garden of one of his direct descendants, Mrs. Louise du Pont Crowninshield, a sister of Henry du Pont of Winterthur and a member of the Tryon Palace Commission from 1946 until her death in 1967.

Somehow, after the tremendous visual assault of the Latham Garden, this is a pleasantly restful place. One can see why naturalism in the garden finally triumphed over the excesses of the mathematical planners, pruners, trimmers, and bricklayers.

The pleached *allée* of yaupon just to the east of Hawks's Allée is another relic of a bygone garden age. This one has a framework over which the holly has been trained. From inside this *allée* and looking south, the arch directs the eye towards the ancient pedestaled stone urn against the background of the River Trent.

Following the map, enter the wilderness area, flanking the great horseshoe-shaped lawn. This part of the palace garden is much more like the gardens of the natural-landscape school in England of the 1770s.

When you reach the stone urn near the river, rest on the seat. Turning away from the river, look back through the pleached *allée* to the gardens beyond—another well-planned vista. In the wilderness, bulbs planted in drifts—daffodils and narcissus, *Nar-*

cissus poeticus—form the flora under heavy plantings of shrubs and trees. Here will be found buckeye (*Aesculus* sp.), azaleas (*Rhododendron* cultivars), gold-dust tree (*Aucuba japonica* 'Variegata'), and southern magnolia (*Magnolia grandiflora*).

THE ENGLISH LANDSCAPE CULT: *The natural-landscape style developed on the great English estates in the 1770s was a severe reaction against the small formal gardens of previous centuries. The whole landscape became the garden. Streams might have to be diverted or dammed to make lakes, artificial hills erected, clumps of trees planted, but even so, nothing was allowed to appear contrived or artificial. No straight lines were permitted (note the curved walks within the Tryon wilderness); even lakes were serpentine (the Serpentine lake in Hyde Park in London dates from this time).*

The great master of the natural-landscape school was Lancelot "Capability" Brown (1715–1783). He was so nicknamed because he always avowed that the particular garden in question had "capabilities." Many of his gardens still exist in England, though they now appear different because exotic shrubs and trees, as they were discovered—rhododendrons from the Himalayas, for example—were gradually incorporated. Winston Churchill's birthplace, Blenheim Palace, had the benefit of Brown's advice.

An anecdote concerning Brown reveals the scope and popularity of this landscape cult in the eighteenth century. When asked to redesign an estate in Ireland, Brown responded, "No, I haven't finished England yet!"

Entering the Kellenberger Garden, we return once more to the late seventeenth century—another delightful *hortus inclusus*. Its charm, however, rests in its relative simplicity. If one had to, one could sketch this garden from memory. (The Latham Garden? Impossible!) This is a privy garden, walled on all sides; it can be viewed from the palace windows. A walk in a north-southerly direction bisects the garden, but the east and west halves are not mirror images as they would have been in the Dutch-English formal gardens of the late seventeenth century. On the west side, the focal point of the four beds is an antique font. On the east, a small fountain is at the center of four differently shaped beds. In both halves germander, *Teucrium* sp., a common herb in Elizabethan knot gardens, forms the edging of the parterres—or should they be called parterres? They are very different from those in the Latham Garden—more like modern flower beds. Flowers dominate these beds; neither the edging nor the shape it outlines is important (in *parterres de broderie*, both are of paramount importance).

The east side is perhaps the more effective. The brick wall is almost covered with vines: English ivy, *Hedera helix*, Carolina jessamine, *Gelsemium sempervirens*, and Confederate jasmine, *Trachelospermum jasminoides* (not really hardy here—it had died during the winter). It all makes a beautiful background for the scarlet globes of the tulips. Two bay laurel shrubs, *Laurus nobilis*, are situated on either side of the wrought-iron "window." In the middle of each parterre on the east is a boxwood shrub —not, however, clipped into topiary. Groups of crown-imperials, *Fritillaria imperialis*, are found at the base of the east and west walls. These fascinating spring flowers, native to Persia, were brought to the colonies by the Dutch in the mid-seventeenth century.

BAY LAUREL: *Today this plant provides the bay leaves used in cooking, but in former times it had a more distinguished role. The Greeks regarded it as sacred to Apollo, while the Romans used its leaves to weave crowns for emperors, victorious athletes, and other honored citizens. The terms "baccalaureate" and "poet laureate" and the expression "resting on your laurels" all stem from this ancient custom.* Laurus nobilis, *native to the Mediterranean, reached northern Europe at the time of the Crusades and was grown in medieval gardens.*

Altogether this is a very pleasant place in which to relax. Benches are provided, so one may enjoy in comfort the spectacle of exuberant colors.

An essential part of an eighteenth-century residence was the potager, or kitchen garden, where herbs, vegetables, and all kinds of fruits were raised. The potager here is well stocked; fruit trees are espaliered against the walls for greater protection from the weather and to conserve space (a dying art in today's world). Apart from the flowering apple, pear, and quince, this is not a spring garden. Summer is the time to browse here. A good clump of Virginia tobacco is grown, which in the old days would have

The Palace—river façade

been cured within the palace. Two brick dipping wells of the period are to be seen—in those days watering was strictly a bucket-carrying process.

Leaving the palace, note the *allée* of magnificent Darlington oaks, *Quercus laurifolia*, leading to the front entrance.

Of the three other houses included in the restoration, the Stanly House has the most attractive garden, at least in the spring. Built about 1780, this house was moved to its present location in 1966, and an appropriately formal "town house" garden was planned for it.

Parterre garden of Stanly House

Darlington oaks punctuate the four corners of the house. At the back and on the west side the two oaks have an underplanting of vivid tulips, surrounded by a circular brick walk that forms part of the rear garden. A low boxwood hedge surrounds the lawn. On the southwest and northwest corners are two decorative gazebos (or "necessary houses"?) of late-eighteenth-century design. Between them on the brick wall is a fountain with shell-shaped basins. Peripheral flowering cherry trees, *Prunus serrulata*, and boxwood, with tulip underplantings, complete the picture.

To the south a small gate leads into the parterre garden. The parterres, edged with yaupon, are not elaborate; some merely enclose box used as a ground cover, topiary boxwood bushes, and tree-trained azaleas (*Rhododendron indicum*) as well as yellow pansies, violas, and tulips. Brick walks separate the parterres, all leading to the central well. Both gardens have attractive benches for contemplation.

At the time of our visit a croquet lawn was being installed on the east side of George Street, opposite the Stanly House. Obviously, like everything else in this restoration, it will be true to the period, well executed, and beautifully maintained.

NORTH CAROLINA
BOTANICAL GARDEN

Chapel Hill, North Carolina

UNIQUE
FEATURES
- A botanical garden entirely devoted to the native flora of the region.
- The finest outdoor collection of carnivorous (insect-eating) plants on public display in the eastern United States.

HISTORY: In 1952 the university board of trustees approved the development of a botanical garden at Chapel Hill, setting aside 70 acres for the purpose. A director of the botanical garden was appointed in 1961. In 1968 the Botanical Garden Foundation was incorporated to receive funds and hold lands (now 307 acres) and aid in the development of the garden. The Totten Center, the garden's first permanent building, was opened in 1976. Further developments are proceeding according to a master plan adopted in 1972. Funding is provided by the university, the foundation, and the state.

- *Admission:* Free.
- *Hours:* Open all year, Monday to Friday 8:00 A.M.–5:00 P.M. Saturday, March 1 through October 31, 10:00 A.M.–4:00 P.M. Sunday, March 1 through October 31, 2:00 P.M.–5:00 P.M.
- *Tours:* Free guided walks on weekends. For information, call (919) 967-2246.
- *Cultural events:* Forest Theater in Battle Park.
- *Plants:* Labeled.
- *Physically handicapped:* Not accessible as yet (1980), but Hortitherapy Program already in operation for outreach work with all types of handicapped groups.
- *Address:* North Carolina Botanical Garden, University of North Carolina—Chapel Hill, Totten Center, 457 A, Chapel Hill, N.C. 27514. Tel. (919) 967-2246.

93

- *Location and directions:* 40 miles from Raleigh, 12 miles from Durham, N.C. From Raleigh, take North Carolina 54; in Chapel Hill, take U.S. 15-501 south in direction of Sanford. Turn left into Old Mason Farm Road (½ mile from North Carolina 54 intersection). Parking lot is on right.
- *Parking:* Free.
- *No gift shop.*
- *No snack bar or restaurant.*
- *Picnicking:* Picnic area nearby on university campus.

This is not the usual kind of botanical garden which puts on displays of foreign plants of particular beauty and rarity. Perhaps the ease of air travel has rendered that kind of garden somewhat passé. Be warned: if you wish to see exotic plants and old-fashioned gardens, you will be disappointed.

The North Carolina Botanical Garden (NCBG) is dedicated to the display, conservation, and propagation of the native plants of North Carolina and the southeastern United States. It is a new theme for a botanical garden, but one in tune with the times. We see the wild flora disappearing before our eyes as the bull-dozers penetrate farther and farther into the countryside. A mission to rescue endangered native plants is one of this garden's major projects. Its rescue team, comprising staff and specially trained volunteers, is in constant contact with the Highway Department, the Army Corps of Engineers, and private developers so that it can appraise the land before it is torn up. Transplanting

The Sandhills Collection

such plant material is a job for experts, and the rescue team has had plenty of experience. Identifying native plants and showing ways to propagate them are two of the free services the NCBG extends to the public.

But what does the garden have to offer the one-time visitor who arrives at the Totten Center? Begin by collecting interpretative leaflets available in the center. You may even be in time to join a free tour. Because NCBG's purpose is the preservation of North Carolina flora—in some respects unique—the display gardens feature plants adapted to the three major habitats of the state: the Sandhills region, the Coastal Plain Savannah, and the Mountains.

THE SANDHILLS COLLECTION

The Sandhills are part of the Piedmont, the plateau that begins at the western end of the Coastal Plain. The Piedmont is the heart of industrial North Carolina; Chapel Hill, Durham, and Raleigh are all on the Piedmont. The Sandhills region, located in the Piedmont foothills, is famous for golf and riding resorts like Pinehurst and Southern Pines. The dominant tree here is the longleaf pine, *Pinus palustris*, together with the turkey oak, *Quercus laevis*. The loblolly bay, *Gordonia lasianthus*, an American member of the tea family, and the sweet bay, *Magnolia virginiana*, are two woody natives of the region. Wire grass, *Aristida stricta*, is very common, and prickly pear, *Opuntia compressum*,

The pond (Sandhills)

sand myrtle, *Leiophyllum buxifolium,* and pyxie moss, *Pyxidanthera barbulata,* also found in the New Jersey Pine Barrens, are typical inhabitants. A man-made pond with resident water snake gives local color, while lizards and bluebirds are not uncommon sights nearby.

THE COASTAL PLAIN COLLECTION

The Coastal Plain, often called savannah, is a much more open region. It yields the rare terrestrial orchids—*Habenaria* sp. and *Spiranthes* sp.—as well as those intriguing animal-eaters the carnivorous plants, or CP, as they are known to aficionados. Among CP enthusiasts worldwide, North Carolina is famous as the only habitat of the Venus's-flytrap, *Dionaea muscipula.* Even within this state, its native habitat is restricted to an area of fifty to seventy-five miles around Wilmington.

CARNIVOROUS PLANTS (CP): *The Venus's-flytrap,* Dionaea muscipula, *is unique even among carnivorous plants in that it behaves in a very unplantlike manner. Its trapping movement is as fast as that of any animal. Once an insect touches the hairlike triggers on the upper surface of the leaf, the two lobes spring shut, trapping the unfortunate prey as effectively as a trap does a mouse. Its struggles stimulate secretion of digestive juices, and all its proteins are assimilated in the course of several days. Then the leaf reopens and the indigestible remains are blown or washed away. In greenhouses the leaves often remain green, but in the natural habitat they are scarlet, possibly attracting victims because they resemble flowers. A pencil point will trigger* Dionaea's *trap, but having been fooled the leaf will not stay closed as long as if it had caught an insect.*

Pitcher plants, Sarracenia spp., *are passive trappers of insects. Curious victims looking into the pitchers find themselves sliding inexorably downward into a fluid in which they drown. Digestive enzymes or bacteria extract the proteins, which are then absorbed by the plant's tissues.*

Sundews, Drosera spp., *may not be such obvious CPs. But if you look closely, you will see that their leaves are covered with hairs, each ending in a sticky blob of fluid, or "dew," that glistens in the sun. The leaves may be round, spoon-*

shaped, or elongated depending on the species. Flies, possibly mistaking the fluid for nectar, become hopelessly glued as they struggle to get free. Slowly the hairs move towards the insect, pinning it against the leaf. Days later, digestion accomplished, the hairs resume their former receptive position.

Why do these plants consume insects? All live in swamp habitats where there is a shortage of nitrates in the soil. Plants cannot utilize the nitrogen in the air all around them, but must depend on nitrates or ammonium salts in the soil for nitrogen from which to manufacture proteins for healthy growth. By digesting insects, the CP obtains the necessary nitrogen in the form of amino acids, from which it can synthesize its own proteins.

In its Coastal Plain Savannah the NCBG has produced a miniature version of the Green Swamp of southeastern North Carolina. This is one of its great triumphs. It is probably the finest display of native CP you are likely to see on public display anywhere in the eastern United States. You may have tried to see them at other botanical gardens, only to be rewarded with pathetic sights. CP do need a great deal of expert attention, and this they have in abundance at NCBG. The garden even has a curator of CP, who supervises their propagation and interbreeding and the as yet experimental propagation of the Venus's-flytrap by tissue culture rather than from seed.

Apart from *Dionaea*, you are likely to see sundews, *Drosera* spp., and several species of the pitcher plant, *Sarracenia*: the yellow form, *S. flava*, the red form, *S. rubra*, and others.

The NCBG warns people not to buy carnivorous plants from commercial sellers of wild flowers unless such companies propagate all their own material. Unscrupulous individuals and commercial dealers are decimating the native CP, especially the now rare *Dionaea*, by unlawful collecting.

THE MOUNTAIN COLLECTION

The mountains of North Carolina reach heights of up to six thousand feet. They include the Great Smokies, the Blue Ridge Mountains, and the Black Mountains. This is the region where America's indigenous rhododendrons thrive, the rosebay, *Rhododendron maximum* being perhaps the most typical. It was from this stock that the so-called ironclad garden rhododendrons were bred in England in the nineteenth century, long before the great

Bluebells

Himalayan discoveries. Mountain laurel, *Kalmia latifolia*, another garden ornamental, comes from this region, as does dog-hobble, *Leucothoe racemosa*. As we stroll along this simulated mountain path in spring, we will encounter such wild flowers as the Oconee-bells, *Shortia galacifolia*, originally discovered in 1790 but then "lost" for over a century until they were rediscovered in these mountains; blue and white bluebells, *Mertensia virginica*; the wild ginger, *Asarum hexastylis*, so called because its roots have a gingery flavor; and the spring-beauty, *Claytonia virginica*. Spring and fall are the best times for seeing wild flowers; few are summer bloomers.

Fern fiddleheads

If you are wondering where the Piedmont Collection is, it is all around you. For closer inspection, cross Laurel Hill Road and follow one or more of the trails. These deciduous woods are typical of the Piedmont's native flora. As yet the plants on these trails are not labeled, but if you enjoy hiking in the woods this may not matter. A garden handbook states that "serendipity is falling upon an unexpected reward while looking for something else." You may experience serendipity along the many trails of this huge botanical garden.

A plant-families or phylogenetic garden was started in 1979 by a group of volunteers. A boon to aspiring botanists, and a feature that should be part of all botanical gardens, it is situated to the left of the Totten Building.

Slightly out of character is the herb garden, a project conceived, implemented, and cared for by another group of volunteers. Undoubtedly it is a response to the nation-wide interest in the growing and use of culinary herbs, part of the backlash against the adulterated convenience foods that are so widespread and so aggressively advertised. You will find this garden informative—it is well labeled—and fascinating. North Carolina's climate is conducive to the year-round outdoor culture of most herbs. Supplemental gardens—a fragrance garden, a medicinal garden, a poison garden, a garden of industrial plants, a knot garden—are, to quote our guide, "in the works." (Braille signs will be incorporated where feasible.)

Obviously, the NCBG is not a garden in the same sense as the nearby Sarah P. Duke Gardens. But considering what has happened to our planet in the last century, perhaps gardens of the future will be portions of wild nature cordoned off and protected from the depredations of human beings. Maybe the Nature Conservancy will be to twenty-first-century Americans what Kew Gardens was to nineteenth-century Londoners or the Tuileries to eighteenth-century Parisians—something unusual and exotic. A pessimistic view? Perhaps. But since the NCBG staff are totally committed to native-plant conservation, they would probably not disagree.

SARAH P. DUKE GARDENS

❧

Durham, North Carolina

UNIQUE FEATURES	• A garden associated with a university, yet not a botanical garden, but one designed for the enjoyment of the public.
	• A dramatically terraced garden in the Italianate manner.

HISTORY: This garden comprises sixty acres, forty of improved loblolly pine forest and twenty of formal and informal gardens. The idea for its development was conceived in 1932 by Dr. Frederick Hanes of Duke Hospital, with financial support from Mrs. Sarah P. Duke. When Mrs. Duke died in the mid-1930s, the financing of the garden was undertaken by her daughter, Mrs. Mary Duke Biddle, who named it in honor of her mother. The designer of the formal terraces, completed in 1938, was Ellen Shipman, a New York landscape architect hired by Mrs. Biddle. A master plan was developed in 1959, part of which has been implemented. An aquatic garden is still to be constructed.

Today the garden is enjoyed by Duke University, the hospital personnel, and patients, as well as by the general public. Although it is occasionally used for teaching, its major function is simply to provide pleasure. Continued support comes from the Mary Duke Biddle Foundation, supplemented by major funding from the university.

• *Admission:* Free.
• *Hours:* Open all year, 8:00 A.M.–6:00 P.M. daily.
• *Plants:* Well labeled only in the Blomquist Garden.
• *Physically handicapped:* By using side paths, visitors in wheelchairs can see the Terraces and most of the gardens.
• *Address:* Sarah P. Duke Gardens, Duke University, Durham, N.C. 27706. Tel. (919) 684-5579.

- *Location and directions:* On west campus of Duke University, beside the Medical Center and University Chapel. From Raleigh, drive west on Interstate 40 into Durham, where it ends. Turn left onto Erwin Road, pass 2 stoplights, then turn left on Anderson Street. Main entrance is 3 blocks ahead on right.
- *Parking:* Free, outside the main gate.
- *No gift shop.*
- *No snack bar or restaurant.*
- *No picnicking.*

If your time is limited, proceed directly to the Terraces. In passing, however, note the splendid maintenance work done here by only seven gardeners and some student help.

After the approach avenue, bordered by a double row of little-leaf lindens, *Tilia cordata*, the hexagonal pergola will appear on the left. This is the entrance to the Terraces. Renaissance garden architects exploited the advantages of a terraced hillside, using stone, water, and plants. Ellen Shipman took full advantage of the topography in the Renaissance manner, but modified that style by using floral rather than foliar embellishments. There is no question that in spring (and probably in fall, because of the chrysanthemum display), this place is intoxicating. One looks down to the dark pool over the heads of battalions of tulips, and across to the Rock Garden. Better still is the view from the Rock Garden across to the ascending Terraces with their riot of color. Two central fountains on the staircase that descends from the

View of the Terraces

A "people" garden

pergola, combined with the pool, provide the third ingredient for a successful garden, namely, water. Flowering cherry, *Prunus* sp., and apple, *Malus* sp., soften the effect of the horizontal stonework. In late April the pergola itself is a focal point, a lavender tent of cascading wisteria, *Wisteria sinensis*, flanked by large box bushes, *Buxus sempervirens* 'Suffruticosa.' This is the garden that makes Sarah P. Duke Gardens out of the ordinary. It is high drama in the world of horticulture.

Unfortunately, the budget is tight—as in most gardens—and at the time of viewing neither of the fountains was working. A pity, though the ornamental rocks and the red goldfish in the dark pool distracted one from the inoperative fountains. One has to agree with the Renaissance gardeners: a hillside needs tumbling water in the form of a water staircase or fountain jets to achieve maximum beauty.

Still, there are other gardens. The Grass and Sky Garden sounds intriguing. An open lawn with a central pool, it provides a counterpoint to the Terraces. The encompassing trees lead the eye upward to the sky. Here the people too are informal, sitting on the grass, munching hot dogs, sunbathing, watching children play. The formal Terraces, on the other hand, are strictly for standing and gazing.

In May, visit the Hanes Iris Garden, and from late May and June on, the Rose Garden. (Neither was seen by the author since these flowers were not in bloom in early April.)

At all seasons it is recommended that you visit the fern glade

in the Blomquist Garden. As you pass through the wrought-iron gate from the parking lot, it is on your left. Its peak season is early May, when the fern croziers, or fiddleheads, have just unfolded and most of the wild flowers are blooming. All the native plants here are labeled—as you would expect them to be in a botanist's garden. This area was chosen because it has the finest stand of loblolly pine, *Pinus taeda*, in the gardens. Like the Grass and Sky Garden, it too is informal, essentially a stretch of native woodland that includes the big-leaf snowbell, *Styrax grandifolia*, and the sweet-bay magnolia, *Magnolia virginiana*. It honors the memory of Professor Hugo L. Blomquist, who taught botany at

Duke for forty-two years and was its fern expert. Funds for the development of this garden have been provided by his friends, students, and associates.

Like all southern gardens, Sarah Duke has a special place for azaleas—the Azalea Court, opposite the wisteria pergola.

Two trees grown here should have special mention. One is the huge dawn redwood, *Metasequoia glyptostroboides*, now fifty to sixty feet high, which was grown from the original seed collected by the Arnold Arboretum in China (see pp. 287–8). The other is a new dwarf cultivar of the Chinese plum yew, *Cephalotaxus fortunei*, an uncommon conifer with light green needles and berrylike fruits which, instead of being bright red and poisonous like those of yew, are dark purple and merely inedible.

Admittedly, the author saw the Sarah P. Duke Gardens on a beautiful spring day, but there is no question that this place gives pleasure to all who visit it. People are everywhere—mothers and babies, students pretending to study or blatantly sunbathing, hospital personnel taking a short-cut or a breather. It is a garden for all the people. In the center of the west campus, beside the chapel and the hospital, it could hardly be better placed.

COLONIAL
WILLIAMSBURG

Williamsburg, Virginia

UNIQUE FEATURES	• A living museum of the gardens of the capital of the English colony of Virginia in the eighteenth century.
	• An authentic exhibit of the Dutch school of gardening (with English modifications) of the late seventeenth century—a more correct representation than any existing in either England or Holland today.
	• A botanical garden of the cultivated plants of colonial Virginia.

HISTORY: The restoration of Colonial Williamsburg, capital of the colony of Virginia from 1699–1781, was the lifelong dream of the Reverend William A. R. Goodwin, rector of Bruton Parish Church. In the 1920s he fired the enthusiasm of the late John D. Rockefeller, Jr., who agreed to finance the project. Neither pains nor money was spared to gather the necessary information for the restoration. Libraries, historical societies, and private collections of documents were searched both here and in England. Archaeological studies and digs at the site were made. (Fortunately for the project, Williamsburg had not grown or developed in the intervening years, but had remained a sleepy little town where many of the old houses survived—with modifications.) Not only were the dimensions of the lots, the materials used, and the architecture of the buildings determined, but the layout and design of the gardens were researched. Letters, notes, and floras written by horticulturists, botanists, and plant explorers of the time, as well as business records of the buying and shipping of plants from the mother country, indicated the species of plants grown in those gardens.

Work began in 1926, and by 1932 the Raleigh Tavern was opened to the public, followed by the Governor's Palace in 1934. The project is still incomplete and will be completed as monies become available. Williamsburg is administered by two corporations: Colonial Williamsburg, Inc., a nonprofit educational organization, and its wholly owned subsidiary, Williamsburg Restoration, Inc., a business corporation. Income from endowments supplied by Rockefeller, together with profits of the Williamsburg Restoration, after taxes, are not meeting the costs in this highly inflationary period. Other funds are being sought from government and from philanthropic foundations as well as from private citizens.

- *Admission:* Buy tickets at information center. Ticket includes admission to all places of exhibition (except Governor's Palace); films, lectures, and exhibits; use of historic-area bus service. Fee increases with length of visit: 1, 2, or 3 days. Special rate for half a day.
- *Hours:* Open daily, all year. Information center: 8:30 A.M.–10:00 P.M. Exhibition buildings: 9:00 A.M.–5:00 P.M. Governor's Palace and Wythe House: 9:00 A.M.– 6:00 P.M.
- *Free bus service:* Daily from information center: every 5 minutes, 8:40 A.M.–5:30 P.M.; every 10 minutes, 5:30 P.M.–10:00 P.M.
- *Plants:* Not labeled in historic area, but labeled around public buildings adjacent to it.
- *Physically handicapped:* Many parts of historic area accessible. Write for free brochure, *A Guide for the Handicapped*, to Miss Betty L. Wiggins, Division of Museum Operations, The Colonial Williamsburg Foundation, Williamsburg, Va. 23185 (includes different kinds of handicaps).
- *Location and directions:* 1 hour's drive on Interstate 64 East from its junction with Interstate 95 in Richmond; 45 minutes from Norfolk on Interstate 64 West. Watch for Colonial Williamsburg signs and specifically for information center. For bus transportation, write or call Greyhound. For trains to Williamsburg, write or call Amtrack.
- *Parking:* Free, at information center. No cars permitted in historic area.
- *Shops:* Information center for booklets; Craft Shop; many small stores in historic area; gift shops at Inn, Lodge, Cafeteria, Cascades Restaurant.

- *Restaurants:* At information center: Cafeteria, Cascades Restaurant. Adjacent to historic area: Williamsburg Inn* and Lodge.* In historic area: King's Arm Tavern,* Christina Campbell's Tavern,* Josiah Chowning's Tavern.*
  (* Reservations needed well in advance—several weeks at popular seasons.)
- *Hotels, motels:* Adjacent to historic area: Williamsburg Inn, Williamsburg Lodge. Adjacent to information center: Motor Lodge. For reservations for rooms and restaurants write Reservation Manager, Colonial Williamsburg, P.O. Box B, Williamsburg, Va. 23185. Or call toll free (800) 582-8976 (in Virginia) or (800) 446-8956 (nation-wide).
- *Picnicking:* Permitted near information center; inquire there.

Before you visit the Williamsburg gardens, it will be helpful to know a little about their historical background.

Eighteenth-century Williamsburg was a stronghold of the Dutch-English school of gardening, developed in England during the reign of William III and Mary (1689–1702). Simultaneously, the mother country was abandoning this particular style, which might be described as the swan song of the *hortus inclusus* concept in European gardening, characterized by geometric symmetry within an enclosed area. In England of the period, interest was turning towards the development of the natural landscape: sweeping lawns, clumps of trees, lakes, streams, and hills. Some of these might be artificial but nothing was to be obviously contrived—no hedges, no topiary, no flower beds, and no straight lines.

For several good reasons, the gardens of eighteenth-century Virginia remained true to the Dutch-English tradition. First was the very practical fact that European fashions, whether in clothes, furniture, or garden art, were slow to reach the colonies. (The gardens of Middleton Place in Charleston, constructed in the 1750s, were based on French garden concepts of the late 1600s; see pp. 61–7.) Secondly, the landscaped gardens of contemporary England would not have appealed to the settlers in Virginia. To them the natural landscape conjured up terrifying prospects of wild and unfamiliar animals and, worse still, hostile Indians. A garden to them was nature tamed, trimmed, enclosed within a picket fence or hedge—boxed in, as it were. Thirdly, there was nostalgia; the colonists tended to repeat the kinds of gardens they knew or their parents knew in the mother country.

Their memories harked back to the gardens that flourished under William III, for whom the capital was named.

D UTCH-ENGLISH SCHOOL OF GARDENING: *Coming to the English throne from Holland, William III and Mary, who were horticulturally inclined, refashioned some of the royal gardens, notably Hampton Court, in the Dutch manner. Dutch gardens of the seventeenth century were more cluttered and confined than those of contemporary France. To a greater extent they used hedges and trees, especially those clipped in topiary fashion or grown in tubs. William was topiary-mad. At Hampton Court he had walks and follies made featuring this form of garden art, all of which have long since disappeared, though William's maze persists to this day (for more on topiary, see pp. 263–4). As far as can be ascertained, Williamsburg never attempted the extreme kind of topiary, which involves the clipping of shrubs into animal forms.*

Mary was more interested in flowers; she sent to Virginia for the "exoticks" that had been described to her. No doubt her influence had filtered back to the small gardens of Williamsburg, where flowers, especially in the gardens of the well-to-do, were grown as much for indoor as outdoor decoration.

Later, while Williamsburg was going "box-crazy," Queen Anne, who succeeded William, was having all the box bushes (Buxus sempervirens) *removed from the royal gardens because she could not abide the smell (it has been said to reek somewhat of tomcats). Still, Queen Anne did not have to dry her own laundry; the housewives and servants of Williamsburg did. Under the hot Virginia sun, the spreading box bushes and hedges were ideal for the purpose.*

It is curious that this small Virginia town has the best examples of the kind of Dutch-English gardens so common all over England in the latter part of the seventeenth century and into the eighteenth. Yet it is understandable: the old is destroyed to make way for the new, and gardens are very transitory art forms. Rarely does a garden come down to us virtually unchanged in three hundred years. (One in England comes to mind: the Topiary Garden at Levens Hall, in the Lake District, dating from 1689.)

The only comparable garden reconstruction undertaken in this century is that of the chateau of Villandry in the Touraine of France. Obliterated in the nineteenth century, the original Renaissance garden, which complements the sixteenth-century chateau, has now been restored to its former glory.

As you look at the plants in the historic area, be aware that they have all been carefully chosen. Only those known to have been cultivated in Virginia gardens during the pre-Revolutionary period are included. No forsythia, no evergreen azaleas, no oriental magnolias, no Chinese wisteria have been permitted. Most plants are attractive natives; a few are exotics, which came directly from England or via England from the Orient. Within the historic area no plants are labeled, but just outside it—around the Inn and the Lodge, for example—they are well labeled.

The tour begins at the information center. Watch the films. If you do not receive a detailed free map, buy one. You may also wish to purchase the soft-cover book *Plants of Colonial Williamsburg*, by Joan Perry Dutton, to help you identify the plants. Mainly a listing of the plants with their common and scientific names, it also includes a map of the trees lining Duke of Gloucester Street. Both are recommended references.

THE GOVERNOR'S PALACE

Catch the free bus and get off at the first stop in the historic area, the Governor's Palace on Palace Green. This building has been entirely reconstructed, having burned to the ground in 1781. By a great stroke of luck the basement survived almost intact. Tour the residence first (there is an extra fee for this).

The gardens, which are at the back (north) of the palace, have been well researched. A plan discovered in the Bodleian Library of Oxford University, and now in the Williamsburg archives, helped enormously. Archaeological digs uncovered the original paths and the gate sites. Artifacts such as broken urns and lead finials indicated the type of decoration employed.

After viewing the interior of the palace, it is not difficult to surmise that the governor led a life befitting a representative of the Crown. Because of this ostentation, disapproving citizens dubbed his residence "the Palace"—a name that stuck. We know

*The Governor's Palace
and ballroom garden*

that one governor paid for some of the work done in the gardens out of his own purse rather than listen to criticism.

The garden directly behind the ballroom is representative of the formal design popular in the late-seventeenth-century gardens of English aristocrats, who copied the royal style. No vistas here of distant landscapes; this is still the *hortus inclusus* of earlier times, an enclosed garden that shut out the surrounding countryside. The wall of rosy brick with its elegant piers and elaborate wrought-iron gates echoes the grand style of the palace.

This garden is strictly geometric. If one regards the central south-to-north walk as the dividing line, it is bilaterally symmetrical. In other words, if you examine one half, you can guess exactly what the other half looks like. Eight diamond-shaped parterres and six cylindrical topiary yaupons, *Ilex vomitoria*, on the west are repeated exactly on the east. Look at the hedgelets enclosing the parterres: this is edging box, *Buxus sempervirens* 'Suffruticosa.' Each parterre encloses a dense growth of periwinkle, *Vinca minor*, and English ivy, *Hedera helix*. The blue flowers of the former are the only note of color in this otherwise green garden. (The Bodleian map clearly showed these diamond parterres.)

Box: Buxus sempervirens *'Suffruticosa,' or edging box, is a small evergreen dicot shrub* (suffruticosa *in Latin means "somewhat shrubby"*), *said to have been first used for parterres by Claude Mollet, a French gardener of the sixteenth century.*

He found it ideal for the purpose; it stood up to summer sun and winter frost and docilely submitted to constant clipping. This is not entirely true of box in the United States; in Florida it is likely to be scorched by the sun, and only a few new cultivars survive the New England and midwestern winters.

Box is a native of southern Europe, North Africa, and Western Asia. The tree form of box, B. sempervirens, is native to southern England, giving its name to Box Hill in Surrey. Buxus means "box" in Latin; the wood of this plant is used for making such items. In the very early days of the colonies box was a link with the mother country, where for so long it had been an important element in garden art.

Yaupon (see p. 86), often used as a substitute for box in topiary and in parterre edging, has here been clipped into twelve cylindrical topiary trees about fifteen feet high. Regularly spaced, six on each side of the ballroom, they are replicas of similar groups of topiary seen on old English estates and called "the Twelve Apostles" (one on the east side seemed less healthy than the others—Judas, perhaps?). Ensconced within huge sheared box hedges are several benches in the popular chinoiserie style of the period. This was a garden meant to be admired from the windows of the palace's upper floor; modern aerial views are especially dramatic.

A broad east-to-west walk divides this green garden from the more colorful but just as geometric lower garden. Again, the area is bilaterally symmetrical, divided into two equal halves by a north-south path. Note the regal decorations in the form of pedestals capped by finely chased lead finials or stone urns containing the Spanish bayonet, *Yucca filamentosa*. In spring and summer gaily colored flowers grow in the large perennial beds. In April masses of red tulips, *Tulipa gesnerana*, contrast with the light-gray trunks of the *allée* of American beech, *Fagus grandifolia*. The pleached *allées* of the same tree at the extreme east and west ends of this garden are especially fine. Opposing branches interlace to form a tunnel without benefit of any kind of supporting frame. Such tunnels, or galleries, as they were called, were a feature of medieval English gardens. In such a climate they were hardly used for shade; more likely their function was privacy. Medieval manors and castles afforded little of this commodity, so that trysts and plots had to be made under such arbors. Here in Williamsburg they were no doubt used as a

*The Palace gardens—
pleached allée of
American beech*

refuge from the sun. The greater number of shade trees grown
on the streets and in gardens reflects the difference in summer
climate between the mother country and the colony. (In England, trees that grow close to a house are often cut down because
they keep out the warming summer sun.)

The two corner gazebos were "necessary houses"—the
eighteenth-century euphemism equivalent to our "rest room."

Wander out of the north gate and climb the mound. This is
a relic of fifteenth-century English gardens; in those days it was
used as a lookout post to survey the surrounding countryside,
or as a vantage point for admiring the parterre patterns. An
elaborate mound with gazebo was once part of the Hampton
Court Garden. Here, it merely insulated the icehouse, a very
necessary adjunct to a residence given to so much entertaining.
The ground cover is periwinkle and English ivy. Using the map,
locate the maze, the parterre garden, and the "falling gardens"
leading to the canal.

The maze, modeled on the one still extant at Hampton Court,
is constructed of American holly, *Ilex opaca* (that in England is
of yew, *Taxus baccata*). Mazes were a form of garden fun in the
pleasure gardens of Renaissance times. Finding your way to the
shady center of this one is not easy. Holly was a good choice—
the prickly leaves preclude cheating.

The parterre garden of boxwood, which in spring encloses
daffodils (*Narcissus pseudo-narcissus*), tulips (*Tulipa* spp.) pansies (*Viola* spp.)—from the French *pensées* meaning "thoughts,"

and periwinkle, has the unusual feature of shade trees, crepe myrtle (*Lagerstroemia indica*, distinguishable in winter by its naked-looking bark and in summer by its beautiful pink inflorescences), yaupon holly, and live oak (*Quercus virginiana*). The trees are again a concession to the Virginia sun; classical parterre gardeners would never have allowed trees to obscure the design.

This kind of garden is not very appealing to modern eyes; to the author it seemed both busy and clumsy. One can understand that people in England had lost patience with all this fussiness. Yet as always, the new fashion for landscape gardens had its own extremes and at times degenerated into silliness; pseudo-Gothic or classical ruins were staged on the bucolic landscape, follies of a different sort from Saint-George-and-the-Dragon-carved-in-box.

The ballroom garden, however, is delightful in its simplicity; nothing could be more effective and dramatic than the repetition of the diamonds in box. The topiary (a little more elaborate in the lower garden) is throughout restricted to simple geometric shapes—no giraffes nor strutting birds. It must have been a very suitable outdoor entertaining room for grand parties. Altogether it is a beautiful example of the best garden art of the period: nothing is overpowering; all is in balance.

The palace gardens of the restoration cover about 10 acres. But in the eighteenth century the governor's land extended for approximately 350 acres, most of which was hunting and fishing country. Water was not a feature of seventeenth-century Dutch-English gardens. The palace was unusual in possessing a canal— the governor had to pay for it himself. Only one other decorative pond can be seen in Williamsburg: that at the Everard House across Palace Green to the east. This was very avant-garde for that time in the colonies.

Williamsburg requires at least three days, if you are to get the most out of your visit. A week would of course be better. The Governor's Palace alone may take at least one day. Whenever possible, tour the house connected with the garden to give you some idea of the people who constructed and enjoyed that garden. As in any museum visiting, the saturation point comes sooner than you expect. Therefore, it is not suggested that you read all of this section on Williamsburg at one sitting (or standing).

THE GARDENS OF WILLIAMSBURG'S CITIZENS

Obviously, these houses belonged to the wealthier members of the colony of Virginia. Ordinary folks would not have been able to afford such residences—we should not forget this fact. Many of them were owned by tobacco planters who, tired of staying at inns and taverns when they visited the capital for the "season," decided to build their own town houses. And so the town grew, but not without careful rules laid down by its first governor, Francis Nicholson (1698–1705), who was one of the first town planners. The houses we see today, each on one acre of land according to the governor's plan, are either restored—repaired and remodeled—or reconstructed—rebuilt from the ground up, none of the original fabric remaining. The tobacco planters turned their town houses into miniature plantations complete with slaves and servants, each having its own vegetable and herb garden (potager), orchard, fowl house, smokehouse, stables, and detached kitchen for reasons of safety.

Note that the gardens are intended to look attractive winter and summer; the brick walks, the decorative benches, the extensive use of evergreens—box, holly, yew, English ivy, and firethorn, *Pyracantha coccinea*, ensure this. Even if your visit is at Christmas, take time to tour the gardens. Fences, enforced by the governor's plan, are attractive and sufficiently low that even if they are closed to the public the yards and gardens can be viewed and photographed, especially in winter and in spring before the leaves unfold. The many shade trees lining Duke of Gloucester Street are American species, with few exceptions, promising good fall colors. The gardens, therefore, are attractive at any season.

First, using the detailed map, locate the seven gardens described below; they can be visited in any order.

Traversing Palace Green, identify the rows of catalpa or Indian bean tree, *Catalpa bignonioides*. It can be recognized by its heart-shaped leaves and clusters of white, purple-flecked flowers blooming in June, later replaced by long bean-shaped pods. A native tree, it was discovered in the Gulf states by Mark Catesby, an eighteenth-century English naturalist. In Europe it is a favored ornamental. Its presence on Palace Green in the eighteenth century is well documented by as famous an eyewitness as Thomas Jefferson, as well as by General Lauberdière of the French army. The crepe myrtle is not documented, but since it reached the colonies in approximately 1747, it is not unreasonable to assume that this highly decorative tree was first grown in the capital of the largest colony. (It is hardy as far north as Washington, D.C.)

GEORGE WYTHE HOUSE: This restored house and garden are open to the public.

George Wythe* (1726–1806) was one of the most influential men of his time. A teacher and mentor of Thomas Jefferson, he was the first professor of law at an American university (William and Mary). Jefferson was a visitor at the house and on one occasion took cuttings of a favored apple tree back to Monticello. Good evidence exists that Wythe was poisoned by his grandnephew, who adulterated his strawberries with arsenic. Wythe lingered on in agony for a week, long enough to disinherit the grandnephew.

The pleasure garden which extends westward from the house is enclosed by picket fencing, boxwood hedges, and at the far end by a pleached *allée* of hornbeam, *Carpinus caroliniana*, with a wooden frame. A bench is placed in the shade of the hornbeams. Stretching from the house is a central brick walk, flanked on either side by narrow lawns on which grow precisely spaced boxwood bushes, clipped into topiary cones. Beyond each lawn are two long rectangular flower beds, filled in April with daffodils, English daisies (*Bellis perennis*), and poppy anemones (*Anemone coronaria*). All is geometric and expected, a miniature, modest version of the palace ballroom garden. Guinea hens wander at will from the orchard, which is as big as the pleasure garden, through the boxwood to the service yard. A huge sycamore, *Platanus occidentalis*—the native species—shades this area. Near the old kitchen, beds of scarlet tulips contrast with the angular shapes of small box bushes.

Plant notes: Until 1800 hornbeam was known in England as hardbeam. In the United States it is still called ironwood. It is easily recognized by its smooth gray trunk, which almost appears to contain contracting muscles or sinews (an alternate name is musclewood). Before iron was commonplace, the wood was used for heavy-duty purposes—wheels, carts, dairy equipment. The famous Elizabethan Epping Forest near London is dominated by ancient lopped-off hornbeams, pollarded (to use the technical

* Wythe rhymes with "Smith."

term) over the centuries to provide fuel. (The English hornbeam is of course a different species, *Carpinus hetulus.*)

TULIPS *were still exotic flowers in eighteenth-century Virginia. Originally discovered in the Crimea, they were brought to Europe in the 1550s by the Austrian ambassador to Constantinople. Because of their resemblance to inverted turbans, they were called "tulbands," from the Turkish word for turban. From this we get the English "tulip" and the Latinized form* Tulipa. *An Austrian botanist eventually took the bulbs to Holland, where he sold them at prohibitive prices. This touched off the Dutch phenomenon called "tulipomania." Bulbs were sold on speculation, like gold and silver, and not for their intrinsic worth.*

One solitary bulb of a coveted kind could, during this wild time, buy two loads of wheat and two barrels of butter. The mania ended in 1637 when the Dutch came to their senses. Tulips probably reached Virginia in the mid-seventeenth century.

English daisies were no doubt grown out of nostalgia. They were and are a common lawn weed in England, blooming almost year-round. The English name comes from the Anglo-Saxon meaning "day's eye"—the flowers open in the morning and close in the evening.

Poppy anemones (*anemone* in Greek means "daughter of the wind") came from the Near East. Some believe them to be the biblical "lilies of the field." Superficially these anemones look like poppies, but they are not even related, belonging to the buttercup family. Native anemones, being small and white, are quite un-poppy-like.

Daffodil bulbs were taken to America by the very early settlers. The common name probably came from the Greek *asphodel* by way of the Dutch *de affodil.* The Latin name recalls the boy of the Greek myth who fell so in love with his own reflection that he turned into a flower.

NORTON-COLE HOUSE: This restored house is privately occupied, but the garden is open to the public. The house was once owned by George Washington's dentist.

A green garden of straight brick walks contrasts with the white woodwork of the house, the well, and the chinoiserie bench. The wide and luxuriant curved box hedges have a border of English ivy, defining the long straight walk. Four topiary boxwood trees, each elaborately clipped into a helix, give character to the precise garden. In spring, look for the perfumed flowers of the yellow jessamine, *Gelsemium sempervirens*, an evergreen vine, climbing the picket fence near the gate. One of America's prized ornamentals, it was introduced into England in 1640. Unfortunately, it is not hardy north of Virginia.

A few deciduous plants grace this otherwise evergreen garden. The oak-leaf hydrangea, *Hydrangea quercifolia*, originally discovered in Georgia by John Bartram, the famous American plant explorer, is easily recognized by its oaklike leaves. It occurs commonly in Williamsburg gardens. The paper mulberry, *Broussonetia papyrifera*, also common throughout the restoration, has a grotesquely gnarled trunk, giving it an aged appearance. The inner bark was used in Japan to make paper lanterns and umbrellas, and in Polynesia to make tapa cloth. Although this strange tree belongs to the mulberry family, it is not closely related to the common mulberry, *Morus rubra*, nor to its Asiatic cousin, *M. alba*, both to be seen here. James I of England attempted to deflect the early colonists from raising that "vile weed" tobacco by promoting a silkworm industry. It failed, but the silkworms' food remained.

ORLANDO JONES HOUSE: This reconstructed house is closed, but the garden is open to the public. Orlando Jones's claim to fame

The Norton-Cole House and garden

is that he was the maternal grandfather of Martha Washington.

The garden is strictly formal, but unusual in having a small oval lawn (lawns were a nuisance in Virginia, where they tended to burn out under the hot sun). A border of white tulips and English daisies edges the lawn. Surrounding the garden is a thick box hedge in which are inset four white garden seats. Farthest from the house and raised on a platform is an elegant chinoiserie bench, flanked by two elegant topiary box bushes, helically clipped. A conspicuous paper mulberry grows out of the center of the lawn, and crepe myrtles are dotted about.

Separated by a picket fence and close to the house is a flower garden of species tulips (i.e., neither sports nor hybrids) and poppy anemones; yaupon is the hedging material, and deciduous trees provide shade.

DR. BARRAUGH HOUSE: Neither this restored house nor its garden is open to the public. The house occupies a corner lot, and being quite small, can easily be surveyed from the outside. (Dr. Barraugh was a physician associated with the college and the nearby hospital.)

In this exceedingly simple but effective garden, again we see a lawn, this time decorated by eight rounded boxwood bushes. A crepe myrtle stands at each corner, and tall trees provide summer shade. The vine climbing the fence is the native white clematis, *Clematis virginiana*. Small and severe, this garden was no doubt reassuring to people only too familiar with the "chaos" of the nearby wilderness.

Plant notes: Clematis is a vine belonging to the buttercup family, Ranunculaceae. Its "petals," often colored in modern hybrids, are really the sepals. The hairy fruits have earned it the common name of "old-man's-beard."

PRENTIS HOUSE: The garden is open to the public but the reconstructed house is not. William Prentis was a prosperous merchant, and his garden was one of the larger ones in Williamsburg. A diary belonging to a family member of that era provided valuable information regarding its design and its plants.

The basic layout is geometric: four square boxwood parterres, exactly alike and symmetrically placed, set the tone. Tiny twin lawns hedged with box and bearing simple round topiary box bushes separate the two pairs of parterres. Note the manner in which the box border of each parterre has been sheared: the effect is to give each corner a point—very contrived. The tree in the center of each bed is a buckeye. All around it colorful spring flowers have been allowed to grow in gay abandon: species tulips, blue and crimson poppy anemones, daisies, and masses of the pale blue spring starflower, *Ipheion uniflorum*. (Since the last is a native of Argentina, it is unlikely that it grew here in Prentis's day.) After so much geometry elsewhere, the wildness of these beds is especially pleasing.

Red tulips, in two flanking rows, run the whole length of the garden. Rough wooden fences bearing espaliered apple trees in full bloom provide effective and useful backdrops. This garden, at least in spring, is one of the most attractive in Williamsburg. It should not be missed.

Before visiting the Alexander Craig House, you may enjoy calling in at the bakery next door to purchase an eighteenth-century snack—a gingerbread cookie, perhaps.

ALEXANDER CRAIG HOUSE: This restored house and garden are both closed to the public.

Some of the original bricks from the house have been in-corporated into the walks of this small, compact, and highly formal garden. It differs from the other gardens in having at its center a round flower bed which is edged, not with box or yaupon, but with bricks and large scallop shells embedded in gravel (shells like these were favorite garden ornaments of the

Garden of the
Alexander Craig House

period). In spring the bed is filled with forget-me-nots, *Myosotis sylvatica.* The surrounding parterres have "billowy" box hedges. A few small box bushes are disciplined into topiary of an elegant shape. Hollyhocks, *Althaea rosea,* adorn the picket fences in late summer.

Plant notes: Forget-me-nots were found wild in the American colonies, as they were and are in England. No doubt the spirit of nostalgia prompted their inclusion in Williamsburg gardens. (The English name is a direct translation from the medieval French.)

Hollyhocks had reached the colonies by the early eighteenth century from China via England. The name comes from the Middle English and means "holy mallow." Why "holy" is not known; "mallow" is obvious because it belongs to the mallow family, Malvaceae, to which hibiscus and rose-of-Sharon also belong. Thomas Jefferson grew hollyhocks in his garden, and it is known from a letter that John Custis (see below) received seeds from England in 1735.

POWELL-WALLER HOUSE: This restored house and garden are closed to the public.

This is perhaps the most photographed of the smaller gardens, and rightly so. In a very small space it illustrates dramatically the compact geometric style so popular at the time. The garden is essentially circular. Two intersecting brick walks cause each parterre to become an exact quarter-circle. In spring, when it is most photographed, beds of salmon-pink tulips are enclosed by hedgelets of box. Benches for sitting and dogwood trees (*Cornus florida*) for shade complete this little horticultural gem. (A carping note: one questions the inclusion of the banksia rose, *Rosa banksiae,* climbing up the outside of the chimney, and of the evergreen azalea, neither of which arrived on these shores until the nineteenth century.)

Final note on the plants: Since the eighteenth century most cultivated plants have changed greatly—have been "improved," we would say. Although still assigned to the same species or genus, they often have an added cultivar name, or the name may now include an X, indicating that it is a hybrid (cross-breed). They are more disease-resistant, often larger, more floriferous (think of the hybrid tea roses blooming all summer). The flowers have changed in the following ways: they are larger, often double, and exhibit a greater range of color; even the shape may have changed (the new snapdragons lack the characteristic "lips"). Therefore, the plants you see in Williamsburg may not be the plants known to the colonists. Today those plants might be difficult if not impossible to find, and this is even more true of fruits and vegetables than it is of flowers. Most probably, they would seem to us too much like the wild flowers of field and forest. One example will suffice. The English daisy grown in the restoration is not the daisy familiar to the colonists. In this century it has been bred to produce bigger plants, bigger flowers. The common weed of English lawns was, no doubt, the colonists' daisy. But in our eyes it would be too insignificant to merit garden status, and so it has been "improved." The African marigold, *Tagetes erecta*, is another case in point.

As already stated, the Williamsburg restoration is not yet finished. Gardeners and plant lovers look forward to the reconstruction of the John Custis House and garden on France Street. Custis (1678–1749) was reputed to have one of the best gardens in the colony. He corresponded regularly with the famous London horticulturist Peter Collinson, from whom he obtained many exotic plants. (Some of this correspondence is in the Williamsburg archives.) When a dry well on the site of his estate was excavated recently, after being sealed for nearly two hundred years, archaeologists found the remains of twenty-one plants, which could be identified. All twenty-one are growing in the restoration, confirming the reliability of the eighteenth-century documents previously studied. Custis's son, incidentally, was Martha Washington's first husband.

As I said before, one could easily spend a week exploring Williamsburg. The space here devoted to it is therefore not disproportionate. A garden symposium is held there every year in April. For details, call the toll-free number.

Note: If you have time, a trip to the nearby Norfolk Botanical Garden is recommended. It came to the author's attention too late to be included in this guide.

GUNSTON HALL

Lorton, Virginia

UNIQUE FEATURES	• A 220-year-old boxwood *allée*, 12 feet high and 280 feet long. • The largest and best-maintained parterre garden of the Dutch-English school in the United States. • A restoration of the garden of one of the founding fathers of our nation, George Mason.

HISTORY: George Mason (1725–1792) is often referred to as the "Pen of the Revolution" because the Virginia Declaration of Rights, which he wrote in 1776, was in 1791 adopted into the federal Bill of Rights.

In 1755, shortly after his marriage, he built Gunston Hall on his prosperous tobacco plantation. Frequent visitors were many of the founding fathers of the young country: George Washington, Thomas Jefferson, Patrick Henry, and James Madison.

Gunston Hall remained in the Mason family until 1866, long after tobacco had ceased to be a profitable crop. Slowly deteriorating, it passed from one family to another until Louis Hertle bought the estate in 1912. Spending lavishly, he and his wife restored the estate to some of its former grandeur, though in the twentieth-century style. On his death in 1949, Louis Hertle bequeathed the entire estate to the commonwealth of Virginia to be managed and supervised by the Colonial Dames of America, his intention being that Gunston Hall Plantation should become a perpetual memorial to George Mason. Major changes had to be made to reconvert the house and gardens back to their original eighteenth-century style. The Garden Club of Virginia undertook the restoration of the grounds, under the direction of Colonial Williamsburg's resident landscape architect. Since 1950 Gunston Hall has been open to the public.

- *Admission:* Entrance fee.
- *Hours:* Open all year, 9:30 A.M.–5:00 P.M. daily. Closed Christmas Day.
- *Plants:* Most of the trees are labeled.
- *Physically handicapped:* Wheelchairs available. Ann Mason Building designed for use by the handicapped. Most gardens are accessible, but not upper floor of the house, unless special arrangements are made.
- *Address:* Gunston Hall Plantation, Lorton, Va. 22079. Tel. (703) 550-9220.
- *Location and directions:* 18 miles south of Washington, D.C., on the Potomac River. May be reached via U.S. 1 or Interstate 95 or George Washington Parkway. From Interstate 95 take Lorton exit (also marked "Gunston Hall and Auto Train"), drive south on U.S. 1; turn left on Virginia 242; 4 miles to the entrance.
- *Parking:* Free, outside the historic area.
- *Gift shop:* In Ann Mason Building.
- *No snack bar or restaurant.* Soft-drink machines beside parking lot.
- *Picnicking:* Picnic tables located near parking lot.

Only twenty miles from Washington, D.C., Gunston Hall is a historic mansion that should not be missed. The gardens are in the Dutch-English style of Williamsburg, only on a huge scale and with the additional advantage of a view. The landscape architect has not exactly jumped over the garden fence (to paraphrase Horace Walpole in 1780), but he has not circumscribed this garden, either. From the gazebos on their ancient mounds one can regard the distant scene, down through the deer park to the Potomac River half-a-mile away and across to the sister gazebo and the woods beyond. Willy-nilly, a suggestion of "Capability" Brown's landscape cult (see p. 89) gives an ambience to the gardens of Gunston Hall that is completely absent from the Governor's Palace at Williamsburg. In spite of the parterres, this is not a *hortus inclusus*. It expands outward to take in the surrounding woods and the river. One has the feeling of being elevated rather than protected and secluded. And it is refreshing. The winds of change are in the air at Gunston, those that will sweep away parterres and fussiness in the following century. At least, that is the feeling engendered by the restoration, intentionally or otherwise.

No real plans of the garden have survived. Its backbone, represented by the magnificent boxwood *allée* (actually a T rather than an *allée*, with the horizontal stroke growing parallel to the house), was all that remained after two hundred years. Two gaps in the *allée* midway to the river view indicated a crosswalk. On the basis of this evidence, as well as a brief written description left by John Mason (1766–1849), the garden was divided into four major sections, or parterres, by Louis Hertle.

Using only plants known to the colonists of the eighteenth century, the Garden Club of Virginia set out to create the kind of garden George and Ann Mason would have enjoyed. Assuredly, Mason was familiar with the Williamsburg gardens. It is not unreasonable to assume that his garden would also have had boxwood parterres, though without the inward look of Williamsburg. The distant Potomac and the stretch of land below the bluff made that impossible. (In Mason's day this land was probably planted with tobacco.)

Purchase your ticket at the Ann Mason Building, making sure you acquire the small map "Welcome to Gunston Hall." After touring the house, turn your attention to the gardens facing the river. At one point you may wish to walk the entire length (280 feet) of the dwarf boxwood *allée, Buxus sempervirens* 'Suffruticosa,' admiring the 220-year-old shrubs. The walk is paved with crushed oyster shells.

The house and right parterre garden

*Boxwood allée looking
back to the house*

The parterre gardens nearest the house are laid out in simple geometric shapes—squares, circles, triangles—all edged with box and enclosing covers of periwinkle, *Vinca minor*, and creeping bugle, *Ajuga reptans*. Here and there a topiary box, *Buxus sempervirens*, or American holly, *Ilex opaca*, a crepe myrtle, *Lagerstroemia indica*, or a tree peony, *Paeonia suffruticosa*, emerges from the center of a bed. As one nears the bluff overlooking the river, the lawn becomes more extensive and the parterres less frequent. Obviously, the intensively parterred section would be nearest the house, where it could be admired from the upper windows. If you have visited Williamsburg, this part of Gunston will remind you of the west parterre garden of the Governor's Palace.

Note that the gardens to the left and right of the boxwood *allée* are not identical, that both the parterre pattern and the shrubs are different. (Compare this with the ballroom garden at the Governor's Palace, described on pp. 110–11.)

In the parterre garden to the left of the *allée*, the trees growing from the squares or triangles are crepe myrtles and tree peony, mainly. Nearest the house an eighteenth-century sundial is the focus of one area of the garden. Along the periphery, trees are planted for accent; predominant among them are eastern red cedar, *Juniperus virginiana*, the fringe tree, *Chionanthus virginica*, and various cherries of the old-fashioned kind, *Prunus* sp.

The garden to the right of the *allée* is a very good example of the cluttered look the Dutch imparted to parterre gardening in

Parterre garden to right of allée

the late seventeenth century—everything seems crowded and somewhat oppressive. Many topiary box bushes contribute to this effect, as do the trimmed American hollies that define the four corners. Red cedar, common lilac (*Syringa vulgaris*), and flowering dogwood (*Cornus florida*) emerge from the parterres. A wide stretch of lawn at the extreme right bordered with garland wreath, *Spiraea arguta*, and cherry adds a pleasing contrapuntal note.

Scattered throughout the entire upper garden are chinoiserie benches, a style fashionable in the eighteenth century and already foreshadowed in the dining room of the house.

When you reach the bluff, the lower garden or terrace can be seen. Here the boxwood *allée* ends in a semicircular mound, which divides the lower garden into two, each a mirror image of the other. Approximately twelve parterres, separated by narrow walks of crushed shells, compose each half. In spring these are enlivened by flowering bulbs, followed by summer and fall annuals. At either end are two elegant gazebos, twentieth-century construction placed on mounts originally there and executed in the chinoiserie manner with pointed Gothic arches. They echo the style of the river-facing porch of the house, constructed by the carpenter William Buckland, whom Mason brought over from England in 1755 and who was a devotee of this latest fashion. Whether the gazebos ever exisited there we shall not know, but they add a great deal of charm and authenticity to this part of the garden. They can be compared with the piers at

Orton Plantation (see p. 80). Entirely different in structure and perhaps more decorative, they are functionally the same: viewing platforms for a lower garden and a distant horizon.

In spring the banks of the lower garden are flushed with red, pink, and white flowering quince, *Chaenomeles lagenaria*, and daffodils. Later the day lilies, *Hemerocallis fulva* and *H. flava* (the former derived from original plants found here and at George Mason's birthplace), and Aaron's-beard St.-John's-wort, *Hypericum calycinum*, make their colorful statements.

As a parterre garden, this terrace is altogether more attractive than the south garden to the right of the boxwood *allée*. Perhaps it is the feeling of space, of vistas reaching out and beyond, that makes the miniature beds at one's feet more appealing. And when the view is enshrouded in mist, as it was on the two days of our visit, the gazebos perched on their promontories give an almost fairy-tale quality to the entire scene.

Brick steps lead down from the mound into the deer park. As in Mason's day, Virginia white-tailed deer still frequent the estate, sometimes roaming the gardens at dusk. The park is a hardwood forest with occasional red cedars and willows, *Salix* sp.

Passing the little schoolhouse, proceed to the Mason family graveyard through the long *allée* of eastern red cedars. Two huge Spanish red oaks, *Quercus falcata*, towering over the gate are estimated to be nearly two hundred years old and were probably planted at the time of George Mason's death. In June, Father Hugo's rose, *Rosa hugonis*, blooms against the brick wall, a

Gazebo on mound with red cedar

Chinese species rose that has given rise to a vigorous modern hybrid, *R. cantabrigiensis*.

Before returning to the front of the house (though it can be argued that it is really the back, since all river plantations faced the water and guests invariably arrived by boat), you may wish to hike the half mile to the Potomac along the Barn Wharf Nature Trail (a self-guide is available at the Ann Mason Building). Since eagles and bluebirds as well as wild flowers may be seen, bird watchers especially may enjoy this walk. The Gunston staff encourage the nesting of bluebirds in the area; you may see various birdboxes scattered around the grounds.

Returning to Gunston Hall and standing in the circle in front of the house, note the two imposing willow oaks, *Quercus phellos* (the common name indicates that the leaves, simple and elongated, are more like those of a willow than an oak). Large as they are, their age is estimated to be no more than eighty years. Behind are two old dogwoods and beyond is the beautiful *allée* of southern magnolia, *Magnolia grandiflora*, all planted in 1922 by Louis Hertle. Parallel rows of eastern red cedar flank the magnolias on either side. In George Mason's time the *allée* consisted of four rows of cherry trees, *Prunus serotina*, a fact reported by one of his sons.

The nearby Ann Mason Building with its modern amenities is not allowed to intrude itself into this historic area. Skillful use of native pines, American holly, and bald cypress, *Taxodium distichum*, provide effective screening.

Gunston is a historic estate where gardens and house complement one another. As much time, money, and research have gone into the gardens as into the mansion—time, certainly: imagine the hours it must take to clip those eighty-eight boxwood parterres! The author felt that this was not true at nearby Mount Vernon, where the house overpowers the garden. For this reason it has been omitted from this guide, which is concerned chiefly with gardens.

DUMBARTON OAKS

Washington, D.C.

UNIQUE FEATURES	• One of the last great private gardens to be created in this century.
	• A brilliant example of the adaptation of classical Italian garden style to American climate and usage.

HISTORY: The first owner of this property was Ninian Beall, who received it in 1702 as part of a land grant. He called it the Rock of Dumbarton after a place in his native Scotland. In 1801 the present house was built. Farms and other outbuildings were part of the estate, since such communities had to be self-supporting. In 1920 Robert Woods Bliss and his wife, Mildred, bought the Oaks, as it was then called. Robert Bliss was a diplomat, so the couple spent much of their life abroad. During the years 1920–1940 the house and gardens were completely remodeled and renamed Dumbarton Oaks. In 1922 Mildred Bliss, who wanted a garden designed to her own special taste, hired Beatrix Farrand as landscape architect. Mrs. Farrand had met with such success that Mrs. Bliss felt confident she could be entrusted with the task while the Blisses were out of the country.

In 1940 the Blisses gave the house and sixteen acres of garden to Harvard University and the other thirty-eight acres to the Department of the Interior. Today Dumbarton Oaks is renowned as the home of the Harvard Center for Byzantine Studies, for its collections of Byzantine and Pre-Columbian Art, and of course for its gardens. Historically, it is famous as the site of the International Conference of 1944 that led to the formation of the United Nations.

- *Admission:* Free November through March. Fee of $1.00 charged April through October.
- *Hours:* Open all year, 2:00 P.M.–5:00 P.M. daily except legal holidays and during inclement winter weather. Museum closed Mondays, so no garden guide and map available on that day (see below).
- *Plants:* Not labeled.
- *Physically Handicapped:* Garden not accessible to wheel-chairs—too many slopes and steps.
- *Address:* Dumbarton Oaks, 1703 32nd Street N.W., Washington, D.C. 20007. Tel. (202) 338-8278.
- *Location and Directions:* Off Wisconsin Avenue at the corner of R and 32nd streets. Museum entrance on 32nd Street, garden entrance on R Street. From downtown Washington, take any bus, nos. 30–37, from Pennsylvania Avenue N.W. between 10th and 15th streets.
- *Parking:* No parking lot, but spaces can usually be found on 32nd Street near museum entrance.
- *No gift shop.* Counter selling garden guide and map, pamphlets, books, and postcards located just inside museum entrance.
- *No snack bar or restaurant.*
- *No picnicking.*

The best seasons for this garden are spring, autumn, and winter. It was designed for outdoor living in spring and fall, for strolling or viewing from the windows of the house in winter. Because of Washington's climate the family did not intend to reside there in summer. But if your only opportunity is in summer, by all means go.

First, purchase the inexpensive guide and map of the gardens within the museum. You cannot enter the gardens from there, so return to R Street; the entrance is only half a block away.

This is a landscape architect's garden. The hilly terrain made the nonliving elements of garden design almost as important as the plants. The gardens near the house are formal in a small, intimate way. There is no great sweep of avenues and flower beds, but instead, a series of very precisely arranged garden "rooms." To achieve this, balustrades, fences, steps, retaining walls, and pergolas are essential. And if these are to contribute to the beauty of the garden, a great deal of skill and artistry has to go into their placement and design. We know that this was the case: nothing was decided until mock-ups had been made, put in place, and voted upon. The judges apparently were Mildred Bliss and Beatrix Farrand. Photographs dating from the early thirties show mock-ups of the urns and fountain that now grace the west wall of the swimming pool.

Mrs. Bliss, who had lived so long in Europe, and Mrs. Farrand, who had visited it often, had the same concept of a garden: it was an outdoor extension of the house, a place for intimate family meals, for entertaining on a grand scale, for quiet reading and meditation, as well as a place for play. Such activities need some sort of confinement. For example, it would be difficult to read with any degree of concentration on one of the great avenues of Versailles; one needs a secluded nook. (Mrs. Bliss actually had a garden book-box designed to hold her favorite volumes.) For entertainment, some enclosure is necessary, else the party breaks up into isolated groups. And tennis players and swimmers need a place to themselves.

Consequently, exploring this garden is like progressing through a large, unfamiliar house, not knowing what sort of room will be encountered next. One passes through a beautifully wrought iron gate or down a flight of steps, ignorant of the pleasures that lie beyond. In this respect Dumbarton Oaks has in abundance one of Harold Nicolson's major ingredients for a successful garden—the element of surprise.

Comfort was also considered. Beatrix Farrand's book* records the thought given to each descent in the garden: Should it be by means of a gently sloping walk or by steps? If by steps, how many is it easy to take at a time? Note the seat on the staircase leading to the Fountain Terrace: two-thirds of the way down one can rest, even though the steps are divided into three flights.

In spite of Farrand's academic qualifications and obvious talents, she always called herself a landscape gardener rather than a landscape architect. Her knowledge of plants, their care, their individual potentialities and idiosyncrasies, far surpassed that of most landscape architects. Both she and Mrs. Bliss wished to simulate traditional European garden art: hence the emphasis on the broad-leaved evergreens—box, holly, and yew. Furthermore, since this was to be a horticultural statement impervious to the seasons, the

* *Beatrix Farrand's Plant Book for Dumbarton Oaks*, ed. Kostial Diane McGuire (Washington, D.C.: Dumbarton Oaks Trustees for Harvard, 1980). Available at the museum.

lavish use of evergreens was indicated. Even so, deciduous trees of character and elegance were not neglected. Farrand used many as living sculptures for winter and spring effects: the silver maple reflected in the Lovers' Lane Pool, the yulan magnolia in front of the Orangery, the beech on the Beech Terrace.

The placing of every major tree and shrub was carefully considered; they oftentimes function as markers to emphasize a transition from one garden to another, or to call attention to nearby specimen trees or to aspects of the house. (For more details, consult Farrand's book.) Note that in this garden there is little of the bilateral symmetry seen at Williamsburg. There is symmetry and balance but no stereotyped answers. As one descends farther from the house, the gardens become less and less formal, until one gets lost in a sea of yellow forsythia and flowering fruit trees—if it is spring—or finds oneself strolling through a tranquil glade of silver maples, an avenue romantically called Mélisande's Allée.

Georgina Masson's "Guide to the Gardens," with its map, outlines an extended tour through the formal and informal areas. Here we shall follow a more limited route, sometimes backtracking, the assumption being that most visitors do not want to see everything. Moreover, much of the informal area—Crabapple Hill and Forsythia Dell, for instance—is exciting only in late March or early April.

We shall start at the Orangery, dating from 1810, easily recognized as the one-story building with a roof balustrade and large

The Orangery

windows to the extreme right (east) of the house. But before entering, identify the huge deciduous yulan magnolia, *Magnolia denudata*, called "The Bride" because of its spectacular display of white chalice-shaped flowers in early April. Small boxwood bushes, *Buxus sempervirens* 'Suffruticosa,' constitute the foundation planting, and in spring the climbing wisteria, *Wisteria sinensis*, forms a wonderful lavender drapery for the rounded Palladian windows. Within, the creeper *Ficus pumila*, dating back to 1860, covers the walls and the supporting beams. French terra-cotta sphinxes give a slightly humorous air to the otherwise empty greenhouse. In winter the potted plants in the courtyard come indoors, as they did in the orangeries of the seventeenth century. Orangeries were North European forerunners of the modern conservatory, and as their name implies, were used for the cultivation of oranges in the houses of the rich.

Immediately to the north of the Orangery is the Green Garden, a formal outdoor entertaining room. Because the party dresses of women guests were supposed to enliven this garden, the planting is muted, confined to trees and evergreens. The huge black oak, *Quercus velutina*, one of the originals that gave Dumbarton Oaks its name, dominates this garden. A small lawn stretches from the trees to the balustrade overlooking the swimming pool and Crabapple Hill. (Note the stone testimonial to Beatrix Farrand in the middle of the balustrade.) The marble consoles are reminders of the days when this terrace was the scene of lavish parties. The potted plants that decorate the terrace during the warmer months include *Citrus* sp., tree ferns, lily-of-the-Nile (*Agapanthus africanus*), and yesterday-today-and-tomorrow (*Brunfelsia calycina*), so called because its flowers turn from purple to white in three days.

Leaving the Green Garden by the west path, do not miss the tiny garden on the left—the Star. This was intended for intimate family meals, especially in spring when a hedge of a white azalea, 'Indica alba' (*Rhododendron mucronatum*), completely surrounds it. This particular azalea has been grown in Japanese gardens for centuries and is believed to be a species, though it has never been found in the wild. On the west wall is a fountain with a bas-relief of Aquarius, and on the ground a paved star, depicting some of the constellations. The circle so formed bears a quotation from Chaucer (see guidebook).

Continuing westward, you will reach the upper terrace of the North Vista. By various tricks known to architects since the seventeenth-century Italians Bernini and Borromini, this vista is made to look much longer than it really is. (Walk the distance and you will agree.) From the terrace of the house the steps leading to the different levels are invisible; they do not intrrupt the view. Yet looking back at the house from the north end, they are highly visible. An unusual feature is their grassy treads, as welcome to the feet as to the eye. Two deodar cedars, *Cedrus deodara*, frame and accent the vista. Close to the house grow southern magnolias, *Magnolia grandiflora*, all severely pruned to prevent their interfering with the view. Various species of yew, *Taxus* sp., flank the sides of the upper terrace.

Retrace your steps past the Star, and just short of the Green Garden descend the staircase on the left. Halfway, it forks to provide space for a charming Italianate fountain—much thought went into its design. Passing through the loggia of the swimming-pool enclosure, take time to admire the fountain, bedecked in spring by two weeping cherries, *Prunus subhirtella* 'Pendula,' and by the same species of azalea seen in the Star. Softening the north and east boundaries are weeping willows, *Salix* sp. (probably a 'babylonica' hybrid).

Originally designed for watching tennis games in the court below, the Pebble Garden Terrace is a perfect viewing platform for the singular Pebble Garden, which has become almost the logo of Dumbarton Oaks. Designed not by Farrand but by her successors, it is a most interesting stone garden. The pebble mosaic incorporates the sheaf of wheat, part of the Bliss family coat

Italianate fountain on steps down to swimming pool

The Pebble Garden from its terrace

of arms. When a thin film of water flowing from the distant fountain covers the pebbles, the whole acquires a glistening patina. It is unfortunate that the plants in the peripheral scrolls are now rather tatty weeds. In a garden where the standard of maintenance is so high, this is something of a shock.

We now ascend the curved path leading south from the Pebble Garden Terrace. On the way up two kinds of box, *Buxus sempervirens* and *B. sempervirens* 'Suffruticosa,' as well as a European hazel, *Corylus avellana*, with dangling yellow catkins in spring, effectively screen the swimming pool below and announce that we are about to enter another "room": the Beech Terrace.

Here the dominating tree is a specimen American beech, *Fagus grandifolia*, underplanted in spring with small flowering bulbs. Beech casts such dense shade that summer ground covers do not prosper beneath it. *Vinca minor*, the periwinkle, however, makes a brave showing. A weeping crab apple, *Malus* sp., marks the northeast corner.

Leave the Beech Terrace by the steps to the east. The Urn Terrace, another delightful and self-contained garden, serves as a prelude to the much more significant Rose Garden. This terrace has been changed since Farrand's day by the introduction of curving beds of English ivy, *Hedera helix*, and pebble mosaics, swirling around the base of the urn (a copy of a French eighteenth-century original, now indoors). Farrand's garden was simple—tiny lawns with edging box. There is an example of her design on the south side of this terrace.

*The Urn Terrace with
Rose Garden beyond*

The climax of the descending sequential approach from the Green Garden, Beech Terrace, and Urn Terrace is the splendid Rose Garden. Here every detail was planned with great care and with no regard for expense. The elaborate garden seat, the stone tablet bearing the family coat of arms, the gates with their pineapple finials, all bear testimony to this. (The pineapple is the time-honored symbol of hospitality, a South American Indian custom adopted by North American colonists.) The large box-wood bushes, unusual in rose gardens, give interest to what would otherwise be a sterile winter garden, and in summer are perfect foils to the texture and color of the rose bushes. The plan is geometric and in the English style. Each bed contains only one kind of cultivar, so the variety is not great. Farrand's original planting plan of 1933 has been discarded as too complicated; all that persists is the west bed with climbers on the retaining wall— roses, clematis, *Clematis paniculata*, wisteria, and winter jasmine, *Jasminum nudiflorum.*

Gertrude Jekyll, a famous English gardener around the turn of the century, did much to put flowers back in their rightful place in the English garden (see p. 256). Her attitude influenced Beatrix Farrand greatly, and this wall planting, together with the beds on the Fountain Terrace, shows that Farrand shared with Jekyll an intense feeling for the juxtaposition and grouping of plants.

The Fountain Terrace marks the end of the east-west progression of terraces. The twin fountains, with their pools set in a grassy lawn, give this garden an Italianate air. The absence of walks and the riot of floral bloom prepare one for the informal gardens beyond. This is the only formal garden featuring flowers as an important design element. In spring the beds are ablaze with tulips, and in summer foxglove (*Digitalis purpurea*), dahlias (*Dahlia* cultivars), snapdragon (*Antirrhinum majus*), pinks (*Dianthus* sp.), and night-scented tobacco (*Nicotiana* cultivars) simulate an English herbaceous border. In Autumn, chrysanthemums take their places. The retaining wall behind the border is covered with creepers: Boston ivy (*Parthenocissus tricuspidata* 'Lowii'), porcelain ampelopsis (*Ampelopsis brevipedunculata maximowiczii*—with apologies!), and woodbine (*Parthenocissus quinquefolia*).

As you pass through the gate of the Arbor Terrace, note the unusual finials—vases of flowers wrought in iron (similar ones act as markers to the Rose Garden seat). This stone-paved patio was originally intended as a herb garden and a *giardino segreto* (see p. 20). Now it is decorated with plants in tubs—*Citrus* spp., oleander (*Nerium oleander*), white azaleas. Along the west wall is a cedar arbor; seats and a wall fountain make this a cool retreat for a sunny day. (Unfortunately, the wisteria at the time of viewing was not very healthy, defeating the arbor's purpose.) Just outside this garden, a line of Kieffer pear trees, *Pyrus lecontei* 'Kieffer,' forms an aerial hedge that frames the view after the manner of early Renaissance Italian gardens.

Return to the Fountain Terrace and leave it by the steps in the east wall. At the division in the path take the left fork, which brings you to Mélisande's Allée, a delight in spring with its drifts of small flowering bulbs, while in summer its avenue of silver maples, *Acer saccharinum*, casts a welcome shade. If you wish to explore it further, turn left (north) and progress to the Camellia Circle (a disappointment).

A right turn takes you to Lovers' Lane Pool, a miniature theater designed after one near Rome. The stage is at the north end, the seating at the south, and the oval pool between adds distance and serves as a sounding board. An audience of no more than fifty can be seated. Baroque columns on the periphery, connected by latticework on which various climbers grow, afford seclusion. The silver maple at the north end, reflected in the pool and seeming to sweep its branches around it, is an effective embellishment.

*The Terrior Column,
with Lovers' Lane Pool
in the distance*

Passing through the gap at the southeast end of the theater, you are immediately in the Terrior Enclosure, a miniature bamboo forest (*Bambusa* sp.). Nothing could be more different from the nearby formal gardens. Close to the Terrior Column (see the guidebook for its story) is a beautifully fashioned bench with a lead chinoiserie roof, surrounded by a few casually placed chairs —as if the family had just left. (All the furniture was designed in 1935 by Farrand.)

Leaving the Terrior Enclosure and walking north, pass through the beautifully arched wrought-iron gate back onto the Fountain Terrace. Return to the Urn Terrace, turn left, and leave it by the steps in the northwest corner. This is the best view of Dumbarton's famous Box Walk. At the far end you can just discern the antique fountain in the center of the Ellipse. The box is edging box and is estimated to be eighty-five to ninety years old. Walk down this slope; the reward at the end is the beautiful Ellipse.

In the center of the Ellipse is an antique Provençal fountain. Two concentric ellipses of hornbeam trees, *Carpinus caroliniana*, form an aerial hedge surrounding the central lawn. Outside them is a third ellipse of American holly, *Ilex opaca*. Originally, the trees marking the Ellipse were box, but in 1958 the whole garden was changed. Since hornbeam is deciduous, this garden now has a very different appearance in winter. In late spring the rusty-colored leaves of the new growth are most attractive, as are their autumnal colors. This little garden is yet another totally unexpected experience, the suspense of the long Box Walk adding to the drama.

Return to the Orangery via the Box Walk, but on your way up, visit the Pebble Garden (on your right) and examine this extraordinary mosaic close to. Unlike Roman mosaics, this one has plants incorporated into the design, and this has made it vulnerable; already attention has been directed to the weedy growth within the scrolls.

Leaving Dumbarton Oaks, note how the trees along the R Street wall have all been most carefully planted to screen out city sights and sounds while presenting an attractive view from the house year-round.

This garden has been described in some detail because, surprisingly, very little has been written about it elsewhere. Yet to the author it seems a significant American garden. Considering its accessibility, it is a pity more people do not know of it—an oasis that might help relieve the stresses and strains of city living.

NATIONAL ARBORETUM

Washington, D.C.

UNIQUE
FEATURES

- Situated in an intermediate climatic zone between the northeastern and southeastern United States, it exhibits an unusually wide variety of woody ornamentals.
- The National Herb Garden, comprising two acres, a joint project of the Herb Society of America and the arboretum (opened 1980).
- Spectacular displays of hybrid and native azaleas in April and May.

HISTORY: The idea for a botanical garden or arboretum in the nation's capital was conceived in 1901. Nothing was done until 1927, when Congress directed the secretary of agriculture to develop a national arboretum. Early planning and the acquisition of land were in the hands of F. V. Colville, principal botanist, and B. Y. Morrison, principal horticulturist, both of the United States Department of Agriculture. In 1951 Dr. Morrison became the first director of the arboretum.

Today this arboretum of 444 acres is one of the largest and most comprehensive in the country, dedicated to the education of the public in matters horticultural and botanical and to plant research, especially the breeding and introduction of new ornamentals. Run by the Science and Education Administration of the Department of Agriculture, it is aided by an advisory council of concerned citizens appointed by the secretary of agriculture. Since 1975, legislation has allowed gifts to be accepted from outside sources.

- *Admission:* Free.
- *Hours:* Open daily, all year. Monday to Friday 8:00 A.M.–5:00 P.M. Saturday and Sunday 10:00 A.M.–5:00 P.M. Closed

Christmas Day. Bonsai Collection: Daily 10:00 A.M.–2:30 P.M. Administration Building and Information Center: Weekdays, 8:00 A.M.–4:30 P.M. Closed weekends except for scheduled events.

· *Plants:* Labeled.

· *Physically handicapped:* National Herb Garden entirely accessible to wheelchairs. Cars may be driven all along the paved road and brief stops made anywhere.

· *Address:* United States National Arboretum, 24th and R streets N.E., Washington, D.C. 20002. Tel. (202) 472-9100.

· *Location and directions:* In northeastern section of District of Columbia. Visitors' entrance on New York Avenue, N.E. By car or taxi: From downtown Washington, take Maryland Avenue N.E. from Capitol to Bladensburg Road. Follow Bladensburg Road to New York Avenue N.E. Turn right and follow New York Avenue to service road and visitors' entrance. Public transport: From central Washington, take metrorail or bus 42 to Stadium Armory Station; then take bus B-2, B-4, or B-5 to intersection of Bladensburg Road and R Street. Walk east on R Street 300 yards to R Street gate. For information on metrorail or bus schedules, call (202) 637-2437.

· *Parking:* Free, within the gates.

· *No gift shop.* Pamphlets, maps, etc. available at administration building and information center.

· *No snack bar or restaurant.* There are restaurants nearby.

· *No picnicking.*

If you have been to nearby Dumbarton Oaks, or plan to go, you will be struck by the contrast between that small private garden emphasizing design and comfortable outdoor living and this large public garden focusing on the plants themselves rather than on their role as elements of design. Of course, this distinction sometimes breaks down: Dumbarton Oaks has specimen trees grown for their own sake, while the National Arboretum uses plants as design features in many areas.

Do not let the lack of a car prevent you from visiting the National Arboretum. You may not see it all, but in the vicinity of the administration building there is enough of interest to occupy two or three hours. The National Herb Garden and the Japanese Garden are in this area, and they in themselves merit a special visit. One great advantage of coming by car is that driving and temporary parking are allowed along all the paved

The Bonsai Collection

road, so that walking energy can be reserved for places of special interest.

In general, the arrangement of plants is botanical. In other words, most of the species of a particular genus are placed together. For aesthetic reasons there are of course exceptions; otherwise the arboretum would not be the thing of beauty that it is. Among the single-genus plantings, the following are outstanding: hollies, camellias, azaleas, magnolias, crab apples, cherries, viburnums, maples, and herbaceous genera such as iris, day lilies, and peonies.

On entering the arboretum, proceed to the modern glass-and-concrete administration building or to the information center to collect a map and look over the various free brochures, available for most of the genera mentioned above as well as for the special gardens like the National Herb Garden. After consulting the blooming dates, select brochures, most of which have detailed maps so that the location of particular species can be easily pinpointed.

The obvious first stop is the Japanese Garden with its bonsai* collection. At the time of writing (1980) the Japanese Garden is not complete; the transition from the western gardens all around is too abrupt to allow one to comprehend the difference in philosophy that separates the Japanese garden designer from his western counterpart (for more on this, see p. 208). Perhaps by 1982 the various planned additions will have been made, so that

* Pronounced "bone-sigh."

the western visitor will experience the change of pace and mood necessary for the appreciation of any form of oriental garden art. In 1980 the highlight is the National Bonsai Collection, magnificently housed in a pavilion specially designed to show off these venerable living treasures to perfection. All are master bonsai, a Bicentennial gift from the government of Japan. The Department of Agriculture leaflet explains in detail what you see here. Maybe it is impossible for a westerner to see these trees in the Japanese way, but that they symbolize the beauty and tranquillity of nature is undeniable. Yet this is paradoxical, for only by man's intervention have they achieved this dwarfed, gnarled, timeless appearance. (Courses on bonsai are offered here regularly. If you are interested, inquire at the reception desk.)

BONSAI: *Each small tree or group of trees is a miniature landscape comprising an exquisite plant form in harmony with its setting. The setting is a combination of container shape, soil, surface moss, and partially exposed roots. That the trees are old (often one hundred years) is incidental; as works of art in Japan, they are judged purely on form. Obviously, a great deal of care, attention, and expertise is needed to produce the prized effect. Judicious pruning, wiring, watering, and fertilizing and meticulous maintenance are involved. Look for a pine tree with short needles: Pinus parviflora, the Japanese white pine. These usually make the best bonsai.*

The National Herb Garden has appeal for everyone. Partly historical and partly ethnobotanical,* it demonstrates the many ways plants have been used by different cultures in times past. (Their vital role as food, however, is not the subject of this display.) A triad of gardens makes up this recent construction: the Specialty Garden, the Knot Garden, and the Historic Rose Garden.

Of the three, the Specialty Garden is perhaps the most interesting. In this oval-shaped area the plants are grouped into ten different categories, each occupying a separate plot. Labeling is clear and comprehensive. For those who have yet to see it, the ten specialties are oriental herbs, industrial plants, fragrance plants, traditional culinary herbs, beverage plants, dye plants,

* Ethnobotany is the study of the ways in which different cultures use plants.

One of the specialty gardens

plants of colonial America, American Indian herbs, plants used in modern medicine, and Dioscorides' medicinal plants. Each garden is on the periphery of the central grassy oval and is delineated from its neighbors by low boxwood hedges (*Buxus sempervirens* 'Suffruticosa') and trees of ethnobotanical significance. Periodically, the species in the plots are changed. But even if books and pamphlets do not keep pace with the changes, the labeling is so museumlike in its comprehensiveness that the visitor should have no difficulty.

Nonetheless, one comment: the tropical periwinkle, seen here in plot 5, has recently been shown to contain two alkaloids with

The Historic Rose Garden

marked ability to suppress the growth of some malignant tumors. Here is a telling illustration of the reason that wholesale destruction of floras not yet studied is tragically short-sighted.

It is not immediately apparent why so much space has been devoted to the other two gardens of the triad, the Knot Garden and the Historic Rose Garden. The Knot Garden demonstrates *parterre de broderie* (see p. 17), which traditionally was executed in low-growing herbs. Here the intricate twists and twirls are done in larger, nontraditional dwarf conifers. It seems a pity that if a knot garden was to be illustrated, it should not have been done in the authentic way, using Elizabethan herbs such as germander, *Teucrium pyrenaicum*, and lavender cotton, *Santolina chamaecyparissus*. If the reason was size, the garden could have been made smaller.

The Historic Rose Garden is fascinating to rosarians. It is not easy to find a garden today that displays the old species roses (but see Mohonk, pp. 256-7). In fact, many here had to be imported from Europe. These are the roses that played such an important role in social history and that are, of course, the ancestors of modern roses. Even for those not so well versed nor so interested in rose lore, this garden will be a visual and olfactory delight in June and early July. Old or species roses, though generally more fragrant than modern ones, bloom only in spring. This garden, when compared with modern rose gardens, is a testimony to the achievements of hybridization. (For more on roses, see pp. 182-4.)

The Gotelli Conifer Collection

In 1980 the trellis walkways were starkly bare. When covered with vines, they should be shady resting spots, reminiscent of the galleries of the "pleasance" gardens of the late Middle Ages.

Apart from the roses, this garden is best viewed in summer and late fall, when the herbs have reached their maturity. (For more on the role played by herbs in past times, see pp. 203–4.)

The National Arboretum is the azalea showplace of the Middle Atlantic states. (Winterthur is its nearest rival; see pp. 157–9.) This is to be expected since its first director, the late B. Y. Morrison, was one of the most successful breeders of azaleas in this country. Within the Morrison Garden four hundred named cultivars of the Glenn Dale series, which he bred and named, are on display. Peak bloom is late April to late May.

Since the arboretum sits in the middle zone between North and South, practically all the azalea hybrids (except the Indica series, which prospers in Florida and Charleston, S.C.) can be grown here, as well as fifteen of the native species and the best of the exotics. In late May to late June visit the Lee Garden, which is reserved for late bloomers—hybrids like the Satsuki series, and species, both native and exotic.

EVERGREEN HYBRID AZALEAS: *The Ghents were among the earliest azalea hybrids. Originally bred in Belgium in the 1820s, they were products of crosses between the evergreen* Rhododendron luteum, *from northern Turkey, and various deciduous American azaleas. This was long before the discovery of the spectacular Asiatic species of this genus.*

Another hybrid series is the Kurume series from Japan, discovered in 1914 by plant explorer Ernest H. "Chinese" Wilson, who brought them to Boston in 1915. The Satsuki hybrids, also Japanese, are prized for their large single flowers and late blooming habit—May, in some localities. (In classical Japanese, Satsuki means "fifth month," referring to the old lunar calendar.)

One of the most successful breeders of hybrid azaleas in this country was the late B. Y. Morrison, first director of the National Arboretum. The Glenn Dale series, bred by Morrison at the Glenn Dale Station of the Department of Agriculture, were developed for the Washington area, though they do well as far south as Callaway Gardens in Georgia. The primary species used in Morrison's breeding program was the evergreen (really semi-evergreen) Japanese Rhododendron obtusum. *Morrison also developed the Back Acre series in Mississippi after his retirement from Washington.*

For more details on the arboretum's azaleas and their locations, see the USDA pamphlet *Azaleas and Rhododendrons*. Note that the collections are all south and west of the information center at the R Street entrance. Be prepared for huge crowds at blooming time. Come on a weekday, if possible.

From mid-March to mid-April and in October and November, the camellias are in bloom at the east end of the grounds. At the limit of their hardiness here in Washington, the two most hardy species are *Camellia japonica* (spring-blooming) and *C. sasanqua* (fall-blooming). Currently, the arboretum is involved in a breeding program whose major goal is the development of cold-resistant hybrids, using the other species seen in the camellia collection, not just japonicas and sasanquas. (For more on these beautiful evergreens of the tea family, see pp. 56–8.)

Magnolias are well represented; they are interspersed within the extensive holly collection on the west side of Holly Spring Road. The early Asiatic species, such as the yulan magnolia, *Magnolia denudata*, start blooming in the first week of April and continue through the entire month. During the second week in May the native species, such as the big-leaf magnolia, *M. macrophylla*, and the sweet bay, *M. virginiana*, follow suit. Like the camellias, the southern magnolia, *M. grandiflora*, is just hardy here in Washington; it produces its large, fragrant flowers in late May and well into June. Some huge specimens of *Magnolia* 'Freeman' can be seen here. These are hybrids, originated in the arboretum from a cross between *M. virginiana* and *M. grandiflora* and looking more like the male parent, *grandiflora*. To locate the magnolia species and cultivars, pick up the USDA leaflet on hollies. Incidentally, the holly collection here is exceptionally fine because of the climate and because the arboretum has for many years conducted a holly-breeding program. Hollies are at their best in November and December when bedecked with their red or yellow berries. (For more on hollies, see p. 246.)

Another species that is tender farther north is the crepe myrtle, *Lagerstroemia indica*. In July and August look for these beautiful flowering trees at the junction of Valley and Beechwood roads, near Heart Pond. Efforts here at the arboretum to produce hybrids more resistant to mildew are meeting with apparent success.

If your interest is conifers, do not miss the Gotelli Conifer Collection at the northeast corner of the grounds. Consisting of some fifteen hundred plants, it was given to the arboretum by William T. Gotelli. Beautifully landscaped, this section is probably best appreciated in winter when almost everything else looks dead. (For more on conifers, see p. 245.)

For those who enjoy natural woodlands, a self-guided trail leads through Fern Valley just off Crabtree Road. (The trail guide is available at the administration building.) For wild flowers the best time, of course, is spring; ferns are probably at their best in summer, when all the fiddleheads have expanded into mature leaves.

The National Arboretum is a wonderful place for the plantsman. Like the Arnold Arboretum, it is a living museum to keep visiting and revisiting, doing the "rooms" one at a time. A most noticeable feature is its excellent state of maintenance. With an adequate budget from the Department of Agriculture, it has nothing of the rundown aspect so common today in public gardens, where money is woefully tight. The fact that in 1979–80 over $400,000 was invested in the National Herb Garden by donations made to the Herb Society of America and matching funds from Congress is welcome and reassuring news to all plant lovers.

NEMOURS

Wilmington, Delaware

UNIQUE FEATURE	· A twentieth-century garden executed in the grand French manner of the seventeenth century—in other words, a miniature Versailles in the Brandywine valley.

HISTORY: Surrounded by a high brick wall studded with broken glass to keep out intruders—"including the other du Ponts"—the Nemours property comprises three hundred acres. Alfred I. du Pont built the mansion between 1909 and 1910, though the gardens were not completed until 1932. The Terrace Colonnade was officially opened, or "housewarmed," in 1931 when it was the scene of Mrs. du Pont's sister's wedding. The gardens were open for only one day in 1932—entrance fee, one dollar. Everyone came, including the other du Ponts, who also paid up. Unrecognized, Alfred directed the traffic and amused himself by watching the reactions of his many relatives to his flamboyant horticultural statement. He and his wife are buried beneath the Carillon Tower.

Today part of the land is occupied by the Alfred I. du Pont Institute, a hospital for the orthopedically handicapped. Both it and the Nemours estate are generously funded by the Nemours Foundation.*

· *Admission:* Entrance fee. Visitors, who must be over sixteen years old, are escorted by a tour guide through the house and into the gardens. There they may wander at will, until ready to return to the parking lot by minibus.

· *Tours:* Gardens open May through November. Visits by guided tour only. Tours Tuesday to Saturday at 9:00 A.M., 11:00 A.M., 1:00 P.M., and 3:00 P.M.; Sundays at 11:00 A.M., 1:00 P.M., and

---

* The *s* in Nemours is silent, except when you say "Nemours Foundation."

3:00 P.M. Tours begin at the reception center on Rockland Road. Visitors should arrive 15 minutes prior to the tour. Reservations recommended for individuals, required for groups. For information or reservations write or call The Nemours Foundation, Reservations Office, P.O. Box 109, Wilmington, Del. 19899. Tel. (302) 573-3333.

- *Plants:* Not labeled.
- *Physically handicapped:* At time of going to press (1981), tours had not yet been adapted for handicapped visitors. Inquiries should be made at address or telephone number above.
- *Directions:* From Wilmington, drive north on U.S. 202, watching for signs for the Alfred I. du Pont Institute. Go west on Delaware 141, then turn left onto Rockland Road. Entrance is on Rockland Road. Request map when making reservations.
- *Parking:* Free, outside gates.
- *No gift shop.*
- *No snack bar or restaurant.*
- *No picnicking.*

Nemours is a sumptuous extravaganza, a garden to impress: in the vernacular, a knockout. The cynical would say the whole place shrieks "money." But from what we know of Alfred I. du Pont, this was contrary to his intention. He sent his son to study garden design in Paris. It is hardly surprising, that Alfred Victor transmitted to his father his enthusiasm for the glories of Versailles and the garden concepts of André Le Nôtre, its famous landscape architect. Alfred Victor, among others, planned the Nemours estate.

ANDRÉ LE NÔTRE: *Appointed garden architect to Louis XIV, the "Sun King," André Le Nôtre (1613–1700) was commissioned to design the garden for the palace of Versailles, which was being transformed from a hunting lodge into a royal residence. The king had seen the excellent work Le Nôtre had done at Vaux-le-Vicomte, the palace of his finance minister, Nicolas Fouquet. (That occasion and its aftermath are a fascinating story of royal envy, but beyond our scope here.)*

Le Nôtre was primarily a mathematician and an architect. In essence, these were his views on garden design: the house itself should be free of clutter—no foundation plantings; the main axis should be a vista stretching off into infinity; all axes, whether

main or subsidiary, should be canals or avenues lined with trees
(allées); parterre gardens should be near the house for the enjoyment of those within; flowers should be used only in the parterres
(flowers played no part in Le Nôtre's "grand design"—though a
contemporary on one visit counted nine thousand pots of blooms
in the Versailles gardens); fountains should lend dignity and
opulence to the entire scene (fourteen thousand jets were erected
at Versailles).

All of this presupposed vast space and unlimited amounts of
water at the disposal of the planner. This is why Le Nôtre's
style has been described as gardening in the grand manner. Space
he always had because his patrons were either royal or rich nobles.
Versailles was his masterpiece; it is inconceivable that any garden
will ever again be constructed on so vast a scale. Though sought
after by most of the kings of Europe, it is believed that he never
ventured outside France.

Although described as a mini-Versailles, Nemours breaks one
of Le Nôtre's fundamental rules: the main axis does not provide
a limitless vista. It stops at the huge Colonnade constructed of
Indiana limestone. Behind this is a sunken fountain garden, a
pond, and a grassy slope leading to the focal point of a second
vista—the Temple of Love. But these cannot be seen from the
house because of the gleaming white colossus built to honor the
memory of Alfred's great-great-grandfather, Pierre Samuel du
Pont de Nemours, and his son.

Vista to the Colonnade

Like Versailles, Nemours is not scaled to the individual human being. Walk around the swimming pool—now called the reflecting pool—which is one acre in size. Stand beside one of the four sculpture groups on its periphery. Don't you feel dwarfed? From the house the Colonnade and the fountain are effective eye-stoppers, but close up they are overpowering.

Garden architecture here is more important than the plants. Framing the vista are horse chestnuts, *Aesculus hippocastanum*, pin oaks, *Quercus palustris*, cryptomeria, *Cryptomeria japonica* 'Lobbii', as well as the cut-leaf stephanandra, *Stephanandra incisa*, a Korean shrub that blooms in June and belongs to the rose family. The edging ground cover is English ivy, *Hedera helix*. Markers for the vista are two rows of marble urns. Immediately in front of the Colonnade is a very self-conscious geometric garden of two kinds of evergreens, no more than two feet high—a Japanese holly, *Ilex crenata*, and American hemlock, *Tsuga canadensis*. This is called the maze, though it is not a true maze, for mazes do not have beds. It functions as a rather fussy carpet for the gilded statue "Achievement"—itself a fitting tribute to Alfred I. du Pont. Somewhat reminiscent of World War II bond posters, it is covered in gold leaf. The square wooden containers for the terrace trees are exact copies of ones designed for Versailles (during *its* heyday three thousand orange trees in tubs like these had to be moved out of the orangery every spring).

Look back at the fountain in the reflecting pool—157 jets are involved. If any are pointing outward, spoiling the effect,

The "maze" garden

"Achievement"

blame the geese whose nocturnal collisions with the jets throw them off kilter. The water in the fountains now recirculates; originally it came from a tributary of the Brandywine.

All the marble statuary in the Colonnade is modern (Art Deco). Only the two urns are antiques, from the Hapsburg Palace in Austria. The elegant Diana in the Temple of Love, dating from 1790, was executed by Houdon.

Behind the Colonnade in the sunken garden and framing the temple vista are hundreds of tulips in beds edged with box, *Buxus sempervirens* 'Suffruticosa.' Approximately fifty thousand tulip bulbs, *Tulipa gesnerana*, are planted in the gardens every fall. In

The Temple of Love

The mansion

this section only the pond and the tiny bridge strike an informal note. Beyond and near the Children's Playhouse is a spring pond presided over by—in this garden of all gardens—Disney-type gnomes. Totally unexpected, but providing comic relief to the nasty-looking marble satyrs and other monstrosities that inhabit the Colonnade and its evirons.

Alfred I. du Pont built Nemours for his wife, who didn't much care for it and rarely lived here. While appreciating its bold sweep, its opulence and ambitious proportions, one can understand why a person might not feel at home here. And in fact, it was used very little for entertaining. Yet its garden predecessors in France were constructed for that very purpose. Only when full of people enjoying themselves did those great gardens become human in scale.

Having experienced Nemours (the verb is used deliberately), it will be well worth your while to see what the other du Pont cousins, Henry at Winterthur and Pierre at Longwood, did with their estates. Nothing could be more different, although both Pierre and Alfred applied their engineering skills in the construction of their gardens. Very early in his life Alfred demonstrated an inventive turn of mind by designing an electric rat trap. The Colonnade—a later statement—and the rat trap are just two of many bizarre incongruities in the life of this remarkable man, recorded in a book by Marquis James.*

* *The Family Rebel—Alfred I. du Pont* (Indianapolis: Bobbs-Merrill Co., 1941).

WINTERTHUR

❧

Winterthur, Delaware

UNIQUE FEATURES	• One of the finest examples in this country of a naturalistic garden, executed in the English landscape tradition. • A pinetum containing the best collection of rare conifers in the eastern United States.

HISTORY: In 1839 James A. Bidermann and his wife, Eveline Gabrielle, daughter of E. I. du Pont de Nemours, bought the estate they called Winterthur (pronounced "Winter-tour") after the Bidermann home town in Switzerland. In 1867 Mrs. Bidermann's brother Henry du Pont acquired the property. From that time it passed from father to son until 1927, when the last private owner, Henry Francis du Pont, inherited the estate. It was Henry Francis who made the greatest contribution to the design and planting of the sixty-acre garden as its exists today. He began in 1902 by planting bulbs along the March Walk. The incomparable collection of azaleas and rhododendrons was his acquisition. In 1951 he gave his home to the Winterthur Corporation, a nonprofit educational foundation established in 1930. Later that year, the Henry Francis du Pont Museum was opened to the public. In 1952 the garden followed suit. Mr. du Pont continued to augment and develop the gardens until his death in 1969. The Quarry, for instance, was completed in the 1960s.

• *Admission:* Entrance fee. Extra fee for escorted open-air tram ride (45 minutes) around the garden; runs mid-April through October (but not on holiday Mondays or July 4).
• *Hours:* Open all year. Tuesday to Saturday 10:00 A.M.–4:00 P.M. Sunday 12:00 noon–4:00 P.M. National holiday Mondays 12:00 noon–4:00 P.M. Closed all other Mondays, Thanksgiving Day, Christmas Eve, Christmas Day, and New Year's Day.

- *Museum tours:* Extra fee and reservations required. Call or write Reservations Office (see below). No reservations necessary for the gardens.
- *Plants:* 50 percent labeled; aim is 100 percent.
- *Physically handicapped:* Adaptations have been made in the parking lot and visitors' pavilion. Alternate routes through the gardens accessible to wheelchairs. Tram, which departs from and returns to pavilion, can accommodate two wheelchairs.
- *Address:* Reservations Office, Winterthur Museum, Winterthur, Del. 19735. Tel. (302) 656-8591, Monday to Friday, 8:30 A.M.–4:30 P.M.
- *Location and directions:* 6 miles northwest of Wilmington on Delaware 52 (Pennsylvania Avenue); turnoff is on right at a traffic light with large green sign. Or take Amtrack train to Wilmington, taxi to Winterthur. (Winterthur is 36 miles from Philadelphia, 138 miles from New York City.)
- *Parking:* Free.
- *Shops:* Gift shop in visitors' pavilion; plant shop open seasonally near pavilion.
- *Restaurant:* In visitors' pavilion; open for breakfast, lunch, and snacks.
- *No picnicking.*

Winterthur is a naturalistic garden. This means that the garden design takes full advantage of the native vegetation and natural topography. The skillful addition of exotics and the judicious felling of trees, producing a parklike effect, has converted the landscape into a garden. Henry Francis du Pont had the vision to see that the virgin forest of beech, hickory, and tulip poplar could form the skeleton of his garden.

Begin with the forty-five-minute tram tour: this gives an overview of a landscape of infinite variety. Enclosed woodland gives way to open parkland, affording vistas terminating in hills topped by gazebos, clumps of specimen trees, or deep valleys carved by winding streams. It all looks perfectly natural. But detailed examination reveals Spanish and Siberian wild flowers growing beneath Japanese azaleas, a Californian conifer standing next to one from China, Himalayan primulas complementing native marsh marigolds. And where have all these glorious azaleas come from? The Far East.

Henry du Pont was a landscape designer who was also a connoisseur of plants. This made it possible for him not only to

"Mexican Hat" archway

create a garden out of a Delaware woodland but to populate it with some of the most beautiful plants from all over the world, and in profusion. When you leave the tram, take a stroll in the woods and farther, if time permits. Beneath a tulip tree is a carpet of Spanish bluebells, *Endymion hispanicus*; across the path may be another of trilliums, *Trillium* sp. Wild nature is no longer like this; perhaps it was a couple of hundred years ago. The picking of wild flowers by generations of "nature lovers" has left most of our woodlands so bare that one enthuses over a single trillium or wood anemone.

Using the map, aim for the Mushroom Seat area. You are now one the edge of the Azalea Woods. Find the figures of George and Martha Washington (in Roman dress!) and the "Mexican Hat" archway. If it is spring, low clouds of the white azalea *Rhododendron mucronatum* 'Magnifica' will be everywhere (this same species is to be seen in the Star at Dumbarton Oaks, p. 133). As you walk through these woods, notice the color scheme: nothing jars, bright reds are muted by white, mauves and purples shade into one another. Very careful consideration went into the plantings. If colors clashed, bushes were moved. Azalea colors are so vivid that they can fight with one another. Many of these original bushes are now too tall; to restore the panoramic view that was part of the plan, they must soon be replaced. Most of these azaleas are Kurume hybrids (see p. 45) which Henry du Pont purchased in 1915 from the original Japanese display in San Francisco. Since then they have been propagated here at Winterthur.

Rhododendron
mucronatum 'Magnifica'

In their understated way the wild flowers, both native and exotic, rival the azaleas in beauty. Here are the Italian anemone, *Anemone appenina*; the dame's-rocket, *Hesperis matronalis*, its lavender flowers echoing the mauve accents of the nearby azaleas; the Virginia bluebell, *Mertensia virginica*; *Trillium* spp. and the Spanish bluebell.

Originally these woods were a nursery for azaleas. About the time of the original purchase of the Kurumes, the native sweet chestnut was dying of the chestnut blight. To fill in the gaps Henry du Pont planted azaleas in a kind of holding pattern. The results were so effective that the nursery became a full-fledged garden. To the azaleas were added true rhododendrons—those with the large evergreen leaves—from the nursery of the late Charles O. Dexter of Sandwich, Massachusetts.

D EXTER'S HYBRIDS: *The hybrid rhododendrons produced by Charles O. Dexter in the 1920s and 1930s have proved more desirable than the old ironclads bred in England in the nineteenth century from native American species. 'Nova Zembla' and 'Roseum Elegans' were two popular ironclads, highly successful in the northeastern United States. All ironclads, however, have a bluish cast to their flower color, producing a "muddy" effect even in the red 'Nova Zembla.' Through the auspices of of the Arnold Arboretum and the efforts of Ernest H. "Chinese" Wilson, Dexter received rhododendrons from the Far East which had no trace of the blue pigment. These species were white,* cream, and red. Using these and others, he proceeded to breed hybrids of clear colors, hardy enough to grow as far north as Massachusetts; some of them have been named. In the thirties many great gardens such as Winterthur bought seedlings from Dexter, making their own selections, for not all of his hybrids were noteworthy. Winterthur has registered one especially lovely biscuit-colored hybrid called 'Tan.' Since Dexter died in 1943, many other American rhododendron breeders have continued his work, using new Asiatic species. However, he was the pioneer in breeding hardy rhododendrons of clear vibrant colors for northeastern American gardens. The pure pink 'Scintillation' is perhaps the most popular of Dexter's hybrids and the easiest for home gardeners to purchase. (For more on rhododendrons, see pp. 249–50.)

As of 1980, Winterthur has constructed a new native azalea garden. If you are interested, ask for directions.

Leaving the Azalea Woods, walk through the Pinetum to the Sundial Garden, laid out in 1914 by Colonel du Pont, Henry's father. Approximately sixty-three species of conifers are represented here, many of them rare and including the comparatively recently discovered dawn redwood, *Metasequoia glyptostroboides* (see pp. 287–8). The somberness of the Pinetum is lit up in spring by early-flowering shrubs such as *Forsythia ovata* and the wonderfully fragrant *Viburnum carlesii*, accompanied by azaleas and flowering quince, *Chaenomeles speciosa*, in shades of red,

The Pinetum from Sundial Garden

white, and pink. If the empress trees, *Paulownia tomentosa*, on the back road are in bloom, it is well worth a climb to the Lookout to gaze back at the purple mist of flowers framed by the green darkness of the tall firs. Although *Paulownia* is a Chinese tree, it was named for Anna Pavlovna, the daughter of Czar Paul I of Russia. Introduced as a novelty for its dramatic flowers, this tree of the foxglove family has now become a weed in many parts of the country. Not a tree for small gardens, here it is positioned just right, as it is in Longwood (see p. 170). The young trees have leaves of almost tropical proportions, presumably an adaptation to the shade in which the seedlings normally start life.

The Sundial Garden is one of the rare formal or semiformal gardens at Winterthur. Originally the site of the family's tennis and croquet lawns, it was designed in the late fifties by Marian Coffin and Henry du Pont. Note the billowy boxwood hedges, *Buxus sempervirens* 'Suffruticosa,' which together with the conifers make an excellent background for the flowering shrubs planted here. In early May a rare Chinese tree, the yellowhorn, *Xanthoceras sorbifolium*, should be in bloom. The showy cream-colored spikes of orange-centered blossoms make such a wonderful picture that it is a mystery why it is not more commonly grown. (Both the Barnes Arboretum and the Planting Fields Arboretum also have specimens.) Another Chinese plant that attracts attention here in May is the snowball shrub, *Viburnum macrocephalum* 'Sterile,' with its large balls of white, infertile flowers. This clone is entirely dependent upon man for its con-

The Sundial Garden

tinued existence and is properly described as a cultivar. In April behind the boxwood hedge is the silver-bell tree, *Halesia carolina*, dangling its dainty pink or white flowers, also another native, fothergilla, two species of which will be seen here: *Fothergilla monticola* and *F. major*, easily recognized by their creamy-white "bottlebrush" inflorescences. This shrub deserves to be better appreciated in its native land. An early introduction from the colonies, it is much more common in Europe. In fact it is called after an eighteenth-century English doctor, John Fothergill.

In 1960 an old quarry was converted into an unusual naturalistic garden featuring bog and rock plants. Streams keep the lower level of the quarry boglike, and here various species of Himalayan primulas grow in profusion. Bloom begins early in April with the globose-headed *Primula denticulata*, followed by various "candelabra" species in late spring and summer. Shrubs, ferns, and wild flowers—both native and exotic—planted among the rocks and under the beeches and oaks make this an enchanting place to sit, especially on a warm day. Early in April the wild marsh marigold, *Caltha palustris*, of the buttercup family grows on the banks of the streams. Clenny Run, a tributary of the Brandywine which flows through Winterthur forming small pools where wild fowl congregate, contributes to the beauty and tranquillity of this place.

Winterthur's only really formal garden is beside the museum. Here will be found garden ornaments, conspicuously absent elsewhere. Steps and flagstones, statuary, fountain, and swimming pool date back to a much earlier period when this was "the sunken garden." The area around the pool is a garden "room" in the sense the word was used at Dumbarton Oaks (see p. 130). Flowering bulbs enliven this area in early spring, while in summer annuals and other tender plants that do not belong in a naturalistic garden can be bedded out here.

Winters in Delaware are relatively mild. Flowers begin to show themselves at Winterthur in March or even February. If you come at that time, explore the March Walk. Follow the path north of the museum towards the area labeled on the map as "Magnolia Bend," and you will be rewarded by the first glimpse of spring. Carpeting the ground are snowdrops—especially the giant species, *Galanthus elwesii*; species crocus like *Crocus tomasinianus* (called tommies in England), which blooms much earlier than the commoner Dutch hybrids; *Adonis amurensis*, a yellow buttercup relative from Siberia; squills, *Scilla* spp.; the spring snowflake, *Leucojum vernum*; winter aconite, *Eranthis hyemalis*, another buttercup relative of bright yellow hue; and many others.

The staff report that around April 4 or 5 early bulbs are at their peak of bloom at Winterthur. So is the Winter Hazel Walk, marked on the map. From the Azalea Woods it can be seen as a haze of pale yellow and lavender. The winter hazels, *Corylopsis* spp., are oriental shrubs belonging to the witch-hazel family, all having pendulous inflorescences of pale yellow flowers before the leaves emerge. The lavender color comes from the Korean rhododendron, *Rhododendron mucronulatum* (not to be confused with *Rh. mucronatum* mentioned earlier). It is a true rhododendron, but deciduous. Hardier than *Corylopsis*, it will grow throughout the United States. Underplantings complement these shrubs; various species of hellebores, *Helleborus* spp. of the buttercup family, predominate. Their decorative evergreen foliage and their white, green, or purple flowers make this also a Hellebore Walk.

By mid-April the drifts of daffodils, *Narcissus* spp., are blooming all over the golf course and around Clenny Run and its pools. Henry du Pont ruled against geometric beds for the daffodils. Instead, he had his gardeners enclose areas of grassland with fallen branches. Within these areas bulbs were planted, the assumption being that the natural curves of the branches would shape beds more in keeping with a naturalistic garden.

For the plant lover there is so much to see here that it is impossible to cover everything. But if you are here in May, do not

Clenny Run

fail to visit the Peony Garden, a wonderful collection of herbaceous and tree peonies (the latter have woody stems so that they do not die down to ground level at the onset of winter—technically, they are shrubs). Peonies have been revered in China since time immemorial. Hybridization has produced some of the most gorgeous cultivars. Professor A. P. Saunders of Clinton, New York, was responsible for all the plants you see here, though some breeding of this genus (*Paeonia*) was done in France and Japan. Peonies are members of the buttercup family, a family that includes some of the most beautiful of cultivated flowers. Like magnolias, peonies are primitive flowers, having the open-saucer (bowl) type of design wherein the sex organs (stamens and pistil) are accessible to all comers—beetles, slugs, bees, or flies.

Obviously spring is the best season to visit this garden. But so much effort has been put into its planning that it is a delight at all seasons. For example, not only foliage color but berried shrubs, carefully selected, make autumn a wonderful time here. The sapphire berry, *Symplocos paniculata*, on the Winter Hazel Walk, with its iridescent ultramarine fruits, is a case in point.

Note: Apropos of the importance of the du Pont family in Wilmington, Delaware, is the following remark overheard by the author in the Azalea Woods: "You think it is not going to bloom? Of course it is—Mr. du Pont would come down here and raise hell if it didn't!"

LONGWOOD GARDENS

Kennett Square, Pennsylvania

<table>
<tr><td>UNIQUE
FEATURES</td><td>· The most spectacular fountains of any garden in the United States.
· The finest and largest conservatories (nearly four acres under glass) in the United States.</td></tr>
</table>

HISTORY: The land on which Longwood Gardens now stands was purchased by a Quaker farmer, George Peirce, from William Penn's land commissioners in 1700. George's son Joshua built the family homestead there in 1732. Joshua's twin grandsons, Joshua and Samuel Peirce, began planting an arboretum near the house in 1798. During the nineteenth century, Peirce's Park became known as the finest collection of evergreen trees in the United States.

In 1906 Pierre du Pont purchased the property from the Peirce family, primarily to save the arboretum, which was about to be felled for lumber. After transforming the Peirce farmhouse into his residence, he proceeded to construct a formal garden which was to become the finest in the United States. His training in engineering and his fascination with garden fountains inspired him to imitate the water gardens of Renaissance Italy and France. Until his death in 1954 he directed the development of Longwood; visitors were allowed in from the beginning, but not until 1921 were the gardens officially declared open to the public.

At his death Pierre du Pont bequeathed Longwood forever to the public use. Permanently and handsomely endowed, it was first operated by Longwood Foundation, Inc., in 1937. Today the responsibility has passed to the Trustees of Longwood Gardens, Inc. Garden receipts constitute approximately one-third of the total budget necessary to take care of three hundred landscaped acres and an additional seven hundred acres of meadow and woodland.

- *Admission:* Entrance fee, which includes brochure with map. Extra fee for Peirce-du Pont house. (Maps also available in French, Spanish, German, Italian, Chinese, and Japanese.)
- *Hours:* Open daily, all year. April 1 through October 31, 9:00 A.M.–6:00 P.M. November 1 through March 31, 10:00 A.M.–5:00 P.M. Conservatories: daily 10:00 A.M.–5:00 P.M. Half-hour displays of the famous illuminated fountains are scheduled two evenings a week at 9:15, mid-June through August. On these dates, conservatories remain open until 10:30 P.M.
- *Cultural events:* Organ music most Saturday and Sunday afternoons 2:00–3:00, October through April. Over 100 performing-arts events each year. Write or telephone for brochure "Schedule of Events," published three times yearly.
- *Plants:* Display labels or brass identification labels located on north side of plant or group of plants.
- *Address:* Longwood Gardens, Kennett Square, Pa. 19348. Tel. (215) 388-6741.
- *Location and directions:* Northeast of Kennett Square on U.S. 1; 30 miles southwest of Philadelphia; 12 miles northwest of Wilmington, Del. Longwood entrance is on U.S. 1 near the Pennsylvania 52 (north) intersection. (Winterthur is 7 miles southeast of Longwood.)
- *Parking:* Free, outside the gardens.
- *Shops:* Gift shop, plant shop at visitor center.
- *No snack bar or restaurant. (A restaurant is scheduled to open in mid-1983.)*
- *Picnicking:* Permitted outside the gardens, April through mid-October.

Those who have absolutely no interest in either gardens or plants visit Longwood and are entertained. In the historic sense, it is a pleasure garden. Longwood satisfies the desire to see flowering plants of all colors and varieties, and in profusion. And as if that were not enough, it puts on a water spectacle, unique in this country, that was inspired by the great pleasure gardens of Renaissance Italy and France.

It has been stated elsewhere that water is an essential ingredient of good garden design. The sixteenth-century Italians carried it almost to excess, as demonstrated by the still existing Villa d'Este and Villa Lante. Intrigued and delighted by their waterworks on visits to Italy, Pierre du Pont also created a garden of fountains.

The fountains in other gardens described in this book have often been disappointing. For some reason or other they worked poorly or not at all. Even Louis XIV in his great park at Versailles had chronic fountain problems. But not Pierre du Pont. At Longwood they work, thanks to modern technology, Du Pont's engineering skill, and money.

In contrast to Winterthur, plants from the greenhouses are bedded out on a large scale beginning in May and continuing throughout the growing season, ensuring peak bloom until October. This is in the Victorian tradition. The most spectacular displays, however, are indoors in the conservatories. At all times and in all weathers Longwood can present a flowering panorama to its public.

Longwood could not be enjoyed from a tram. It is a garden for walking, for inspecting, for sitting. Plan to spend the best part of a day. Bring a picnic lunch to enjoy in the designated picnic area, or plan to visit one of the nearby restaurants—though a picnic is recommended as less time-consuming. Begin by watching the orientation slide show at the comfortable visitor center.

Before you start out from the visitor center, consult the map and note that there are three choices of direction: you may go east (to the right), west (to the left), or north (straight ahead). Your decision may be influenced by the weather. (If it is rainy, you should know that the conservatories will take up at least one full hour.) The three sections may be done in any order; that followed here is not necessarily the best. The assumption here is that the weather is warm—May to October. The emphasis of this description is less on plant identification and more on style and design. This is because of Longwood's stated policy that the plants displayed are selected for their aesthetic qualities rather than for their botanical interest. The bedding-out display methods involve constant change, seasonally and from year to year. Besides, in contrast to many gardens, trees and shrubs are meticulously labeled (if trees are planted in an *allée*, you may have to search for the one specimen that is labeled, but you can depend on finding it).

EASTERN SECTION

Starting out to the right from the visitor center, aim for the Open Air Theatre, by way of the Theatre Garden. In passing, note the Rose Arbor, which from June onward has its trellises covered with cascading blooms of the climbing or pillar-type roses. The Theatre Garden features Mediterranean-type plants, those which can stand up to moderate drought. Found here are various types of succulents, predominant among them the Spanish bayonet, *Yucca filamentosa*, one of the very few that is hardy at this latitude.

Immediately to your right, beyond the large stone wellhead, note the row of bald cypress, *Taxodium distichum*, originally part of Peirce's Park. Those who have seen bald cypress growing in Florida or South Carolina may be surprised to find such vigorous specimens here, and without their usual watery environment. However, this native species is highly adaptable; it can live in regular soil and grow as far north as Boston. Note the lack of "knees" (for more on this tree, see pp. 71–2).

The Open Air Theatre, dating from 1913 and inspired by the theater at the Villa Gori near Siena, Italy, was intended for the entertainment of the du Ponts' guests. Today it is used for benefit performances held throughout the summer. Its seating capacity is 2,100. Forming the backdrop of the stage are hemlocks, *Tsuga canadensis*, and Kentucky coffee trees, *Gymnocladus dioicus*, while the wings are meticulously clipped arborvitae, *Thuja occidentalis*. What is remarkable about this theater is its waterworks. The "curtain" is a line of jets spaced six inches apart; the two-level stage conceals hundreds of illuminated fountains, which give their own performance at the close of dramatic or musical evenings. Dressing rooms are under the stage and lawn.

The Flower Garden Walk is Longwood's original flower garden. Plantings were begun here in 1907. Now framed by mature evergreens, it is highly formal with its brick walk, central fountain, and end seat. Its plantings are changed frequently with specimen plants from the greenhouses and nursery so that it is colorful and eye-catching from early spring until autumnal frost. This is the Victorian style at its best, depending upon huge back-up greenhouses.

From the fountain of the Flower Garden take the south walk to the small garden room called the Square Garden. Enclosed by walls of clipped arborvitae and featuring a fountain in a square pool, it is usually planted with pansies in spring. Except for the flowers, this is a Renaissance-type garden. Flowers played no role in those gardens, probably because the Italian climate and soil were not particularly kind to small flowering plants.

Return to the bald-cypress walk and passing the Ornamental Grass Section, walk towards the lake. Here is another demonstration of a style: the landscape garden of eighteenth-century England. The tranquil lake, the magnificent trees, the naturalistic ambience, evoke the ghosts of "Capability" Brown (see p. 89) and his less aggressive successor, Humphrey Repton (p. 180). The love temple completes the picture. Such classical artifacts used to excess were to make such gardens ridiculous, but in the early days, used with restraint, they served as focal points in the green symphony of trees, grass, and their own watery reflections. Here the love temple serves exactly that purpose. Goldfish, geese, and other wildfowl complete the bucolic scene.

Returning to an earlier stage in this mini-history of garden style, we next encounter a small Italian Renaissance garden of the sixteenth century. Inspired by the water-parterre garden of the Villa Gamberaia near Florence (also a Renaissance "copy"), it outdoes it in hydrotechnics—if there is such a word—by the addition of a water staircase and scores of fountain jets placed in the six water parterres. As in all such gardens, plants are unimportant. Clipped hemlock forms the end wall, and an *allée* of clipped lindens, *Tilia cordata*, substitutes for the Italian cypresses of the original. The stonework, always an integral part of such gardens, is Italian, but modern. Gardeners in warm countries have from time immemorial realized the importance of water in producing a psychological cooling effect. Additional

The Italian Renaissance Garden

sensuous dimensions are the play of light on the moving liquid and the accompanying soothing sounds. Viewing this delightful spot, one is forced to agree with those early garden architects. (It is noteworthy that Winterthur manages to be successful without water ornamentation.)

We now glimpse Longwood's natural area. Cross over the bridge that spans the lake. Around you is the meadow, mowed once a year to prevent the natural process of succession from transforming it into a woodland. In summer and fall, wild flowers enliven this area, but in spring, the wood is the place to search for them. The native deciduous trees here are tulip poplar, *Liriodendron tulipifera*, beech, *Fagus grandifolia*, hickory, *Carya* spp., and various oaks, *Quercus* spp. Other plant communities to be explored are pine barrens, marshes, and limestone out-croppings.

Wend your way back to Peirce's Park. This is the original arboretum planted by the Peirce brothers at the turn of the nineteenth century. Near the lake is a large Kentucky coffee tree, easily recognizable in summer by its bipinnate leaves. A member of the pea family, it is native mostly west of the Appalachians. Nearer the Peirce house is a huge pagoda tree, *Sophora japonica*, also a member of the pea family but native to China and Korea and introduced in 1747. Its common name comes from the fact that it was often planted around Buddhist temples in China. It is a highly desirable ornamental, producing white inflorescences in late summer. Close to the house are other specimen trees planted around 1800, notably a huge cucumber tree, *Magnolia acuminata*, a native magnolia with greenish flowers and cucumber-shaped fruits. Two ginkgos, *Ginkgo biloba*, are easily identifiable by their fan-shaped leaves that turn bright yellow in the fall. The ginkgo, discovered by Europeans near Japanese temples in the seventeenth century, is a primitive conifer that once was widespread (fossil ginkgos have been found in England) but is now native only to a small habitat in eastern China. Ancient as it is, it is one of the few trees that stands up to urban air pollution. Yet perhaps it is this toughness that has enabled it to survive on earth for 200 million years.

A visit to the Peirce house, built in 1732, is worthwhile. Pierre du Pont added to it in 1914 by building another wing and enclosing the space between to make the conservatory you see today. This was Longwood's first display greenhouse.

NORTHERN SECTION

Leaving the Peirce house, take a little more time to explore Peirce's Park. Turn right and then west along an *allée* of copper beech, *Fagus sylvatica* 'Atropurpurea.' This is a cultivar of the English beech. Although its leaves are dark red, the vital chlorophyll necessary for photosynthesis is present, its green color masked by the red pigment anthocyanin. This is true of all red-leaved varieties, such as the Japanese maple, *Acer palmatum* 'Atropurpureum.' In the fall anthocyanin, manufactured by the dying leaves, turns our maple forests scarlet.

At the first intersection in the path, turn left along the east side of the Topiary Garden. This is an *allée* of empress trees, *Paulownia tomentosa* (see p. 160). If it is May, you may wish to walk the entire length, admiring the lavender flowers that bloom in advance of the leaves. Today the wood is much sought after for the manufacture of Japanese dowry boxes.

THE CONSERVATORIES: Although not an architectural landmark like the New York Botanical Garden's conservatory, Longwood's conservatories are a revelation of what triumphs horticultural science and art can accomplish. The original greenhouse, the so-called Orangerie, was opened in 1921. It is now the Main Conservatory. Since then additions have been made, the most recent being the Azalea House with its modern lamella-arch roof. Today nearly four acres of vegetation flourish under glass. The architecture of the Orangerie is reminiscent of similar Palladian buildings in Europe. Originally, it and the adjacent ornate ballroom, housing the magnificent organ, were used for entertaining, the Peirce–du Pont house being too small for lavish parties.

Two kinds of displays are mounted here: the permanent collections, which are mainly educational and the kind one would find in a major botanical garden; and the wonderful floral spectacles housed in the Main Conservatory and the Azalea House, which change with the seasons and are especially breathtaking at holiday times. Spring bulbs and lilies are featured at Easter, thousands of chrysanthemums of all types at Thanksgiving, and poinsettias, paper-white narcissus, and cyclamen at Christmas. Alternating with these are other "shows": azaleas and rhododendrons in March and begonias in the summer. Every bloom is pristine; as soon as it begins to fade, new plants are substituted from Longwood's huge back-up greenhouses. This is true throughout the glasshouses. Maintenance is of a very high order, based on an adequate staff to do the job. This is in contrast to most public gardens, where lack of funds prohibits first-class maintenance.

The Main Conservatory constitutes a florist's dream, while the Azalea House is more "gardenesque." It is currently planted as an indoor garden with a lawn and a serpentine pool; the plants stand out clearly and individually, chosen for their form and texture as well as for their colors (the Gertrude Jekyll approach —see p. 256). The Main Conservatory, however, is planned for massed color effects, the individual plants often getting lost in the process.

Before leaving the Azalea House, do not fail to visit the educational annex. Displays here are intended to provide help and ideas for the average home gardener. The 1981 demonstration is a simulated town-house duplex, illustrating ways to decorate it with plants and solve the lighting problems posed by such an environment. Attached to the "kitchen" is a solar greenhouse.

Like the trees and shrubs outdoors, the plants of the permanent collections are well labeled. The following are the most important:

- Orchids. A display features those specimens at peak bloom from among Longwood's five thousand plants (for more on orchids, see pp. 9, 34).
- A desert house of cacti and succulents from the American deserts, such as agave, yucca, and prickly pear, and of succulents from Africa, such as jade plant, various euphorbias, and "living stones," *Lithops* spp.
- A rose garden. At all times Longwood's visitors can see roses in bloom.
- A fern passage, demonstrating various types of these ornamental, nonflowering, non-seed-bearing plants. Among them are epiphytes (see pp. 32–3), climbers, and terrestrial species (for more on ferns, see pp. 227–8).
- Carnivorous plants, both native and exotic. Among the most impressive are the pendulous pitchers of the tropical *Nepenthes maxima*—the nearest we can get to a man-eating plant. This creature has been known to digest a mouse—not here but in the wild! (For more on these plants, see pp. 96–7.)
- Economic plants. Here is a chance to see the climbing vanilla orchid, *Vanilla planifolia*, with its succulent leaves; the choco-

late tree, *Theobroma cacao*, from Mexico; giant herbaceous banana "trees," *Musa* spp.; and a breadfruit tree, *Artocarpus altilis*, the crop the notorious Captain Bligh of the *Bounty* was taking to the West Indies at the time of the mutiny.

· Palms. Surrounded by an elevated walkway, the Palm House is designed so visitors can get an unusual bird's eye view. (For more on palms, see pp. 5–6.)

Do not miss the outstanding collection of water lilies on display between June and October in the outdoor pools between the conservatories. Prominent among them is the Brazilian giant water-platter, *Victoria amazonica*. The upturned margins of its leaves, which can attain a diameter of up to six feet, distinguish it from water lilies of the genus *Nymphaea*. Air spaces in the veins enable its leaves to float and support a weight equal to that of a child. Seeds of this plant reached England in the nineteenth century, and, not unexpectedly, it was first named *Victoria regia*. The arrangement of the leaf veins is supposed to have been Sir Joseph Paxton's model for the steel framework in the Crystal Palace, built in London in 1851.

Other aquatic plants here are a species of *Canna* and the lotus, *Nelumbo nucifera*. Both of these plants have aerial leaves. The lotus, related to the water lilies, is easily identified by its round leaves with centrally attached petioles. Buddhists, who regard it as sacred, often plant it in temple gardens.

WATER LILIES: *To the botanist, water lilies are beautiful examples of plants adapted to an amphibious life. While flowers and upper leaf surfaces are aerial, the rest of the plant flourishes under water. Unlike those of most plants, all the stomates are concentrated on the upper leaf surface. Air that enters them passes down the plant by a system of air channels. Note*

the water-repellent nature of the leaf surfaces: the shiny, waxy coating is designed to rid the surface of water, which, collecting in droplets, slides off or evaporates. Blocking of the stomates is thereby avoided. Water lilies belong to the Nymphaeaceae, a family of primitive flowering plants related to the magnolias and the buttercups. The flowers are geared to beetle pollination, like those of magnolias.

Water-platters

WESTERN SECTION

THE MAIN FOUNTAIN GARDEN: The most impressive garden at Longwood, this was obviously Pierre du Pont's pride and joy. This is a formal garden. In its strictly geometric lines it shows a Le Nôtrean influence; the powerful fountains, defying all laws of nature, are also Le Nôtrean. Yet the exuberance of the fountains, the decorative stonework—walls, statues, urns—and the subdued but pervasive greenery hark back to earlier days, to the garden architects of sixteenth-century Italy.

After observing it from the terrace, walk through this garden, noting the details. In the center is an "island" of billowy boxwood, *Buxus sempervirens* 'Suffruticosa,' surrounded by a moat. On three sides are *allées* of Norway maple, *Acer platanoides*; the low accenting hedges surrounding the lawns are Japanese holly, *Ilex crenata*. Various conifers serve as markers at the north corners. Note the exquisite detailing of the statues in niches along the walls; though fabricated in Italy, these are of the twentieth century.

The greenery and the stonework, however, are merely self-effacing companions to the magnificent collection of fountains, which vary in power from the modest sprays in the foreground to the crashing crescendos of the tallest jets, which send water 130 feet into the air. Their evening performances are worth a return visit: ten thousand gallons of air-borne water recirculated each minute, illuminated by multicolored lights (for times and

The Main Fountain Garden

dates see p. 165). With respect to Italian Renaissance gardens, Sir George Sitwell remarked, "The Italians played with water as a Sultan with his jewels." One has the feeling that had he seen Longwood, Sir George would have said the same about Pierre du Pont.

In the Topiary Garden three species of yew, the traditional topiary material of the seventeenth century, are used: English yew, *Taxus baccata*, Japanese yew, *T. cuspidata*, and a hybrid between the two, *T. media*. Most of the forms are geometric—cones, "cakestands," bulbous disks, octagons, and columns. (For more on topiary, see pp. 263–4.)

The Topiary Garden

The northern end of this garden, marked by a curved yew hedge, accommodates Pierre du Pont's analemmatic sundial, installed in 1937. A complicated device (except for an engineer), it consists of two scales—one for A.M., the other for P.M.—shaped like a figure 8, which incorporate the declination of the sun and the equation of time for each day of the year.

South of the Topiary Garden lies the Rose Garden. Instead of one large outdoor rose garden, lying dormant for half the year, Longwood has three: one indoors, for the edification and pleasure of winter visitors; this collection, beautifully accented by its dark evergreen background but modest in scope; and the Rose Garden in the Idea Garden.

From the Rose Garden walk south to the canopied building housing the Eye of Water. This is the newest and perhaps the most intriguing of Longwood's aquatic attractions. Not one of Pierre du Pont's brain children, it was inspired by the "Fuente de Ojo de Agua" near San Antonio de Belén, Costa Rica. Every minute five thousand gallons of water glide over the sculptured "eye." The water comes from the main water reservoir, used for the Main Fountain Garden. After gushing through the "pupil," it flows along a channel to cascade over the nearby waterfall.

West of the Eye of Water is a naturalistic area devoted to conifers, rock-garden plants, and heathers and other members of the heath family, Ericaceae. The dominant features of the landscape are the man-made waterfalls. These need to be very cleverly designed if they are to appear part of the natural landscape, which presumably is the intention here. Somehow, this one does not quite come off. It may be too flamboyant and too exuberant for the setting. To get a panoramic view of the gardens, it is worthwhile to climb the Tower.

The best time for a visit to the Rock Garden is spring when the small alpines, gentians, anemones, and primulas are in flower. These mountain species are all adapted to rocky soils and cold, exposed habitats. The garden is beautifully designed, looking as if it were indeed part of a mountain slope. However, no mountain slope would or could display the elegant dwarf conifers and maples seen here.

Summer is the best time for the Heather and Heath Garden, for then most of its species are in bloom. The soil here has to be rendered quite acid to encourage the growth of these acid-loving plants, at home on the infertile soils of moors and mountains. Both the true heather, *Erica* spp., and the bell heather, *Calluna vulgaris*, are found here. The roots of the members of the Ericaceae—and this includes rhododendrons, azaleas, mountain laurel, and leucothoe—are intimately associated with fungi, which help the plants extract mineral salts from these infertile soils. Presumably it is this fungus partnership, called mycorrhiza, that enables them to survive in such habitats. The fungus also benefits from the relationship, probably by obtaining carbohydrates. These somewhat tender plants need a good snow cover in winter. To protect them Longwood has even tried a snow-making machine, but this was less than successful. (As stated before, Longwood's maintenance practices are of a high order.)

If you are a home gardener, you may wish to inspect the Idea Garden. One of Longwood's newest, it features not only recommended flowers but vegetables and fruit that will grow successfully in local backyards. The new Food Gardening Example Garden is scheduled to open here in June 1982.

Longwood has an extensive educational program. The two-year graduate course in ornamental horticulture given in conjunction with the University of Delaware is unique. Its uniqueness lies in the fact that it emphasizes the management and administration of public gardens. In today's world of intense competition and soaring costs, administrative experts are required for these institutions. Longwood's graduates are prepared to meet these challenges.

Summing up, Longwood is America's greatest horticultural garden. In style it is eclectic, combining elements from Renaissance Italy, seventeenth-century France, and eighteenth-century England. Its methods of extensive bedding-out are Victorian, based on huge supporting greenhouses and plenty of labor. Its floral and aquatic spectacles remind us that gardens are intended for pleasure, something we often overlook today as we ferret for labels, scribble notes in makeshift notebooks, or rush through the gardens at a jogging pace.

Note: For comparison, try to visit the two other du Pont gardens nearby: Nemours (pp. 149–54) and Winterthur (pp. 155–63).

MORRIS ARBORETUM

Philadelphia, Pennsylvania

UNIQUE
FEATURES

- One of the best collections of oriental woody plants in the northeastern United States.
- A landscaped setting with vistas and follies after the manner of early-nineteenth-century England.

HISTORY: In 1887 John T. Morris and his sister Lydia, having made their money in the family ironworks, bought the 175 acres that are now the arboretum. After the building of the mansion, Compton, and the landscaping of the grounds, this land became their country estate. John Morris died in 1915, Lydia in 1931. She bequeathed the estate to the University of Pennsylvania as a public arboretum and center for research and educational activities.

Today the arboretum is financed partly by the Morris bequest endowment and partly by membership dues and fund-raising events. Its affiliation with the University of Pennsylvania still continues for joint educational activities, but the arboretum receives no revenue from the university.

- *Admission:* Entrance fee.
- *Hours:* Open daily, all year. April 1 through October 31, 9:00 A.M.–5:00 P.M. November 1 through March 31, 9:00 A.M.–4:00 P.M. Wednesdays, June 1 to August 31, 9:00 A.M.–8:00 P.M. Closed Christmas Day.
- *Tours:* Free tours with admission, every Saturday and Sunday at 2:00 P.M. from Hillcrest Pavilion. For special tours, call (215) 242-3399.
- *Plants:* Labeled. Grid location (see map) for every labeled plant is available in complete plant list at Hillcrest Pavilion.
- *Physically handicapped:* Visitors in wheelchairs can park just outside Hillcrest Pavilion. Most roads are accessible to them.

- *Parking:* Along Hillcrest Avenue.
- *Address:* The Morris Arboretum of the University of Pennsylvania, 9414 Meadowbrook Avenue, Philadelphia, Pa. 19118. Tel. (215) 247-5777.
- *Location and directions:* In the Chestnut Hill suburb of Philadelphia, about 15 miles from downtown Philadelphia via Germantown Avenue. Public entrance on Hillcrest Avenue*; classrooms and offices on Meadowbrook Avenue. Best route is from Pennsylvania Turnpike. Take Interchange 25, drive east on U.S. 422, turn left on Hillcrest Avenue at intersection with Germantown Avenue (about 4 miles from Turnpike).
- *No gift shop.* Brochures and guidebook with map on sale at Hillcrest Pavilion.
- *No snack bar or restaurant.*
- *No picnicking.*

This is an arboretum which is also a garden in its own right. The original garden, constructed by the Morrises, was landscaped in the English style of the early nineteenth century.

The hallmarks of the eighteenth-century landscape garden, made fashionable by "Capability" Brown (see p. 89), were rolling lawns, clumps of tall trees, and serpentine lakes. In Victorian times this style was modified to include flower beds, shrubberies enclosing small gardens, and architectural features

* This may change in 1982 with the implementation of the new Master Plan. Phone (215) 247-5777 for advice.

such as follies, lookouts, and fountains. Humphrey Repton, who died in 1818, was the greatest influence in bringing about these modifications. Through his books, published between 1795 and 1807, his ideas were widely disseminated, and they persisted long after his death. The Morrises were apparently much influenced by Repton's principles of garden design, one of which was unity: a single theme without distracting elements. When this principle was ignored, the typical Victorian garden became an eclectic jumble of parterres, bedded-out exotics, and elaborate conservatories. Fortunately, the Morrises, by their choice of the Reptonian style, made easy the conversion of their garden into an arboretum. And an arboretum within an already landscaped garden makes for a more attractive whole.

Quite unawares, the Morrises laid the foundations for the arboretum in the early years of the twentieth century by planting many oriental trees discovered by "Chinese" Wilson and others during plant-exploration trips in the Far East. They were able to obtain these new species through the Arnold Arboretum, for which Wilson was working. The Morris Arboretum therefore is not the best place to study native trees, unless you explore the woodland trails near Wissahickon Creek. Rather, it is for the study of ornamental exotic woody plants. And because the Far East is richer in species than Europe (for reasons explained on pp. 284–5), the trees and shrubs here are from China, Japan, and Korea.

"CHINESE" WILSON: *Ernest H. "Chinese" Wilson (1876–1933) made four trips to China and two to Japan, Korea, and Formosa during the years 1899–1917. He collected and introduced to the gardens of the West more than one thousand new species, a greater number than any other plant hunter. At the beginning of his career, Wilson worked for a nursery in England; later, for Professor C. S. Sargent of the Arnold Arboretum, where he eventually became curator (for Wilson's later career, see pp. 280–1).*

At the Hillcrest Pavilion purchase the "Guide to the Grounds," and also the "Blooming Calendar" to see what is currently in flower. The guide includes a detailed map, which is essential for locating particular trees. If you wish to see the tropical ferns, inquire here how to get the key to the Fernery greenhouse.

After leaving the pavilion, turn left. Take the circumferential road, which soon passes on the right one of the garden ornaments, the water staircase—not functioning, but a pleasant idea. Nearby is a large specimen of the Siberian elm, *Ulmus pumila*, from North Asia. It does not look like an elm, but on examination its leaves reveal lopsided bases, a characteristic of all elms.

The John Morris Rock Garden is a kind of Japanese garden, distinguished by the large standing flat rock with Chinese characters and the rare trident maple, *Acer buergeranum*, from China and Japan. Note the three-lobed leaves, like a trident. To construct this garden and the other Japanese garden, John Morris engaged gardeners from Japan.

The English Park is now on the right. This is simply a wide expanse of lawn, essential to the design of an English landscape garden. It can be best surveyed from the Seven Arches Lookout, a little farther on. Italian in origin, this is another garden folly or ornament, completely nonutilitarian except as a viewing platform. In the vicinity look for the rare *Pteroceltis tartarinowii* from China, related to our native hackberry, *Celtis occidentalis*, both of them in the elm family. Another rather rare tree nearby is *Pterostyrax hispida* from Japan, the epaulette tree, valued for its fragrant white flowers appearing in June. It is related to *Halesia*, the silver-bell tree.

The Mercury Temple—now somewhat the worse for wear— was erected in 1913 by the Morrises to mark the twenty-fifth anniversary of the estate. To us it seems pretentious: why not a tree instead? Anyway, it is to be restored, as part of the master plan. In the Morrises' time it commanded an excellent view, but by mistake witch hazels were planted in front of it, which are now tall enough to spoil the vista. *Hamamelis vernalis*, the native witch hazel, and *H. japonica*, the Japanese species, are the first shrubs to bloom; their yellow flowers, each with four strap-shaped petals, are a welcome sight in February. The autumn-flowering native witch hazel, *H. virginiana*, is at the other side of the arboretum. Witch hazel is one of the few plants that have fruits that explode, violently shooting out their seeds.

Continue on until you reach the T-junction in the road. There take the left fork, which immediately passes over a small stream. Just before the bridge, leave the road and walk east to find "Lydia's Retreat," a small rustic cabin used by Miss Morris to seclude herself and enjoy the natural scenery hereabouts. Return to the road. Cross the bridge. Soon a grove of the dawn redwood, *Metasequoia glyptostroboides*, appears on the left. The dawn redwood was discovered in the wilds of China in 1941 after scientists, having studied fossils of it, decided that it was extinct. The Arnold Arboretum obtained seed and distributed it to various gardens and arboreta. The trees here came from this original seed. (For more on this tree, see pp. 287–8.)

The Medicinal Garden, at the time of viewing, was not worth a side trip, so I suggest you continue along the road until you reach a quaint-looking greenhouse on the right—the Fernery. Built by the Morrises, this reflects the Victorian mania for tropical ferns. In fact, their cultivation developed into a kind of cult. This was before the advent of central heating, when the home environment was more conducive to the growth of these delicate plants. Their popularity declined when houses became warmer and drier. (For a description of ferns, see pp. 227–8.) If you do not have a key, staff members working nearby may be able to let you in.

Just beyond the Fernery, a path on the right leads you to the Rose Garden, which dates back to the Morris era. It is the only formal geometric garden on the estate. The low hedges of English yew, *Taxus baccata*, resemble the parterres of earlier times. Accentuating the formality are a central fountain and a balustrade. From June to October All-American roses may be seen here. Every year the arboretum receives new roses to test for the All-American trials (see pp. 39–41).

ROSES: *About 150 species of roses occur in nature, all of them native to the Northern Hemisphere. An account of the origins of modern roses from these wild ancestors would fill a book.*

The symbolism associated with the rose has played no small part in history. Venerated in the "paradise" gardens of Persia (see pp. 196–7), the rose was introduced by the returning Greek conquerors into Asia Minor and Greece. It eventually reached Rome.

One of the most popular flowers of ancient Rome, the rose was cultivated in greenhouses to induce winter bloom. Among other things, it was associated with the God of Silence. A rose was hung above council tables to encourage secrecy; hence the expression "sub rosa," meaning "in confidence."

The early Christians rejected the flower as a symbol of the pagan goddess Venus. Even so, throughout the Dark Ages rose culture was carried on clandestinely in monasteries by monks who loved flowers (see p. 199).

At the beginning of the nineteenth century the best collection of cultivated roses was in the garden of the Empress Josephine at Malmaison, near Paris, recorded in the beautiful paintings of Redouté. Reputedly the empress, who had bad teeth, always carried a bouquet of roses to help disguise her halitosis.

Fragrant roses, of course, have always been very important to the perfume industry. Attar or oil of roses comes from Bulgaria, the Black Sea region of the Soviet Union, and Turkey. It is so precious that the Bulgarian government hoards containers of it in banks around the world, just as other nations hoard gold. Bulgaria's rose fields are planted, not with cultivars, but with the heavenly-scented species rose Rosa damascena, *the damask rose, so called because it supposedly came from Damascus. Three tons of roses gathered from four to five acres yields approximately two-and-a-half pounds of attar, the oil from the petals. Byproducts of this industry are rose-petal jam, rosewater for flavoring, and rose-hip syrup, all of which are encountered in the cuisine of Eastern Europe and the Near East.*

Modern roses have a greater color range than the species roses. In recent years the rage has been for orange-vermilion; the hybrid tea 'Tropicana' is the most popular. As yet, no true blue roses have emerged, but pale-lilac varieties like 'Sterling Silver' suggest that a blue rose may be just around the corner. "Rose" is synonymous with "pink," and obviously most roses are pink. Among these look for the gorgeous floribunda 'Queen Elizabeth,' a recent hybrid. Rose breeding continues unabated in most countries where roses grow well (they will not grow in the tropics).

The name "hybrid tea" may be puzzling and should be explained here. In the late nineteenth century wild roses from China came to be used in European breeding programs. These roses had a fragrance reminiscent of fresh tea leaves (not dried ones). Because they were important parents of modern, large, single-flowered cultivars, which often inherited the tea perfume, the modern roses were dubbed "hybrid teas."

Unfortunately, in contrast to species roses, only a few of the new cultivars have a pronounced perfume. 'Peace' is practically scentless, though the pink 'Tiffany' is a notable exception. Rose breeders now realize that in the past too little attention was paid to fragrance; color, hardiness, and pest resistance were higher priorities. Today this is being rectified. 'Typhoo Tea,' 'Fragrant

*Cloud,' and 'Double Delight' are recent strongly fragrant intro-
ductions. And 'Sutter's Gold' actually has the tea scent of the old
Chinese species.*

The map will help you find the Mansion Site. All that is left of
Compton is a horseshoe-shaped staircase similar to the one at
Dumbarton Oaks (p. 134), but without the fountain, and the
rock-garden wall. The alpines on the wall bloom in spring,
making it easy to find at that time. The garden was planned
around the mansion, built on high ground so that the various
interesting features could be admired from the windows. Incidentally, the hilly nature of the entire estate made it highly
adaptable to landscaping in the English eighteenth-century tradition. Near the site are two large trees, the Bender Oak, *Quercus
benderi*, and the weeping form of the European beech, *Fagus
sylvatica* 'Pendula.' The latter form was discovered in Switzerland
in the 1660s. All present-day individuals are clones of this original
Swiss "sport," or mutation.

If it happens to be the blooming season for the magnolias, a
visit to Magnolia Slope is recommended as the next stop. The
oriental species begin blooming in early April and continue
through the month and into May. The Morris Arboretum has a
good collection of species, cultivars, and hybrids. The native
magnolias, which flower in mid-May, are not so spectacular.
Their blossoms have not the chalice form of the orientals, and
they are partly obscured by the leaves, which have now emerged.
The exception is the evergreen southern species *Magnolia
grandiflora*. One cultivar of this, 'Edith Bogue,' is hardy here, its
leaves coming through the winters intact. It blooms in mid-July.
(For more on magnolias, see pp. 55, 191.)

Walking towards the Oak Allée, you will encounter a magnificent tree with multiple trunks and heart-shaped leaves. This
is the katsura tree, *Cercidiphyllum japonicum*, which the Morrises
obtained through the Arnold Arboretum. It is sufficiently different from other trees as to be the only member of its botanical
family. The Oak Allée was planted as a vista and a feature to be
admired from the Mansion Site.

In the Azalea Meadow are hybrid azaleas as well as species,
both native and exotic. The hybrids are mainly Ghent, developed
in Belgium in the 1820s, and Skinner, latter developed at the
United States Arboretum. The arboretum is about (in 1980) to
patent its own cultivar, called 'Morris Gold.' Unless sprayed,

Katsura tree

azalea flowers are very susceptible to a fungus disease called petal blight, which spoils their appearance. The year 1980 was a bad one for the disease, and since the arboretum had not sprayed, the azaleas looked rather woebegone. Blooming in the native species begins in late April and continues through May. The last to bloom is the native plumleaf azalea, *Rhododendron prunifolium*, in late July. (For more on native azaleas, see p. 46.)

Continue walking west through the Azalea Meadow. Just before you reach the Swan Pond, a pine with a curious, peeling bark will attract your attention. This is the lace-bark pine, *Pinus bungeana*, a rare species from China prized for its multicolored trunks.

Lace-bark pine

The Love Temple

Slightly to the right is a grove of trees that looks natural but is actually part of a second Japanese garden—rather nondescript, it must be admitted. Since the 1890s, as our knowledge has increased, our tastes in oriental gardens have become more sophisticated. The arboretum has plans to restore and improve this garden—part of the master plan slated for 1982.

Near the Love Temple is the Chinese elm, *Ulmus parvifolia*, a more attractive tree than the Siberian species. The leaves are smaller than those of our familiar elms, and the whole tree has a daintier appearance. Neither of the Asiatic species is susceptible to the Dutch elm disease, which has decimated the elm populations of the United States and, more recently, England.

The area around the Swan Pond is one of the most pleasing in the entire arboretum. This is English picturesque landscape design at its best. The small lake with wildfowl, the reflections, the attendant specimen trees, together with the antique Tuscan temple, make this a delightful miniature landscape.

Crossing the stream, you are now back at the Hillcrest Pavilion.

Except in the spring, the Morris Arboretum is not for everyone. Rather, it is for the sophisticated gardener or plantsman who admires beautiful trees. Of course, the average visitor can appreciate the understated garden design, but the lack of floral displays at times other than spring may be disappointing.

ARBORETUM OF THE
BARNES FOUNDATION

Merion, Pennsylvania

· Displays, within an area of only twelve acres, 290 genera of woody plants from all over the Northern Hemisphere, belonging to about ninety plant families.
· Offers the dual attraction of an art collection and a woody-plant collection, both of high caliber.

HISTORY: The twelve-acre estate belonged to Joseph Lapsley Wilson from 1880 until 1922, when it was bought by Dr. Albert C. Barnes, a chemist, physician, and art connoisseur. Mrs. Barnes had the gardens professionally landscaped, adding to the original collection of trees and shrubs planted about 1880. In this way the Barnes Arboretum was born. Meanwhile Dr. Barnes added to his art collection, which is now nationally famous. As an educational institution, currently giving courses in botany, horticulture, and landscape architecture, the arboretum dates back to 1922, when it received its charter. Today it is funded by the Barnes Foundation, a nonprofit, privately endowed institution.

· *Admission:* Free. Admittance to arboretum by appointment only. To obtain passes, write to Director, 57 Lapsley Road, Merion, Pa. 19066, or call (215) 664-8880. No appointment necessary for art collection.
· *Hours:* Open all year. Grounds open Monday to Friday 9:00 A.M.–4:00 P.M., Saturday 9:00 A.M.–12:00 noon. Closed Sundays. Art collection open Friday and Saturday 9:30 A.M.–4:30 P.M., Sunday 2:00 P.M.–4:00 P.M. (closed July and August).
· *Plants:* Labeled.
· *Physically handicapped:* Paths not suitable for wheelchairs.
· *Address:* For information, write The Arboretum of the Barnes Foundation, P.O. Box 128, Merion Station, Pa. 19066.

· *Location and directions:* At 57 Lapsley Lane in Merion, a suburb 5 miles west of downtown Philadelphia. Art collection entrance at 300 Latch's Lane, off City Avenue. Public transportation: From center city (Suburban Station, 16th Street and Kennedy Boulevard), take Conrail, Paoli local train, to Merion station; then take Septa Bus no. 44. From Germantown (Germantown and Chelten Avenues), take Septa Bus E.
· *Parking:* Free.
· *No gift shop.*
· *No snack bar or restaurant.*
· *No picnicking.*

This is a garden for those who enjoy looking at plants and learning their names. One real advantage the Barnes Arboretum has over many other arboreta is that you do not have to trudge over a vast landscape designed by Olmsted to find them. In just twelve acres you can study a good sample of the best woody ornamentals the temperate zones of the world have to offer. Moreover, as some plants have been admitted that are not woody—wild flowers, hardy ferns, and alpines—the appearance is that of a garden rather than an arboretum. Still, the special gardens such as the Rose Garden, the Rock Garden, and the Vine Collection are all subsidiary to the marvelous collection of woody perennials.

If you are especially curious, jot down the names of any that intrigue you. Consulting the books dealing with trees and shrubs

in the Bibliography, you will be able to learn more about them. These books may be available in your local library or in that of a botanical garden or horticultural society. If you live nearby, consider joining classes at Barnes; the arboretum is used for field work. Of course, you may be content with just looking at the plants, admiring them and making comparisons.

Barnes has wonderful collections of certain families and genera. These are physically close to one another, so that comparison is easy. For example, north of the greenhouse are beds devoted to woody shrubs of the rose family, Rosaceae. One is amazed at the number of variations on the rose type of flower structure, giving rise to so many different genera. Hollies, viburnums, boxwoods, and magnolias are also well represented.

Mrs. Barnes spared no pains nor expense in procuring exotic and rare specimens, in order to make this arboretum as cosmopolitan as possible. However, as in any assemblage of temperate-zone woody plants, species from the Far East predominate. Here, near the administration building, you will find the fascinating dove tree or handkerchief tree, *Davidia involucrata.* "Handkerchief tree" is perhaps the apter description, for when the blossoms fall after flowering in early May, the ground beneath appears to be littered with Kleenex.

THE DOVE TREE: Davidia involucrata *was first seen in China in 1869 by Father David, a French missionary. Eventually seeds reached France in 1897, and the "doves" were seen in 1906 when the plant flowered. Each flower is subtended by two white "petals," one about three inches long and the other six inches. Actually, these "petals" are bracts—leaflike parts often associated with flowers—like those of the dogwood. The dove-tree flowers have no true petals. Although they look like dogwood flowers, the two plants are not related.* Davidia *belongs to the same family as our native tupelo or black gum,* Nyssa sylvatica.

Ernest H. "Chinese" Wilson, the great English plant explorer, also discovered the dove tree some years later, not knowing that the French had already found it. The seeds he collected, however, were from a different variety. The French discovery, D. involucrata vilmoriniana, *is hardier, growing as far north as Boston. Both varieties can be seen in the Barnes Arboretum.*

Rose Garden entrance

Many other plants discovered by Wilson in the Orient at the turn of the century are to be seen here. Among them are the spring-blooming beautybush, *Kolkwitzia amabilis*; the Korean boxwood, *Buxus microphylla* 'Koreana'; the small, rather rare paperbark maple, *Acer griseum*, with its leaves of three leaflets (like those of the box elder, *A. negundo*) and its handsome peeling, chestnut-colored bark, reminiscent of the birches.

Two other small oriental trees, rarely seen but growing here, are the bee-bee tree, *Evodia daniellii*, which belongs to the citrus family, Rutaceae, and the raisin tree, *Hovenia dulcis*, with small edible fruits. Presumably, the bee-bee tree is so called because its

Magnolia sieboldii

small black seeds look like BB shot, as well as for the fact that it attracts many bees in August when nectar-bearing flowers are few.

The collection that should not be missed is that of the genus *Magnolia*. From early April through July one or another species is blooming. Oriental and American species grow side by side. The early spring species, blooming before the leaves unfold, are the most spectacular; among them are the star magnolia, *M. stellata*, from Japan and the yulan magnolia, *M. denudata*, from China. The summer-blooming species often have beautifully sculptured flowers like the Korean *M. sieboldii*, pictured here, with its deep-crimson stamens. The latest bloomer is our own native southern evergreen magnolia, *M. grandiflora*, several cultivars of which grow here. In Philadelphia it is close to the limit of its hardiness.

MAGNOLIAS: *In the wide-open magnolia blossoms, note the abundance of sticky pollen. This open-plan type of flower allows access to beetles, the only pollinating insects around when these primitive flowering plants first appeared on earth. Beetles visit the flowers to consume pollen, which they chew with their strong, biting jaws. There is no nectar. Bees that visit these flowers carry away pollen to feed the young larvae in the hive. If the time is autumn, look for the large conelike seed pods. The many compartments open to reveal large red or orange seeds, attractive to squirrels. Their large furry buds and smooth gray bark make these trees interesting even in winter. The larger buds contain the flowers for next spring.*

The tree peony collection is also very fine, most of them blooming in late May. The beautiful yellow *Paeonia lutea* is displayed here, as well as many of the Moutan cultivars, *P. suffruticosa*.

The various cultivars of the European beech, *Fagus sylvatica*, on the left of the drive leading up to the Gallery should be examined: 'Roseo-marginata,' with its pink leaf-margins; 'Rotundifolia,' with spoon-shaped leaves; and the fern-leaf variety, 'Laciniata.' Beech is easily recognized by its perfectly smooth gray bark. In May a nearby Chinese fringe tree, *Chionanthus retusus*, in full bloom indicates their location. It is to be seen on the edge of the drive on the left.

Araucaria araucana

Most visitors wonder at the strange conifer near the administration building, shaped like some weird piece of sculpture and having large, fierce-looking pointed leaves. This is the monkey-puzzle tree from Chile, *Araucaria araucana*, its scientific name referring to the Araucarian Indians, on whose land it was found. Its cones at maturity can be as big as coconuts. Like the southern magnolia, it is near the limit of its hardiness at this latitude. In Chile it can grow to a height of eighty feet.

Obviously, the best times to visit this miniature gem of an arboretum are spring for the flowers and autumn for the colored foliage. To the author, it is much more appealing than the Arnold Arboretum, where great distances have to be traveled on foot to see many of these same species—though that may change in the near future.

DUKE GARDENS

Somerville, New Jersey

UNIQUE	· A garden entirely under glass.
FEATURES	· Eleven small gardens, displaying the history of garden art in many different cultures.

HISTORY: A conservatory for growing fruits and flowers for the estate was constructed at the turn of the century by James Buchanan Duke. Later his daughter, Doris Duke, converted it into the series of eleven gardens we see today. In 1964 she turned over the gardens and twelve acres of land to a well-endowed nonprofit foundation, Duke Gardens Foundation, Inc. The foundation's responsibility is to operate the gardens for the enjoyment of the public.

- *Admission:* Entrance Fee. Advance reservations required; call (201) 722-3700, or write to address below.
- *Hours:* Open October 1 through May 31. Daily 12:00 noon– 4:00 P.M. Wednesday and Thursday evenings 8:30 P.M.–10:30 P.M. Closed Thanksgiving Day, Christmas Day, and New Year's Day.
- *Plants:* Not labeled.
- *Physically handicapped:* Not equipped for visitors in wheelchairs.
- *Address:* For information, write or call Duke Gardens Foundation, Inc., Somerville, N.J. 08876. Tel. (201) 722-3700.
- *Location and directions:* 40 miles west of New York City, 17 miles north of Princeton, N.J., 22 miles south of Morristown. From New York City: New Jersey Turnpike to exit 10, Interstate 287 north to U.S. 22, west to U.S. 206, south to Somerset Shopping Center. Continue south on U.S. 206; at third traffic light, turn right into gardens (1½ hours). Parking lot is on right.

From Princeton: North on U.S. 206. After Hillsboro Shopping Plaza, turn left at third traffic light for entrance to gardens (30 minutes).

From Morristown: South on Interstate 287 to U.S. 206 south. Then proceed as if coming from New York (see above) (35 minutes).

· *Parking:* Free, within the gardens.
· *No gift shop.* Pamphlets, slides, and postcards available at visitor center.
· *No snack bar or restaurant.*
· *No picnicking.*
· *Note:* Cameras and high-heeled shoes not permitted in the gardens.

Under one acre of glass Duke Gardens presents a historical and cultural view of gardening as a fine art. In the course of an hour one can "walk around the world," seeing gardens of Japan, Indo-Persia, and France, or wander back in time to view an Edwardian conservatory and gardens of Elizabethan England and colonial America.

A group of twelve to fourteen people is conveyed from the parking lot by minibus to the visitor center, where a trained guide is waiting. Within the conservatory the guide directs your eye to salient elements of garden design, rather than to the individual plants that create the effect. If you are interested in plant identification or in taking home lists of desirable house plants, you should be aware that this is not a botanical garden, else you will be disappointed. The tour is intended to be an aesthetic experience, an introduction to garden art which, though three-dimensional, is miniaturized for comfort and practicality. Only a half-mile of walking is required.

Of the eleven tiny gardens, nine demonstrate the kind of design favored by particular cultures at various points in time, while two—the desert and the tropical forest—are exhibits of plants with special and contrasting adaptations. Three are particularly noteworthy:

THE FRENCH GARDEN: This is a replica of part of a seventeenth-century Le Nôtrean garden. Extremely formal with its parterres in fleur-de-lis patterns, its antique statuary, and its surrounding treillage, it demonstrates the contemporary desire to tame nature,

disciplining it into geometric forms. The parterre edging consists of Japanese holly, *Ilex crenata* 'Helleri,' on the outside with some box in the interior of the garden (box, *Buxus sempervirens*, does not prosper in this year-round heat). Flowers fill the parterres and are changed seasonally. The decorative ivy here is jet ivy, a cultivar of *Hedera helix* developed at Duke Gardens.

So that the parterres may be admired from above in the traditional manner, there is an upper garden of seasonal flowers around the "Majesty" statue. (For more on French gardens of the period, see pp. 150–1.)

THE ENGLISH GARDEN: This garden incorporates four different styles:

- A topiary garden of the type popular at the end of the seventeenth century. The figures here are executed in yew, *Taxus baccata*, and *Junipers* sp. (For more on topiary, see pp. 263–4.)
- A herbaceous border. Such borders became popular in England at the turn of the century as an alternative to Victorian carpet-bedding and are still popular today. The flowers, offset by the traditional lawns, are colorful, exuberant, and redolent of summer: delphinium, four-o'clock (*Mirabilis jalapa*), schizanthus, and oxypetalum. The tropical fig, *Ficus pumila*—actually out of place here—creeps over the wall.
- An Elizabethan knot garden. The gray lavender cotton, *Santolina chamaecyparissus*, is planted to mimic intertwining

knots that surround beds of rosemary, parsley, sage, and other useful aromatic herbs. (For more on herbs, see pp. 203–4.)

· A succulent garden. Small exotic succulents from arid foreign sources, planted in patterns like this one (called a sunburst), were characteristic of eighteenth-century gardens in England and France. Since working greenhouses were lacking, such tender plants had to be imported every year and hence were seen only in the gardens of the rich.

THE INDO-PERSIAN GARDEN: This is perhaps the most beautiful of all the Duke gardens. Certainly, it is unfamiliar; this kind of garden is seldom re-created in the United States. Going back thousands of years, it is called a paradise garden, from *pairidaeza*, the old Persian word for a walled garden, which became the Latin *paradisus* and ultimately the Middle English *paradis*. Shown here are its essential elements: the straight watercourses, the brick-patterned tiles (copies of those in the Shalimar Gardens at Lahore, India), the geometrically planted trees, the whole surrounded by a protective wall, represented here by the Islamic arches and screens. The intersection of the two water canals symbolizes the four rivers of life, dividing the earth into four equal quarters. The central fountain represents the sacred mountain. This symbolism is extremely ancient, part of the religions of the Near East, whose origins are lost in prehistory.

In the Near East water was and is a precious commodity. It is not surprising, therefore, that it became an essential embellish-

ment. In the dry summer heat fountains and waterfalls cooled the air; walkways were raised, as they are here, to divert every drop of rain or floodwater into the watercourses and flower beds. Statues like those seen in French and Italian gardens were taboo because the Islamic religion regards the depiction of human beings and animals as idolatry.

The Duke garden is a miniature of the kinds of gardens created by the Mughal emperors who invaded and settled in northern India in the sixteenth and seventeenth centuries. The trees are cypress, *Cupressus sempervirens*, which represents eternity, and grapefruit, *Citrus paradisi*, which represents life and rebirth. Cherry, peach, and plum were the traditional fruit trees, but they need a period of cold and would not survive indoors. The rose garden recalls the Mughal-Persian veneration of the rose. Other flowers seen here are the passion flower, *Passiflora* sp., the gloriosa lily, *Gloriosa superba*, and the tropical *Medinilla magnifica* with its gorgeous flowers.

As you walk through the conservatory, note its immaculate appearance; the kind of meticulous maintenance and supervision practiced by the staff here is rare today in gardens open to the public.

Finally, in the cold, dark months of the New Jersey winter, Duke Gardens injects a breath of perpetual spring. The extravagance of bloom everywhere lifts the spirits, an aesthetic and emotional experience needed at this time of year.

THE CLOISTERS

New York City

UNIQUE FEATURES	· Three cloister gardens, planted in the manner of the Middle Ages, in two instances using plants that would have been grown at the time.
	· One garden devoted to the plants depicted in the medieval tapestry series *The Hunt of the Unicorn*.

HISTORY: This medieval museum, owned and operated by the Metropolitan Museum of Art, was built in 1938. The money for its construction, for its principal collections, including the famous fifteenth-century tapestry series *The Hunt of the Unicorn*, and for the purchase and shipment of five medieval cloisters came from John D. Rockefeller, Jr. Even the park and the land immediately opposite The Cloisters on the other side of the Hudson River were purchased by Rockefeller. The Palisades property was acquired to prevent high-rise buildings from marring the view across the river.

· *Admission:* Entrance fee (amount of contribution suggested). Senior citizens free. Free brochure with map.
· *Hours:* Tuesday to Saturday 10:00 A.M.–4:45 P.M. Sunday and holidays 1:00 P.M.–4:45 P.M. Sunday, May through September, 12:00 noon–4:45 P.M. Closed Mondays. Outdoor gardens closed December 1 through March 31.
· *Plants:* Labeled only in the Herb Garden.
· *Physically handicapped:* Gardens not accessible to wheelchairs.
· *Address:* The Cloisters, Fort Tryon Park, New York, N.Y. 10040. Tel. (212) 923-3700.
· *Location and directions:* Within Fort Tryon Park in upper Manhattan, at 193rd Street. By subway: Eighth Avenue A train (IND) to 190th Street/Overlook Terrace stop. Then take no. 4 bus, "Fort Tryon Park–Cloisters," to museum entrance. By bus:

Take Madison Avenue no. 4 bus, "Fort Tryon Park–Cloisters," to museum entrance (1-hour ride from 42nd Street). By car: Take Henry Hudson Parkway north. After George Washington Bridge, take first exit on the right.
- *Parking:* Free, along road beside entrance (inside the park).
- *Gift shop:* In museum.
- *Snack bar and restaurant:* Outside the museum but within the park, about a 5-minute walk south along bus route.
- *Picnicking:* Facilities in Fort Tryon Park.

A member of the staff who is a professional horticulturist takes care of the gardens. This relatively recent change ensures displays that are both horticulturally pleasing and authentic for the late Middle Ages. For the history buff, interested or not in plants, the three outdoor gardens will be utterly fascinating. The gardener also should find them interesting and unusual, especially the Herb Garden, where everything is carefully labeled.

Although the winter displays in the Saint Guilhem Cloister are attractive, especially the Christmas show, for the plant lover the best months for a visit are April through November. August and September are probably the best months for the Herb Garden.

Using the map, find the Cuxa Cloister, which has been reconstructed here with stonework, half of which is original, from the twelfth-century French monastery of Saint-Michel-de-Cuxa in the eastern Pyrenees, once a way station on the Crusade route. (Incidentally, all three cloisters considered here are from this southern region of France.)

THE CUXA CLOISTER

This enclosed garden of four quadrants with a central fountain and a tree in each quadrant is typical of the period. The fountain or pool was used for watering or washing; sometimes it was replaced by a piscina, or fish pond, from which Friday's dinners might come. Purely ornamental—monks liked flowers even if the laity thought of them as pagan—it was separate from the utilitarian gardens where food and herbs were grown. The trees, however, were usually fruit trees. Here you see a pear, *Pyrus* sp., a crab apple, *Malus* sp., a hawthorn, *Crateagus* sp., and a cornelian cherry, *Cornus mas*, not a cherry but a European ornamental of the dogwood family, prized for its tiny yellow flowers produced in March long before the leaves emerge.

The Saint Guilhem Cloister

The plants here are not meant to be historical. They are chosen for their fragrance, display, and time of bloom to ensure flowers from April through October and even November. Thus both the spring-blooming crocus and the autumn saffron crocus, *Crocus sativus* (not to be confused with the poisonous *Colchicum autumnale*, a member of the lily family with six stamens, not three), will be found here.

Conspicuous here is the long-blooming blue sage, *Salvia superba*. The madonna lily, *Lilium candidum*, both fragrant and decorative, probably would have been grown in medieval cloisters because it symbolized the purity of the Virgin Mary. Tussocks of Cheddar pinks, *Dianthus gratianopolitanus*, the small yellow *Coreopsis verticillata*, and verbena, *Verbena hybrida*, give color in summer, offset by the tall spikes of the foxglove, *Digitalis purpurea*. This is one of the few plants that is still grown for the drug it makes in its leaves: digitalis, a cardiac medicine. The common name is a corruption of "folk's glove," conferred presumably when a belief in the fairies or "little folk" was widespread. Lilyturf, *Liriope muscari*, looking like a grass, makes an attractive edging; however, the purple flower spikes it puts up in the fall declare it a member of the lily family. The flowers of the turtlehead, *Chelone* sp., also appear in autumn—note the uncanny resemblance to its namesake.

Next seek out the Hall of the Unicorn Tapestries, south of the Cuxa Cloister. Six tapestries are complete; the fifth has only two surviving fragments. Woven around 1500, they are known to have belonged in 1680 to François VI de La Rochefoucauld of Paris, where they adorned his bedroom. Stolen during the Revolution, they were recovered and restored. When John D. Rockefeller, Jr., bought them in 1922, they were still in the hands of the La Rochefoucauld family. Rockefeller created a special room for them in his New York City house. In 1935, when the Cloisters were built, he agreed to give them to this museum, which seemed designed for them.

Briefly, the story told by the tapestries is as follows: The lord and his huntsmen set out to capture the legendary animal. Miraculously finding him, they watch with awe while he dips his horn in the stream. Wild creatures wait around to drink the water, the horn supposedly having the magical property to purify water made poisonous by venomous creatures during the night. Coming to their senses, the huntsmen now cruelly pursue the animal, which defends itself by spearing a dog. Ultimately, they realize that the unicorn cannot be taken by force. Only the caresses of a virgin maid can render him vulnerable. This accomplished, he is killed and brought to the castle on the back of a horse. The seventh and final tapestry shows the animal alive and well, but in captivity. This simple story has secular and religious symbolism. It can be interpreted as the courtship and capture of a lover-bridegroom, or it can symbolize the Incarnation, Crucifixion, and Resurrection of Christ, the seventh tapestry depicting either the ensnared lover or Christ inside Paradise. (For more on this, purchase the booklet entitled *The Unicorn Tapestries* from the gift shop.)

The first and the seventh tapestry scenes are enacted against a fantasy of flowers. Known as "millefleurs," it represents the medieval adoration of the flowers of forest and meadow. All the seasons are brought together; flowering daffodils and fruiting pomegranates appear in the same scene. Our concern is the amazing detail with which the surrounding flora is depicted, to such a degree that trees and flowers can be identified. Understandably, there are some botanical lapses: the pomegranate tree in the center of the seventh tapestry is hardly recognizable (compare it with the living specimen in the Trie Cloister). The fruits were probably familiar to the designer of the tapestries, but not the entire plant, since it is native to the shores of the Mediterranean. Contrast the pomegranate with the violets, irises, and strawberries, all well known to the designer and all accurately depicted.

If you have time, see how many plants you can recognize, realizing that none will be endemic to America. The oaks are the European *Quercus robur*, the holly the English *Ilex aquifolium*, the marigolds, not the familiar Mexican *Tagetes* sp., but the pot marigold, *Calendula officinalis*.

Now descend to the Trie Cloister on the lower level.

THE TRIE CLOISTER

This cloister was reconstructed from parts of a late-fifteenth-century Carmelite convent near Cuxa. A fountain in the form of a wayside cross stands in the center of this new "Unicorn" garden (new as of 1980). The plants growing here are some of those depicted in the tapestries—its flora come to life, so to speak. Even if you cannot name them, you will probably recognize them from the tapestries.

The following are the most important species growing here:

· *Trees:* the European oak, readily identified in the tapestries by its leaves; the European linden, *Tilia europaea*; the hazelnut tree, *Corylus avellana*; the European plum, *Prunus domestica*; the English holly (both male and female trees to ensure berries), and the pomegranate, *Punica granatum*, not hardy in New York City and so grown in a tub. (This plant figures so prominently in the tapestries because it was a symbol of fertility in the Middle Ages.)

The Trie Cloister

- *Shrubs:* the cabbage rose, *Rosa centifolia*, the "rose of a hundred petals," not the rose of the tapestries since the cabbage rose dates from a cross made in the seventeenth century. The tapestry rose is probably *Rosa gallica.* (This illustrates the difficulty of procuring those old-fashioned species today.)
- *Non-woody plants:* violets, *Viola* spp.; yellow flag, *Iris pseudacorus*; pot marigold; cornflower or bachelor's-button, *Centaurea cyanus*; madonna lily; English bluebell, *Endymion non-scriptus*; and wild strawberry, *Fragaria vesca.*

Note: All of the dyes in the tapestries were of course plant-derived, the principal ones being woad, *Isatis tinctoria* (blue), weld, *Reseda luteola* (yellow), and madder, *Rubia tinctorum* (red). Woad and weld together make green.

THE BONNEFONT CLOISTER

Two sides of this cloister are the original thirteenth-century vaulting from the abbey of Bonnefont-en-Comminges near Trie. The cloister so formed is the site of the famous Herb Garden of the Cloisters, dating back to 1938 and specializing in useful plants that would have been grown in medieval monasteries.

HERBS: *Herb plantings in the Middle Ages would have been greatly influenced by a much-publicized list drawn up by the Emperor Charlemagne (742–814) for the imperial farms in Germany. Monasteries and convents specialized in the growth and study of medicinal herbs. The knowledge acquired made such institutions the centers of healing during both the Dark and the Middle Ages.*

Apart from their medicinal uses, herbs (pronounced either "erbs" or "herbs") were of much greater importance than they are today. A source of perfumes, flavors, dyes, love potions, poisons, and pesticides as well as of amulets against plague, the herb garden was indispensable not only to the monastery but to the castle and the manor. Our senses would receive a rude shock could they encounter the medieval environment: air reeking with stenches resulting from poor sanitation and personal hygiene, bad-tasting food due to inadequate methods of preservation—all of this exacerbated in winter. Furthermore, spices from the Far East, which in future times would take over some of the functions of herbs, were too rare and costly prior to 1500 to play any important part in daily life. A pound of ginger, for instance, cost as much as a sheep.

The plants in this garden are labeled (so there is no need for botanical lists here) and segregated into beds according to their functions. Thus, that at the northeast corner contains medicinal herbs. The thorn apple, though poisonous, yielded a drug that helped asthma; motherwort tea was said to help women in labor; dittany promoted the healing of wounds.

Herbs used in seasoning grow in the southeast corner. A few are unfamiliar, such as the salad burnet and borage; perhaps they were ousted by the eastern spices as these became more commonplace.

Aromatic plants are concentrated in the southwest corner. The madonna lily, peonies, and meadowsweet are not strictly speaking kitchen herbs but flowers of strong fragrance. Of course, many of the herbs used in seasoning had also an aromatic function. Strewn on floors and beds, they disguised unpleasant human smells and helped to control fleas and lice.

Fresh vegetables were extremely important when food preservation was either nonexistent or poor—especially the leafy varieties rich in vitamin C, like dandelion, horseradish, lovage, orache, good King Henry, and sorrel. Many have disappeared from our diets, replaced by the ubiquitous spinach. Look for them in the northwest bed. Root vegetables like beets, skirret, onions, and

The Bonnefont Cloister

garlic were also popular, the latter two functioning as effectively as herbs in disguising the taste of spoiled food. Note the absence of potatoes, green peppers, kidney beans, and string beans—all American plants unknown in Europe until the sixteenth century. (The only native European bean is the fava or broad bean, *Vicia faba.*)

Quince trees like the four grouped around the well are uncommon today, but in medieval times the yellow, pear-shaped fruit was, like the pomegranate, a symbol of fertility and often seen at weddings. Today it is used to make a delicious jelly. The medlar, its near relative in the rose family, growing beside the grapevine on the east wall, is also little seen today, as its strange-looking fruits cannot compete with apples and pears for flavor. The grape was of course extremely important: wine was often safer to drink than water.

The tender plants in tubs—the orange, the fig, and the bay laurel—are Mediterranean plants, probably brought back by the Crusaders. The orange, the most tender, could not be of much importance until the development of glasshouses (orangeries) in the seventeenth century made its year-round culture possible.

Note that the rosemary growing here, though tender in New York City, would have survived French and English winters. It too is a native of the Mediterranean.

The dye plants featured in the middle northern bed would have colored medieval clothes. Not until the seventeenth and eighteenth centuries were dyewoods imported from Brazil, and chemical dyes were discovered only in the nineteenth.

These cloister gardens take us farther back in history than any others reviewed in this book. Their medieval setting serves to heighten our interest and deepen our understanding of the role of plants in a society so far removed from our own.

BROOKLYN BOTANIC
GARDEN

New York City

UNIQUE FEATURES	• One of the best representations of Japanese gardens in the United States.

UNIQUE
FEATURES
- One of the best representations of Japanese gardens in the United States.
- The best collection of Japanese flowering cherry trees in any botanical garden.
- A seasonal display of bloom remarkable in an urban botanical garden.

HISTORY: As early as 1897 a group of interested citizens enlisted the help of the New York Assembly in creating a botanical garden in Brooklyn. In 1910, fifty acres of waste land close to Prospect Park were made available for its development. Generosity on the part of many private citizens made possible the acquisition of plants and the construction of special gardens within these acres. Three outreach stations are now part of the garden, two in Westchester and one in Nassau County, each a gift from a generous benefactor: the Kitchawan Research Station, established in 1956; the Teatown Lake Reservation, acquired in 1965; and the Fanny Dwight Clark Memorial Garden, dating from 1966. The city still holds title to the original fifty acres, but three-quarters of the Brooklyn Botanic Garden's operating budget now comes from private funds.

- *Admission:* No fee for grounds; nominal entrance fee on holidays and weekends for Ryoanji–Roji–Tallman Dwarf Plant Garden Complex, Japanese Hill-and-Pond Garden, and conservatory.
- *Hours:* Open all year. May 1 through August 31: Tuesday to Friday 8:00 A.M.–6:00 P.M.; weekends and holidays (including holiday Mondays) 10:00 A.M.–6:00 P.M. September 1 through April 30: same as above, except closes at 4:30 P.M. Conservatory

(year-round): Tuesday to Friday 10:00 A.M.–4:00 P.M.; week-ends and holidays 11:00 A.M.–4:00 P.M.

- *Physically handicapped:* About 75 percent of the garden is accessible; the administration building, not at all; the Conservatory, possibly on uncrowded days.
- *Plants:* Labeled.
- *Address:* Brooklyn Botanic Garden, 1000 Washington Ave., Brooklyn, N.Y. 11225. Tel. (212) 622-4433.
- *Location and directions:* Adjacent to Brooklyn Museum and Prospect Park.
- By car from Manhattan: South on East Side Drive to Brooklyn Bridge; center lane to Atlantic Avenue; turn left onto Atlantic Avenue, then right onto Washington Avenue. Cross Eastern Parkway. Brooklyn Museum parking lot immediately on the right, behind museum.
- By subway: IRT 7th Avenue Express to Eastern Parkway–Brooklyn Museum station. D or M train to Prospect Park Station. IND 8th Avenue train to Franklin Avenue; change to BMT shuttle to Botanic Garden station.
- By bus: Lorimer Street B-48 south on Franklin Avenue, north on Washington Avenue. Tompkins Avenue B-47 via Empire Boulevard (last stop). Flatbush Avenue B-41 to Empire Boulevard. St. Johns B-45 to Washington Avenue. Culture Bus II (weekends and holidays only) to Empire Boulevard (stop no. 8).
- *Parking:* Parking lot north of the garden, between it and the Brooklyn Museum.
- *Gift and plant shop:* Within administration building.
- *No snack bar or restaurant.* Nearest restaurant is within the Brooklyn Museum.
- *No picnicking.*

For the city dweller the Brooklyn Botanic Garden is a delight, an oasis in a concrete jungle. It is miraculous that such an exciting garden can flourish in the midst of so much air pollution. Its compactness and controlled access—the gates are manned, only one or two being open at a time—make it a relatively safe city park. Schoolchildren are not allowed to enter unless accompanied by adults. Picnicking is forbidden. The visitors are here to enjoy plants in diverse settings.

The advantages of a small botanical garden where everything is within easy reach are here apparent. It is hard to get lost, paths are well delineated, directions are clear, and the topography permits a view of nearby attractions.

Ask at the administration building for a map to guide you to the gardens described below—all worth a visit, depending upon the time of year.

THE JAPANESE GARDENS

If your time is limited, visit these gardens first. The Brooklyn Garden is justifiably proud of its interpretations of Japanese gardens and horticulture.

JAPANESE GARDENS: *The Japanese approach garden design from an entirely different viewpoint. For them a garden is not a showplace for beautiful flowers but rather a place for the quiet contemplation of nature. Plants may or may not contribute to this end. For example, plants are lacking in the famous Zen garden in Kyoto—the Ryoanji—a replica of which you will see here. The aim of most Japanese gardens is to "capture nature alive." Western gardens, with their complex of terraces, geometric design, fountains, and sculpture, seem almost artificial by comparison, but this is because they serve a different function. To occidentals, a garden is a place for outdoor living, one in which they can enjoy the air, chat with friends, and picnic while admiring the flowers and the scenery. The medievals summed it up by speaking of a "pleasance" or pleasure garden.*

This is a far cry from the thoughts of the Japanese artist as he plans a garden. As you explore these gardens, keep in mind the fact that veneration of nature in all its forms is the ultimate goal. Remember also that the worship of nature is an integral part of Japanese religion.

Broadly speaking, Japanese gardens may be of two types: one to be experienced by the perambulating visitor—a stroll garden; the other, a static garden to be viewed like a painting from a seated position.

HILL-AND-POND GARDEN: This garden provides a series of spatial experiences during a stroll around the lake.

Water, or the simulation thereof, is a very important ingredient in Japanese garden design. Here, in the form of a lake that has the stylized shape of the Chinese character meaning "heart" or "mind," water adds a dimension of changing reflections. The red

*The Hill-and-Pond
Garden*

gateway—the torii—directs the eye to a shrine on the hill above
the waterfall dedicated to Inari, the Shinto god of the harvest.

Listen to the waterfall. In creating a mood, the sound of water
is also considered important. The landscape architect Takeo
Shioto, who designed this garden in 1914, took particular pains in
arranging the tiers of the waterfall. Not until the music of the
cascade met his approval were the rocks cemented in place.

Stones form the skeleton of the Japanese garden, setting its
initial mood and atmosphere. Consequently, great care goes into
the choice of their shapes and positions. The arrangement of the
stepping stones is intended to suggest a flight of geese. All the
rocks contribute to a severely contrived naturalness. In harmony
with them, the shrubs—azalea, barberry, quince, and maple—are
meticulously sheared and pruned to attain an over-all effect of
perfect proportion. (In the classic Japanese garden the azaleas
would not be allowed to bloom—blossoms would detract from
the mood of subdued elegance.) The bridges, the stone lanterns,
and the artificial island in the shape of a turtle (a symbol of
longevity) play significant roles in enhancing and augmenting
this miniature landscape. The type of lantern beside the lake is
described as "snow-viewing" because it looks best when capped
by snow. The Japanese designer visualizes his garden in all
seasons and at all times of the day; even moon-viewing is taken
into account.

Since this garden is a traditional landscape garden, it has a
roofed waiting pavilion and a teahouse with an open verandah

overhanging the lake. The tea ceremony, a Zen ritual involving the host and his guests, would be performed in the teahouse. The waiting pavilion would accommodate the guests while the host and his assistant made the necessary preparations. The purpose of the ritual drinking of tea and partaking of light refreshments among friends is to induce calmness and reflection for a short time within the bustle and confusion of everyday life. Unfortunately, in modern Japan the use of the tea ceremony is declining.

Although the Hill-and-Pond Garden is closed in winter, enough of it can be seen even in that season to make a visit worthwhile.

ROJI GARDEN: A roji is a miniature stroll garden. It originated in the sixteenth century as the approach to the teahouse. *Roji* means "dewy," and this garden would be sprinkled with water before and during the tea ceremony. Quiet, subdued beauty is the mood the roji seeks to inspire—the kind of feeling one would experience walking along a lonely mountain path. Flowers would be out of place. Note that the shrubs are mainly somber evergreens— rhododendron, andromeda, *Pieris japonica*, Japanese laurel, *Aucuba japonica*, and pines. Ferns and liverworts form the ground cover. Because the ground supposedly is always wet, the walk is stone-paved (some roji have stepping stones), and to give the illusion of length, it is also winding. Two other important features of this type of garden are seen here—the lantern to provide light for early morning and evening ceremonies, and the stone water basin. Besides its purely practical cleansing function, the water helps contribute to the mood of deep serenity. Squatting down before the basin, guests wash away worldly stains from their hands and mouth (note the bamboo ladle) before entering the teahouse.

Since this particular roji does not lead to a teahouse, it is really a facsimile of a courtyard garden. Such gardens were later adaptations of the roji for use in tiny, shady urban spots. The presence of a water basin, stepping stones or a curved stone walk, and a lantern indicates their origin. What is so fascinating about this miniature stroll garden is that within such a small enclosure, using so few "props," the meditative, subdued mood the Zen priests strove for is readily evoked. And this is true even in the center of a big city.

RYOANJI GARDEN: In contrast to the two other Japanese gardens, the Ryoanji is intended to be viewed from a static position, a verandah being provided for the purpose. To western eyes this

Entrance to Roji Garden

garden is very strange and initially incomprehensible. It consists of fifteen rocks arranged in five separate groupings, reposing on a flat surface covered with gravel meticulously raked in rippling designs. There are no plants except for the moss that grows on the rocks. (Any other plants that establish themselves are assiduously removed.) What we see here is a replica of the five-hundred-year-old garden adjacent to the Ryoanji Buddhist Temple in Kyoto. It was constructed in 1963 under the supervision of a Japanese landscape architect. The rocks, the tiles for the enclosing walls, and the carved entrance all came from Japan. No one knows who was responsible for the original nor what was

The Roji Garden

its purpose. Clearly, it is a religious garden, one that induces philosophical meditation which goes far beyond mere physical beauty. To appreciate it fully one should probably be a Zen Buddhist, but even a nonbeliever can be transported by ideas that take flight from the five "islands" peering out of a tranquil "sea." To the Japanese observer the vacant space within the garden is just as important as its physical components, allowing the observer to fill it in or even to expand it. In this respect it is somewhat akin to modern abstract art, which also calls upon the viewer to find his own meaning by allowing the stimuli provided to release his own imagination. It seems as if the Zen artist of the Ryoanji is compelling us to do this. And should we heed his bidding, perhaps in the middle of Brooklyn we shall experience some tranquillity of the spirit.

Note: At this point you may wish to inspect the bonsai collection in the conservatory. Bonsai are dwarfed trees grown in containers, an art that is purely Japanese. The Brooklyn Botanic Garden's bonsai collection is second only to that of the National Arboretum (see p. 143).

THE WESTERN GARDENS

A visit to a typical western garden will present a remarkable contrast. The Cranford Memorial Rose Garden followed by the Osborne Memorial Section would be good choices. If it is spring or summer, the beauty of the flowers, their vivid color and scent, the activity of the pollinating insects, the great contrasts of light and shade, are indeed striking; so also is the essentially geometric layout of the garden. Should it be winter, how dull they will appear—at least to the untutored eye, though the sophisticated may appreciate the "architecture" of the trees. Even so, it is difficult to escape the feeling that the garden has been "put to bed." This is never true of a Japanese garden, constructed as it is for all seasons.

Such comments are not meant to disparage western gardens but rather to re-emphasize the different functions gardens serve in different cultures. If a garden is a place to admire beautiful flowers and if it is also outdoor living space, then winter is the time to move elsewhere to await the rebirth of spring. The great glasshouses of the nineteenth century *had* to be a western phenomenon: they provided a place for the garden in winter.

TALLMAN DWARF PLANT COLLECTION: Modern city and suburban gardening puts a premium on dwarf shrubs and trees. As a practical aid, this garden displays those that are readily available from nurseries. Some are deciduous, but most are evergreen, and all are labeled. Related plants—those in the same genus—are grouped for better comparison: for instance, all the juniper cultivars are side by side.

City dwellers should be aware that deciduous plants stand up better to air pollution than evergreens. After only four months of active life, deciduous leaves are dropped in the fall to be replaced in spring by brand-new ones. Evergreen leaves, often needle-shaped, may persist for as long as three years, collecting grease and noxious gases all the while. Still, evergreens have more year-round appeal, so one has to balance the advantages.

Even though you are not in search of plant information, you will still enjoy this garden. The absence of floral flamboyance makes it a fitting neighbor to the Roji Garden—the subdued mood of the latter is not immediately dispelled.

CRANFORD MEMORIAL ROSE GARDEN: In late spring and summer the riot of floral form and color is a testimony to human ability to improve on nature. Practically all the roses here originated as crosses (hybrids) between wild species or cultivars or as "sports" (mutations) in nature. They are perpetuated by human agency. In practically all respects, except possibly fragrance, they are improvements on nature. Most impressive is their lengthy blooming period. Species roses, which have been taken from the wild and improved in our gardens by breeding and selection, bloom only once: in June. Cultivars bloom continuously from June through October. Species roses are indicated by two scientific names: e.g., *Rosa rugosa*. Cultivars bear the name of the genus followed by a varietal name in single quotes: e.g., *Rosa* 'Peace.'

Arranged for inspection are nine hundred species and cultivars of roses. They include the floribundas, the grandifloras, the hybrid teas—the most recent introductions in each of these classes—as well as some of the old-fashioned species roses. All are labeled. This is a place for the serious rosarian as well as for the casual visitor seeking a temporary refuge from urban blight.

The pollinating bees are not gathering nectar for honey but pollen to make bee-bread for their young. Roses, like magnolias, have no nectar but instead offer copious amounts of sticky pollen.

Actually, not a great deal of seed is set in this garden because many of the cultivars are sterile hybrids—"vegetable mules," as the early botanists called them. Species roses, however, are fertile. So, in late summer look for the attractive red seed cases (rose hips) that have replaced their blossoms. During World War II rose-hip syrup made from wild roses provided the much-needed vitamin C to citrus-deprived Britons. (For more on roses, see pp. 182–4.)

OSBORNE MEMORIAL SECTION AND FAWCETT MEMORIAL TERRACES: You are now looking at a small version of a formal landscaped western garden. It has little in common with the Japanese gardens. Note the geometric layout, the large, dominant fountain, the obelisk, the specimen trees, the banks of flowering azaleas, and the pergolas. This is one evolutionary version of the "pleasance" garden of medieval days. The pergolas, draped in spring with pendent wisteria, are especially reminiscent of the "galleries" of the old gardens. Another reminder is the topiary junipers on the Fawcett Terrace. Clipping shrubs into shapes of animals or objects introduces a comic or at best a geometric note that would seem to be the antithesis of the Japanese concept. (For more on topiary, see pp. 263–4.)

RHODODENDRON GARDEN: Though tucked away behind the Native Plant Garden, this collection of ornamentals (four hundred species and cultivars) should be visited at peak bloom in late May. (For more on rhododendrons, see pp. 249–50.)

THE HERB GARDEN: This is an example of the earliest type of western garden, dating back to feudal times, when its function was purely utilitarian. Herbs were of great value because of their scent and flavor and for their use as medicines, love potions, and poisons.

During Elizabethan times decoration crept into the kitchen garden. Elaborate designs were fashioned by clipping tiny hedges of herbs to look from a distance like green garlands tied in knots. Hence it was often called a knot garden. To get the full effect of this pattern, reproduced from a sixteenth-century design, climb the steps to the west. (Originally, the knot garden was meant to be viewed from the castle windows.) Only certain herbs lend themselves to this kind of pruning. Here we see germander, *Teucrium lucidum,* used for the cure of gout and as a strewing herb,* and santolina, or lavender cotton, *Santolina chamaecyparissus,* used in the treatment of ringworm. Note the effective use of gravel as a contrasting background for the green garlands.

On the periphery of the knot garden you will find most of the culinary herbs familiar to you as dried or ground-up leaves available in the supermarket. You may also find a few unfamiliar types like lovage, *Levisticum officinale,* used today as a flavoring in stews and salads, but in medieval times as a nostrum for all manner of "pestilential disorders." (For more on herbs, see pp. 203–4.)

THE SHAKESPEARE GARDEN: Originally located within the Children's Garden, this fascinating garden of plants mentioned in Shakespeare's plays is now accessible to the general public. It lies north of the Fragrance Garden.

Sit here in this summer garden and imagine yourself back in the English countryside of four hundred years ago. You are now looking at the plants Shakespeare would have known. Great efforts have been made to acquire the wild species or the old-fashioned variety of the time rather than use a modern "improved" cultivar.

Shakespeare makes more references to plants by name than any modern playwright.** This we would expect: he came from a society in which plants had roles far surpassing their value as food. Most Elizabethans lived in villages, or at least close to the land. Every good housewife was schooled in the use of wild plants and cultivated herbs to treat illnesses of mind and body, to perform superstitious rituals, and to concoct love potions and amulets. Thus, references to individual herbs would have had, for Elizabethan audiences, meanings that now escape us. Today we would not understand Ophelia's speech in *Hamlet* (act 4, scene 7) in which she says, "There's rue for you; and here's some for me; we may call it herb of grace o' Sundays." In Shakespeare's day holy water was sprinkled from brushes made of rue before the Sunday celebration of High Mass. Rue, *Ruta graveolens,* with its unpleasant smell and bluish-green leaves, was a cultivated herb

---

* A herb that was strewn on floors to disguise bad smells.
** See Jessica Kerr, *Shakespeare's Flowers* (New York: Thomas Y. Crowell Co., 1969).

of many uses: to improve the eyesight, as an antidote to poison, to ward off witches (probably Ophelia's intention), and to kill fleas.

Many of us remember Oberon's speech from *A Midsummer Night's Dream*:

> I know a bank whereon the wild thyme blows,
> Where oxlips and the nodding violet grows
> Quite over-canopied with luscious woodbine,
> With sweet musk-roses, and with eglantine:
> There sleeps Titania . . .

Here we see all the plants mentioned: woodbine is honeysuckle, *Lonicera periclymenum*; oxlip, a species of primrose, *Primula elatior*; eglantine, a rose species, *Rosa rubiginosa*. All grow wild in Britain except the musk rose, *Rosa moschata*, and would be in flower on June 21—Midsummer Night—with the possible exception of the oxlip.

THE FRAGRANCE GARDEN: Originally constructed for the blind, this tiny garden of scented plants has attracted the sighted perhaps even more. It is the only garden where plants may be handled. With beds raised to waist height, it is easy to smell a flower, crush a tiny segment of a leaf to savor its fragrance, feel the texture of a petal or a leaf, while reading the English and Braille signs (the latter give more information than the English ones). For flowers pollinated by insects, which as a class of animals has a very good

The Fragrance Garden

sense of smell, scent is paramount for the fulfillment of their biological function: the production of seeds. It is indeed fortunate that the scents attractive to bees, moths, butterflies, and beetles are also attractive to us. Scentwise we do not see eye-to-eye with carrion flies. Flowers that have adapted themselves to these insects stink. Have you ever smelled the starfish-shaped blossoms of the succulent *Stapelia*, or those of the skunk cabbage? Fortunately, evil-smelling flowers are rare. (None will be found in this garden.)

Most of the plants in these raised beds owe their fragrance to their leaves, the biological significance of which is not altogether clear. It is possible that the odors repel attacks by vegetarian insects—the garden marigold seems a case in point—but evidence for the theory as a whole is slim. Many scented leaves are used as culinary herbs, such as mint, thyme, sage; some, in perfume manufacture, such as the rose-scented geranium, *Pelargonium graveolens*; some, such as wormwood, *Artemisia absinthium*, to flavor alcoholic beverages.

One bed is devoted to plants with interesting textures. The nonsighted person has the sense of touch highly developed, so that feeling a plant and its texture imparts more information than it does to the sighted. Feel the velvety leaf of the peppermint geranium or the woolly betony, the slippery waxy leaves of the camellia. Hairs protect plants from water loss and are an adaptation to dry habitats. (All the geraniums are native to the dry veldt of South Africa.) Very smooth shiny leaves also provide the same biological advantage: the thick, waxy coating reduces desiccation.

THE MAGNOLIA PLAZA: This formal garden is a fairyland of bloom in late April and May. Species and cultivars of magnolias from the Orient and the southern United States, hardy in this latitude, are on display here. Oriental magnolias are the more dramatic because they produce their large globular flowers before the leaves expand; the native members of the genus flower only after the leaves have emerged.

The Brooklyn garden has a breeding program for magnolias. In the last twenty-five years two highly desirable cultivars have been patented. (For more on magnolias, see pp. 55, 191.)

The daffodils on Boulder Hill make a perfect backdrop for the spring-blooming magnolias. After blooming the daffodil leaves, though untidy-looking in the grass, are left unmown. For several

Zelkova sinica

months the leaves must continue making food (photosynthesis) to ensure the production of next year's flowers.

Autumn brings color again to Boulder Hill, the hedge composed of the burning bush, *Euonymus alata compacta*, and the sorrel tree, *Oxydendrum arboreum*, turning a brilliant red.

THE LILY-POOL ESPLANADE: Two rectangular lily pools and a fountain grace the plaza in front of the conservatory. Hardy water lilies will be found in the south pool, blooming from May till frost. Most are species native to the area. The north pool contains the larger tropical cultivars (with labels), which are planted out each year in June. To prolong blooming into November, the north pool is artificially heated. (For more on water lilies, see p. 172.)

On the conservatory side of the esplanade is a perennial border, but for floral display *par excellence* look at the opposite beds. In spring thousands of Dutch tulips form a foreground to flowering crab apples and cherries. In summer the tulips are replaced by a variety of colorful annuals, many of which are new All-American trial cultivars.

THE CONSERVATORY

The plant collections of this comparatively modest conservatory, though small, are well tended and well labeled. There is usually a floral display or special exhibit in the cool house (to the right after you enter) during October through April. In recent years the conservatory has been the site of temporary special exhibits, thanks to private and public funding. Additional information is provided by films and lectures running concurrently in the auditorium.

For its size, the tropical rain forest contains a surprising number of economic plants—cacao, mango, cassia (also known as Chinese cinnamon), ylang-ylang (for perfume)—which are well identified.

Tucked into another small section is an impressive collection of bromeliads, members of the pineapple family. These are epiphytes or air plants of tropical jungles which obtain the necessary light by perching on the topmost branches of trees, using their roots only as anchors. Here a dead tree serves to display the variety of species and cultivars in this family, ranging from our native Spanish moss, *Tillandsia usneoides*, to the exotic *Aechmea* and *Billbergia* spp. with their decorative flowers and gray foliage. (For more on epiphytes, see pp. 32–3.)

Other displays worth investigating are the ferns (pp. 227–8), the orchids (pp. 9, 34), the cycads (p. 8), and the small but comprehensive collection of desert cacti and succulents (pp. 228–9).

Do not leave the conservatory without seeing the bonsai exhibit. As you might expect from its involvement with Japanese horticulture, the Brooklyn Garden has one of the best collections of these Japanese dwarfed potted trees. As a result of private generosity some heirlooms have come from Japan; others have been created by the garden's experts.

You will see only a dozen or so bonsai, a small fraction of the collection. As with any other form of art, space is needed for their full appreciation. Consequently, the members of the collections are periodically rotated. (For more on bonsai, see p. 143.)

THE CHERRY ESPLANADE

Brooklyn's flowering cherry display in early May is second only to that of Washington, D.C. The trees, a gift from Japan, are a double-flowered pink variety of the oriental cherry, *Prunus serrulata* 'Kwanzan.' The extra petals that make the blossoms so roselike are sterile replacements of the stamens. Lacking these male organs, which produce the pollen, the flowers are of course sterile. Fruit does not follow flowering, which is perhaps fortunate.

The trees are planted in two double rows flanked on the outside by the red-leafed maple cultivar *Acer platanoides* 'Schwedleri.' To get an aerial view of the scene, the elevated Ginkgo Walk just south of the Brooklyn Museum parking lot makes a perfect viewing platform. After the cherry blossoms fall, the area looks as if a pink blizzard had hit the garden.

Since blossoming is so weather-dependent, it is best to telephone before making a special trip. These trees bloom at least three weeks after the Washington cherries.

Brooklyn has some fine and rather rare specimen trees. Two especially fine species should be noted: the dove or handkerchief tree, *Davidia involucrata*, of which there are two specimens opposite the Rose Garden and one opposite the Children's Garden; and *Zelcova sinica*, which has no common name but is a relative of the common elm with a strange form of growth (see photograph), and is to be seen near the monocot bed opposite the Rock Garden. Both are Chinese species.

With a subway at its front door, this is a most accessible garden. Besides being a delightful retreat for pavement-weary New Yorkers, it is a major attraction for tourists interested in the plant world. At any season the Brooklyn Botanic Garden will reward you with beauty and tranquillity.

NEW YORK BOTANICAL GARDEN

Bronx, New York

UNIQUE FEATURES	· The recently restored Enid A. Haupt Conservatory.
	· One of the best institutional rock gardens in the country.
	· The only uncut climax hemlock forest in New York City.

HISTORY: Nathaniel Lord Britton, a botany professor at Columbia University, founded the New York Botanical Garden in 1891 so that the United States might have a garden comparable to England's Kew Gardens. It was chartered by the state of New York to advance botanical science and teach horticulture while also serving as a place for "entertainment and recreation." When Britton raised the sum stipulated by the commissioner of parks, 250 acres were given over to the garden. The first president of the board of managers was Cornelius Vanderbilt, its first vice-president, Andrew Carnegie. The conservatory, modeled after the great glasshouses of Europe, was completed in 1902. By 1973 it was so dilapidated that there were plans to tear it down and replace it with a new, climatically controlled "climatron." Whereupon the city declared it a Bronx landmark and promised half the funds for its restoration. Subsequently, the financial situation of the city deteriorated and the garden realized it would have to bear the entire cost alone. Thanks to the generosity of Mrs. Enid A. Haupt, it was able to do this, and in 1978 the restoration was opened to the public. Like all museums and botanical gardens in New York City, the New York Botanical Garden has gone through a period of great financial hardship. Today less than one-third of its revenue comes from the city, the rest from private funds.

- *Admission:* Free to the grounds; entrance fee for Haupt Conservatory.
- *Hours:* Open daily, all year. June 1 through September 30, 8:00 A.M.–7:00 P.M. October 1 through May 31, 10:00 A.M.–5:00 P.M. Conservatory: Tuesday to Sunday and holiday Mondays, 10:00 A.M.–4:00 P.M.
- *Physically handicapped:* Accessible; most walks in cultivated section paved. Tractor-tram should be helpful. Conservatory possible, but difficult in some houses because of fiber-covered floors.
- *Plants:* Trees in grounds labeled; some plants in Haupt Conservatory labeled.
- *Parking:* Two parking lots, one in front of Watson (administration) Building, one in front of Haupt Conservatory. Parking fee.
- *Address:* The New York Botanical Garden, Bronx, N.Y. 10458. Tel. (212) 220-8700.
- *Location and directions:* Bronx Park, 200th Street and Southern Boulevard.
  By train: Conrail local to Botanical Garden station, 20 minutes from Grand Central Station (schedule available at latter).
  By subway: IRT no. 4 to Bedford Park Boulevard; or IND D train to Bedford Park Boulevard; then walk 8 blocks east.
  By bus: From Manhattan, take BXM 11, with stops along Madison Avenue. Go to Pelham Parkway stop, then walk 3/10 of a mile; or to Gun Hill Road stop, then transfer to 55X to Bedford Park Boulevard and Webster Avenue. Call (212) 881-1000 for stops and schedule. From Westchester, take no. 60 from White Plains.
  By car: Exit from Pelham, Bronx River, or Moshulu Parkway or Southern Boulevard. Then follow signs to garden—enter from Southern Boulevard.
- *Garden Shop:* In museum building. Open 10:00 A.M.–5:00 P.M. Sells plants, gifts, books.
- *Snuff Mill Cafeteria:* Open all year, in center of garden, 10 minutes' walk from Haupt Conservatory.
- *Picnicking:* Picnic area near Snuff Mill (see map).

The scientific reputation of the New York Botanical Garden (NYBG) is high. Unfortunately, in recent years its size, combined with budget cutbacks, has made it impossible for the diminished gardening staff to make this the horticultural showplace it once was. Collections of particular trees, such as magnolias and conifers, are low-maintenance items and therefore still impressive, but the beds of annuals and spring bulbs have disappeared under grass. Apart from the Rose Garden, floral displays are now virtually confined to the Enid A. Haupt Conservatory, where understandably most of the horticultural effort and expertise is concentrated.

Obviously 250 acres cannot be covered in one visit. But by 1982, when private cars will be banned from the grounds, a tractor-tram will make frequent trips around the entire garden, providing an over-all view of its natural and man-made beauties. The superb landscape setting is due to activities of the last Ice Age, which carved out the Bronx River Gorge and left various huge rocks (erratics) in its trail.

Highly recommended for detailed exploration are the Thompson Rock Garden, the Native Plant Garden, the Haupt Conservatory with its adjacent gardens. All are within the garden's high-security zone, and not too much walking is involved. Nature walks are conducted in the hemlock forest every Saturday afternoon, and periodic courses on the local flora incorporate field trips into the natural areas (make inquiries at 220-8748).

Plan your visit to the Haupt Conservatory during October through April, as summer inside this glasshouse can be very hot. Note that it is closed most Mondays, except holidays.

The best time for the Rock Garden flowers is mid-April through June, although the garden itself is beautiful in all seasons, as is the adjacent Native Plant Garden. For the gardens around the conservatory, the Rose, Herb, and Irwin Memorial gardens, June to September are the best months.

At the main entrance security booth, the Watson Building foyer, or the museum, pick up a map of the grounds as well as the guide leaflet to the Rock and Native Plant gardens (both are free).

The Rock and Native Plant gardens are within the same enclosure just west of the hemlock forest and five minutes' walk from any of the main gates. (It is assumed for the purposes of this description that you have the leaflet to hand.)

THE THOMPSON ROCK GARDEN: Rock gardening began about a century ago when the Alps and other mountainous regions were first explored. In these bleak habitats plants are extremely slow-growing, forming cushions and rosettes and flowering just as soon

Entrance to Thompson Rock Garden

as the snow melts. Shrubs are usually dwarfed or prostrate. More recently, rock gardens have come to incorporate other dwarf plants from equally unfavorable places, such as deserts, tundras, cliffs, bogs, and moors.

The adaptations required for life in these harsh habitats have made their floras unique. This is part of their appeal and fascination. The leaves of alpines are small, hairy or waxy, and often overlap each other, adaptations that reduce water loss in windy, exposed places. Moss campion, *Silene acaulis*, is a good example seen here. Shrubs are small evergreens with leaves that are sometimes tough and leathery (rhododendron), sometimes tiny and needlelike (heather). Because the growing season is so short in alpine regions, flowering must occur as early as possible in the spring to allow seeds to form promptly. For this reason April to June is the best time to see a rock garden. The conspicuous flowers, the gentians and anemones, are related to the paucity of insects on windy mountains. Dramatic advertising is necessary if they are to get pollinated. Practically all are perennial. A seed has a very limited food reserve as compared with a bulb or root. Only a large food store can ensure rapid growth in spring.

That such miniature plants with such delicacy of floral structure can triumph over supremely hostile environments is part of the appeal of rock-garden plants. The challenge of growing them is another factor. If you wish to know the extent of their popularity, attend NYBG's Rock Garden Festival in mid-April.

Accenting the beauty of this garden is the graceful birch culti-

var, *Betula papyrifera*, while the ancient sturdy oak, *Quercus velutina*, near the waterfall gives it character. The leaflet lists the small plants, many quite rare, many difficult to grow. One point, however: the numerous species of primrose, *Primula* spp., in this garden, from Europe, Japan, and the Himalayas, do not look like alpines. Yet their rosettes of leaves, pressed close to the ground, often protected by leaves of neighboring plants, are a good adaptation for survival in exposed places. The heathers, *Calluna vulgaris* and *Erica* spp., seen at the north end are not alpines but moorland inhabitants. Like many of the plants here, they need an adequate snow cover for winter protection. Summer is the time to see their flowers. In its native Scotland, *Calluna vulgaris* turns the hills purplish in August. (For more on heathers, see p. 176.)

The labeling here is thorough—so thorough that one small girl, visiting for the first time in early spring, asked if it were a pet cemetery! The fact that there are more labels than plants testifies to the difficulties of cultivating these rather demanding species.

THE NATIVE PLANT GARDEN: In contrast to the Garden in the Woods (see pp. 266–73), the plants growing here are restricted to natives of the northeastern United States; there are no exotics. Four major habitats are displayed: a deciduous woodland, a limestone outcropping for lime-loving plants, a pine barrens (see p. 271), and a meadow, both damp and dry. For details consult the leaflet.

The Thompson Rock Garden

Well cared for and instructive, this is a very pleasant oasis. This woodland is much richer in species than the natural one beyond the fence, which has been picked and trampled upon for eighty years.

ENID A. HAUPT CONSERVATORY

At the door on the northwest side, obtain the map and brief guide to the eleven houses that make up this Victorian glasshouse, a charming anachronism in this city of skyscrapers. The gardening staff has to do what it can to adjust the temperature and humidity in the different houses to the needs of the plants. That this conservatory is not a "climatron" is well demonstrated in summer, when every house is equally hot.

The over-all theme is ethnobotanical rather than strictly botanical. The relationship of plants to man is emphasized throughout, and more especially in houses 1, 2, 4, and 5. There is something here for everyone, although the botanist seeking information may at times feel thwarted. Unfortunately, many plants are still unlabeled. Since its opening in 1978 the minuscule staff have been fighting a losing battle in this arena.

House 4 is reserved for seasonal displays of flowers: poinsettias at Christmas, lilies at Easter, begonias in summer, and chrysanthemums in the fall. The Palm Court displays orchids in winter and impatiens in summer. Otherwise the houses are static, except for house 1, which is reserved for major exhibits funded by grants

Enid A. Haupt Conservatory from Herb Garden

and lasting one to two years. The present exhibit (1980) concerns the living food plants that contribute to the processed foods we see in the supermarket.

The staging for all these displays could not be improved. The ambience of this huge crystal palace built in the grand manner of the nineteenth century is exciting in itself, especially when snow blankets the Bronx. The following houses deserve special mention.

THE PALM COURT (HOUSE 6): Architecturally, the drama and beauty of the conservatory reside here. Until the nineteenth century, greenhouses were brick, Palladian-windowed structures (as at Dumbarton Oaks, p. 133). We owe the concept of the light, airy structure of steel and glass seen here principally to Sir Joseph Paxton, who erected the Crystal Palace in London in 1851. Inspiration for its construction supposedly came to him after studying the veins in the leaf of the giant water-platter, *Victoria amazonica*. This plant may be seen in the heated circular tank in the courtyard. (For more on the water-platter, see p. 172).

The garden under the dome represents a grove of palms in a desert oasis. The seventeenth-century fountain from Damascus, surrounded by pots of myrtle, *Myrtus communis*, recalls the Moorish gardens of southern Spain. The variety of palms collected here, from all over the world, is impressive. For a description of their botany and economic importance, see pages 5–6.

THE FERN FOREST AND SKYWALK (HOUSE 8): This exhibit is designed to display to best advantage a variety of tropical and subtropical ferns in a forestlike setting. The trees here are native to tropical forests. Locate the kapok tree, *Ceiba pentandra*, whose seeds provide stuffing for mattresses, cushions, and life jackets. It shows the characteristics of such trees: thin bark, broad evergreen leaves, and a fluted, buttressed trunk. Some flowering plants have been added for color—small gesneriads tucked into niches in the "volcano" (for more on gesneriads, see pp. 33–4) and some aroids, like the flamingo-flower, *Anthurium scherzerianum* (for aroids, see p. 27).

FERNS: *Lacking flowers, ferns are valued as ornamentals for the beauty of their leaves; even the young uncoiling leaf— the crozier, or fiddlehead—has its own beauty and symmetry. They exploit all niches in the tropical forest. Look around you and you will find some that are trees, looking superficially like palms. Others, like the staghorn fern,* Platycerium *sp., are epiphytes (for more on epiphytes, see pp. 32–3; on* Platycerium, *see p. 32). A few are climbing vines, twining around supports on either side of the exit door. A few are aquatic, like the small species in the water tank at the foot of the stairs, as well as the leather fern,* Acrostichum aureum, *growing in the pool under the waterfall. Small terrestrial ferns grow in the soil in shady spots, among them the maidenhair fern,* Adiantum *sp.*

Ferns are less common in drier and colder habitats. They are not, therefore, conspicuous inhabitants of a temperate deciduous forest.

Look for brown patches on the backs or tips of the leaves. These patches, called sori (singular, sorus), when viewed under a microscope are seen to consist of many tiny spore cases. When mature, the cases burst, setting free millions of dustlike reproductive bodies or spores, which become airborne. Since they germinate only in damp places, many are lost. They are not seeds. A seed contains an embryo plant and a food store encased in a protective coat, whereas a spore is usually a single cell and shortlived because it readily dries up. Ferns preceded seed plants on this planet by some 50 million years.

From the botanist's and the fern fancier's viewpoints this is perhaps the most impressive gallery in the conservatory. A multitude of ferns has been cleverly accommodated in a relatively small space to simulate a natural habitat. The ingeniously designed skywalk allows a more intimate view of the "forest." Labeling here is meticulous.

THE DESERT HOUSES (HOUSES 10 AND 11): In their native environment the plants of these houses have to cope with one major problem: low rainfall—approximately 5 inches per year as opposed to 42 inches in New York City. Lack of shade, cloudless skies, and low humidity aggravate the situation.

DESERT PLANTS: *To survive in the desert, plants must reach a compromise between their need for carbon dioxide to carry on photosynthesis and the vital necessity to cut water loss. The carbon dioxide passes into the leaves and stems through tiny pores called stomates. But inevitably, water passes in the opposite direc-*

tion from the damp leaf cells to the outside air. A compromise is achieved, but at the expense of growth—desert plants are notoriously slow-growing.

Most of the plants are short and squat—no lush vegetation such as is seen in the tropics. Their coloring is different, the green being muted to gray by a coating of wax or hairs that reduces water loss from the surface (also, pale plants absorb less heat). Other adaptations are succulence—fat stems or leaves distended with water; lack of leaves, the green stems taking over photosynthesis; spines, which deter thirsty animals; stomates that open only at night.

In house 10, old-world desert flora are collected: plants from arid but not necessarily desert habitats. The trees are Australian, natives of the dry Outback. The rest are succulents from the South African desert. Some, with leafless, spiny succulent stems, look very much like cacti, the same environmental conditions having evoked similar adaptations even though the plants are unrelated. These African plants are euphorbias belonging to the poinsettia family, Euphorbiaceae.

Not all are euphorbias. Look for the aloes, *Aloe* spp. of the lily family, with their rosettes of gray succulent leaves. The juice of one species, *Aloe vera*, reduces the pain of burns and insect bites; it is used in lotions and creams. Do not miss the "living stones," *Lithops* spp., perfectly protected by their pebblelike appearance from the eyes of thirsty beasts, revealing their animate nature only when they flower.

House 11 features plants of the American desert. It has been designed to re-create different mini-habitats typical of the Sonoran desert, whose flora is represented here.

The arroyo is near the entrance on the right. In the real desert, flash floods would sweep down this channel when it rained. Even though the stream bed is dry most of the year, its soil retains moisture. Consequently, the plants growing in this model arroyo lack any obvious adaptations to drought. Known as "drought evaders," they complete their short life-cycles before severe drought sets in. Only after heavy rains do their seeds germinate.

The seep is on the left as you descend into the tunnel. Underground springs in certain areas allow the development of a flora quite atypical of deserts. The most conspicuous plant of this model seep is the slender, yellow-flowered shrub *Nicotiana glauca*. Like the arroyo, this mini-habitat is watered fairly frequently, the rest of the house only once or twice a year, usually in winter.

All the plants growing in the model of the desert proper are drought-resistant. The huge cactus is the giant saguaro (pronounced sa-WAR-o), *Carnegiea gigantea*, named for Andrew Carnegie by Nathaniel Britton. This specimen is over a century old. Plants can live as long as two hundred years and weigh as much as eight tons, most of which is water. It is therefore not surprising that they can live for two years without rain. Note the entire absence of leaves, typical of the Cactaceae. The saguaro skeleton here is estimated to be a lot older than a century. The woody veins of which it is composed were used by Indian tribes for all kinds of construction. An endangered species, the saguaro is now protected in the Saguaro National Monument. Many smaller cacti will be seen nearby, all with fat stems, fierce spines, attractive flowers, and often edible fruit (the fruit of the saguaro and prickly pear are relished by humans and other animals). Cacti are native only to the New World.

The century plants, *Agave* spp., and the yuccas, *Yucca* spp., are American succulents resembling the aloes of Africa. Leaves clustered together in a rosette effectively reduce water loss (the same habit is seen in mountain plants and serves the same purpose). The century plant is so-called because it was formerly believed that it flowered and died only after one hundred years. Now it is known that it can flower after as little as five years. In all cases, however, death follows flowering. Both yuccas and agaves have been used by people for their sugary sap at flowering time and for their tough leaf fibers.

The creosote bush, *Larrea divaricata*, is the most drought-tolerant species in the American desert. In extreme dought its leaves die or shrivel and the whole plant appears dead, remaining in this dormant state for long periods. When rain returns *Larrea* revives; the leaves turn green and resume photosynthesis. Its foliage is sticky and does smell somewhat of creosote.

The ocotillo (pronounced o-ko-TEE-yoh), *Fouqueria splendens*, is another typical Sonoran desert shrub. Its leaves are deciduous for most of the year, photosynthesis being carried on in its green, thorny stems. Several specimens prosper in this house, some with leaves, some without. Its flowers are a brilliant red.

This collection of desert plants is perhaps the finest on the east coast. If cacti and succulents are your favorite house plants,

The Herb Garden

visit this exhibit, not just for the plants but for the unique and attractive mode of presentation.

Before leaving the conservatory, explore the pools in the court-yard, which exhibit native and exotic water lilies, the lotus, *Nelumbo nucifera*, and an aquatic *Amaranthus* sp. The latter two are called "emerging aquatics," because they have aerial leaves but aquatic roots. A unique feature is the floating walk-ways, which enable visitors to get a more intimate look at the pool's flora and fauna.

The Rose Garden, the Irwin Memorial Garden, and the Herb Garden, on the north side of the conservatory, are all worth a visit. The Rose Garden, moved to this location in 1972, is now beginning to look well established. A good display of modern roses may be seen here (for more on roses, see pp. 182–4). The small Herb Garden, cared for by the American Herb Society, features an Elizabethan knot garden. Incidentally, you are allowed to open the gate and walk in, which many visitors seem not to realize. (For more on herbs and herb gardens, see pp. 203–4.) At present the Irwin Memorial Garden is in the process of construc-tion. It should be completed by 1982.

OLD WESTBURY
GARDENS

❧

Long Island, New York

UNIQUE FEATURES	• A house and gardens that are compatible and complementary in style. • A historical exposition of a way of life that vanished with World War II.

HISTORY: This Stuart-style mansion and gardens were built in 1906, designed by the English architect George Crawley for John S. Phipps, sportsman and financier. Mrs. Phipps's English background (she grew up in Battle Abbey, Sussex) is reflected in the design of the gardens and the furnishing of the house. In 1959 the estate was opened to the public, under the aegis of the Old Westbury Gardens Foundation, to maintain the garden as an arboretum and horticultural collection and the house as a museum. The purpose was to preserve for posterity a great estate of the early twentieth century. Today 40 to 50 percent of the budget comes from the foundation, the remainder from membership dues, gate receipts, and fund-raising programs. Expansion of these programs is indicated by the appointment (in 1980) of a director of development. The gardens and house are administered by a board of trustees, which includes some members of the Phipps family.

- *Admission:* Entrance fee; additional charge for house.
- *Hours:* Open May 1 through October 31, Wednesday to Sunday 10:00 A.M.–5:00 P.M. Also open Memorial Day, July 4, Labor Day, Columbus Day, and Veterans' Day.
- *Plants:* Most are labeled.
- *Physically handicapped:* Wheelchairs can negotiate 75 percent of the paths; see map for recommended route. House accessible via ramps.

- *Address:* Old Westbury Gardens, P.O. Box 420, Old Westbury, Long Island, N.Y. 11568. Tel. (516) 333-0048.
- *Location and directions:* Approximately 25 miles from New York City on the North Shore of Long Island. By Car: Queens Midtown Tunnel from New York City to Long Island Expressway. Exit at Glen Cove Road (39S). Continue east on service road 1.2 miles to first road on right, which is Old Westbury Road. Continue ¼ mile to gardens. By train: Long Island Railroad from Pennsylvania Station to Westbury (45 minutes). Taxi to gardens (taxis meet all trains).
- *Parking:* Free.
- *Gift shop:* Open weekends only. Pamphlets, postcards, and slides may be purchased weekdays in mansion foyer.
- *No snack bar or restaurant.* Soft-drink machine in gardens (see map).
- *Picnicking:* Permitted in designated area under beech trees of North Allée.

Westbury presents the ideal setting for all kinds of romantic events. It is the dream garden that comes to mind on a winter evening, as one peruses nursery catalogues. In fact, it is used for weddings, movies, and fashion stills.

It cannot be classified in any particular school of landscape design, nor attributed to any period. Perhaps, because Mrs. Phipps was English, it developed from a sense of nostalgia for the English gardens of Victorian times. Indeed, parasols, swirling skirts, and picture hats would seem appropriate here. Constructed in 1906, the older gardens seem suspended in time. Only as we pass to the modern demonstration plots does the dream evaporate. In this respect Westbury is truly evocative of an era that will never return.

The "estate" period in America, of which this is a beautiful example, was consequent upon the phenomenal rise in wealth in the second half of the nineteenth century. Nothing comparable happened in Europe. It was the inevitable outcome of rapid development in a country with unlimited resources—or so they seemed then. Fortunately for us, the public that has inherited Westbury and other great estates, great riches often went hand in hand with good taste. At Planting Fields, another great estate now in public hands, efforts were directed toward a horticultural showcase, whereas at Westbury the goal was a pleasure garden.

One of the features of Westbury that makes it such a successful and popular garden is the artistic balance between the architecture—house and garden—and the vegetation. One does not outdo the other. An extreme example of a garden that is out of balance is Versailles. One remembers only the fountains, the long avenues, the urns—the plants are merely incidental.

But we must be on our way. The map is essential, and the prescribed route is the one to follow. It is assumed that the time is spring. It is recommended that you first tour the house. It will give you the flavor of the period and a feeling for the family who lived here.

From the north terrace of the mansion look north towards the *allée* of European beech, *Fagus sylvatica*. Originally, 286 trees were planted. Now 280 mature specimens are alive and thriving, the largest collections of such trees in the entire state of New York. This section is reminiscent of the parkland of an English country estate. Skirting the glassed-in loggia on the left (west), pass under a magnificent American beech, *F. grandifolia*, and descend the grand staircase to the small lake below. Pause on the stairs to admire the Boxwood Garden in the distance, a prospect both formal and romantic: formal in its symmetry and romantic in its aura of enchantment, which can be perceived from afar.

On either side of the staircase, rhododendrons are massed, among them ironclads and Dexters (see pp. 158–9) which John Phipps originally acquired. It is indeed fitting that recently, under the aegis of the Rhododendron Society of New York, some of his brother's hybrids have been added to the collection. Howard Phipps, Sr., of Old Westbury was a breeder of rhododendrons for some seventy years. Using Exbury hybrids from England, Dexters from Cape Cod, and certain Asiatic species, he produced new hybrids, hardy on Long Island yet free of the muddy pigments so prevalent in the ironclads. That he was successful is evident from the display here. At the end of May look for the vibrant red 'Ananouri' and the deep pink 'Mrs. Howard Phipps.' (For more on rhododendrons in general, see pp. 249–50.) With the lake behind you, the Boxwood Garden looks very like a stage set. Huge European beeches form the background, one on the left being of the weeping variety, *Fagus sylvatica* 'Pendula.' The foreground is a gracefully curving colonnade featuring a statue of Diana the huntress (perhaps because her domain was the woodland, she crops up more often in gardens than any other deity). The main focal point is a small rectangular pool with a

The Boxwood Garden

central fountain, accented by tubs of deep blue lily-of-the-Nile, *Agapanthus africanus*. The "wings" are spreading boxwood, *Buxus sempervirens* 'Suffruticosa,' which were old bushes when they were placed here seventy years ago. On the edge of the lake note the especially beautiful Japanese dissected maple, *Acer palmatum* 'Atropurpurea Dissectum.' The whole is understated but utterly successful. One could relax here by the hour, listening to the fountain and contemplating the reflections in the pool. (The "cute" swan boat moored in the lake was used by the family to reach the garden.)

Leaving the Boxwood Garden and aiming towards the Lilac Walk, look for a shrub with paired leaves and deeply etched veins. Called leatherleaf, *Viburnum rhytidophyllum*, it is a rather rare Asiatic shrub, an evergreen member of a genus that is mainly deciduous. Numerous varieties of lilac, pink, purple, maroon, and white, are to be found along the walk, most of them cultivars of the common *Syringa vulgaris*. If they are not blooming, it is better to press on—lilacs out of bloom are the least interesting of shrubs. In bloom, however, their perfume alone is sufficient to commend them.

Viewed through the filigree gate, the Walled Garden with its floral palette of all the colors of the rainbow is the epitome of enchantment. The herbaceous borders, a mixture of annuals and perennials, and the rosy brick walls declare its English ancestry, while the elegant antique gates, the Italian cypresses, *Cupressus sempervirens*, and the pseudo-well create a Mediterranean atmosphere (it was originally known as the Italian Garden). In early spring it is aglow with tulips, *Tulipa* spp., accompanied by pansies, *Viola tricolor*, and English daisies, *Bellis perennis*. In late spring a riot of blooms takes over—peonies, *Paeonia* spp.; astilbe, *Astilbe arendsii* cultivars; columbine, *Aquilegia hybrida*; poppies, *Papaver* spp.; the Japanese iris, *Iris kaempferi*; sweet William, *Dianthus barbatus*; and zinnias, *Zinnia* spp.—all well labeled. Many are bedded out from the greenhouses after the decline of the tulips. Espaliered on the brick walls are the southern magnolia, *Magnolia grandiflora*, hardy in this sheltered position and blooming; the Japanese dogwood, *Cornus kousa*; firethorn, *Pyracantha atalantoides*; and the Japanese yew, *Taxus cuspidata*, accompanied by natural climbers like roses, clematis, hardy fuchsia, *Fuchsia magellanica*, and the tender leadwort, *Plumbago capensis*.

At the south end of this garden is a rather beautiful semicircular ornamental pool with a fountain, hardy water lilies, *Nymphaea* spp., and lotus, *Nelumbo nucifera*. South of it a semicircular wisteria pergola, sheltering a statue of Ceres under a beehive-shaped excrescence, is something less than successful. Inappropriately rococo, it is the only place at Westbury, in the author's opinion, where decorative zeal overlaps itself.

Before leaving the Walled Garden by the east gate, look beyond to the distant statue surrounded by a high clipped hedge— a surprise vista.

Outside the gate turn left (north) and enter the somber pleached *allée* of hemlock, *Tsuga canadensis*, which simulates the Ghost Walk in Battle Abbey, known to Mrs. Phipps as a child. There each yew represented the soul of a departed monk.

The Rose Garden

The Rustic Arbor

As you emerge into the sun again, you will confront two metal peacocks planted with yellow pansies and partially enclosed by a semicircular hedge—one of the many surprises in store for the visitor here. (For the role of surprises in garden design, see p. 53.)

Now continue though the pinetum to the Rose Garden. Formal and English in design, its beds are edged with Japanese holly, *Ilex crenata*, and its walks with old red brick. Floribunda and hybrid tea roses grow here in profusion, creating a charming picture, but the variety of cultivars is not great. It is an ornamental garden rather than one designed to disseminate information. A tall, many-sided sundial marks the geometric center. Leave the Rose Garden by the north exit.

The old brick used in the Rose Garden paths is continued in the Primrose Path, under a rustic arbor of climbing roses. Beneath are azaleas, primroses, *Primula* spp., and forget-me-nots, *Myosotis* spp. Here is the charm that comes from simplicity. (The pergola in the Walled Garden, by contrast, is pretentious.)

Turn right at the end of this walk and aim for the Cottage Garden. The pseudo-Tudor English thatched cottage was formerly used as a children's playhouse and has been restored and refurnished. A beautiful silver maple (*Acer saccharinum*), so-called because its leaves have silvery hairs, towers over it. Within the white picket fence a charming little garden, shaded by pink and white dogwood, is particularly resplendent in spring.

Continuing eastward, cross the magnificent *allée* of European lindens, *Tilia europaea*, only six-and-a-half feet in height in 1906 when they were planted. A thick hedge of hemlock within each row of lindens gives added breadth to the *allée*. This north-south *allée*, which is continued north of the mansion by the beech *allée*, marks the main axis around which all the subsidiary gardens are designed. At the Governor's Palace in Williamsburg the main axis divided the garden into two completely symmetrical halves. This geometric exactitude is now unfashionable. Since the eighteenth century some leeway in symmetry has been considered desirable, and is exemplified at its best here at Westbury.

The Demonstration Gardens are the educational part of Westbury, but owing to clever and ingenious plantings one would never guess it. In fact, these are some of the most endearing small gardens so far encountered in this garden odyssey. Each is provided with a pedestaled map, showing the positions and names—both common and scientific—of all the plants therein. (One carping criticism: specific epithets tend to be capitalized indiscriminately.) Three gardens stand out in the memory:

- The Herb Garden. Two appealing antique stone lambs, sitting in front of tufts of deep purple lavender, *Lavandula* sp., guard the entrance.
- The Shade Garden. Shade is cast by a magnificent fern-leaf beech, *Fagus sylvatica* 'Laciniata,' a tulip tree, *Liriodendron tulipifera*, and a red or swamp maple, *Acer rubrum*. Among the perennials featured are the spotted dead nettle, *Lamium maculatum* (note that "immaculate" means "unspotted"); foam-

Entrance to Herb Garden

South terrace of the mansion

flower, *Tiarella cordifolia*; epimedium, *Epimedium* spp., with heart-shaped leaves; Spanish bluebell, *Endymion hispanicus*; astilbe; and the popular plantain lily, *Hosta* spp. The trees are deciduous. These perennials start growth early in the spring, often flowering early also. In this way they adapt to deep summer shade, their period of intense food-making activity coming before the trees leaf out.

· The Green Garden. This is a garden entirely without flowers which can function as an outdoor room for summer living. Under the large apple tree the white wrought-iron furniture contrasting with the shade and the greenery is both useful and ornamental. The minimal lawn area surrounded by interesting shrubs makes this a low-maintenance garden, the living area being bricked over. Adaptable to town or country—provided that in the former, care was exercised in the choice of woody plants and the lawn eliminated.

East of this area a Japanese garden is planned for the future. Southeast are the vegetable test gardens (not viewed by the author).

If it is May, a walk through the Bluebell Wood is recommended. Bluebells, *Endymion non-scriptus*, are English wild flowers that grow in such profusion as to suggest that a blue haze has settled in the ground. On a recent trip to Britain, Mrs. John H. Phipps purchased 20,000 bulbs and presented them to Westbury. *E. non-scriptus* differs from the Spanish bluebell, *E. hispanicus*, in having yellow stamens and recurved petal tips.

Return to the linden *allée* and walk across the magnificent lawn to the mansion. The imposing terrace with its twin balustraded staircases is supposedly modeled after the seventeenth-century garden of the Villa Garzoni in Tuscany, Italy. Climbing wisteria, *Wisteria sinensis*, great urns of geraniums on the balustrades, statuary, and topiary shrubs embellish this splendid façade. (For more on topiary, see pp. 263–4.) Mounting the staircase, you come face-to-face with a pair of life-size sphinx.

Proceeding east along the terrace, descend the steps to the swimming pool. In 1969 its loggia was transformed by the execution of intricate shell mosaic on its walls, recalling the shell decorations of grottos in seventeenth-century Italian gardens. The grotto was a cool, shady retreat; the shells evoked a cold, watery marine environment. Copied in English gardens, grottos were less than successful. Dr. Johnson remarked that they were fit only for toads.

Beyond is a large lake, a walk around which is delightful in spring or fall. In spring one is rewarded by Wordsworth's "hosts of golden daffodils"; in autumn, by the foliage colors of beech, maple, and sweet gum, *Liquidambar styraciflua*.

Autumn at Westbury is no less enchanting than spring; a muted, mellow beauty takes over. The Walled Garden is ablaze with asters and chrysanthemums, the woods with fiery colors of fall.

Westbury rivals the best of European gardens. Do not fail to see it when in the vicinity of New York. Devote a day, if possible. Another day should be reserved for that other great estate nearby, Planting Fields Arboretum.

PLANTING FIELDS

Oyster Bay, Long Island

UNIQUE	· Majestic trees in a parkland setting.
FEATURES	· The finest collection of rhododendrons and azaleas in the East.
	· A synoptic garden—desirable ornamental shrubs arranged in alphabetical order, with comprehensive labels.

HISTORY: "Planting Fields" was the Indian designation for the land which today is the arboretum. Originally fertile farmland, worked first by the Indians and later by the colonists and their descendants, it became in 1904 the estate of a wealthy New York family, the James Byrnes. In 1906 the Byrnes built a large brick house, with various outbuildings, on the site of the present Coe Hall. The formal gardens near the present house date back to that time. In 1913 William Robertson Coe bought the estate, adding to it so that its size totaled 409 acres. Of English origin, Coe was a highly successful insurance executive and financier. After a fire destroyed the Byrne house in 1918, he had the present Coe Hall built in the "Tudor Revival" style, modeled after Sydenham House in England.

The Olmsted Brothers of Boston, the firm that designed Central Park, landscaped the grounds after the manner of an English park of the early nineteenth century. William Coe's interest in rare and unusual trees turned Planting Fields into a horticultural showplace.

In 1949 Coe deeded his entire estate to the people of the state of New York to be used for educational purposes, primarily horticultural. It became known as Planting Fields Arboretum. After Coe's death in 1955, part of his estate established the Planting Fields Foundation for the preservation and development of the arboretum.

A crisis came in 1971 when Planting Fields was transferred from the state university budget to the State Department of Parks and Recreation, which was then unequipped to deal with this additional financial burden. For a year the arboretum was closed to the public. Meanwhile, a voluntary organization, "The Friends of Planting Fields," was formed in the community to rescue and maintain the arboretum. Today Planting Fields derives three-quarters of its revenue from the state. The Coe foundation and the "Friends" contribute the remainder.

- *Admission:* Entrance fee, which includes free tours Saturdays and Sundays at 10:30 A.M. You must register beforehand by calling (516) 922-9200. Extra fee for tour of Coe Hall (summer only); call same number for tour schedule.
- *Hours:* Open all year, 10:00 A.M.–5:00 P.M. daily. Greenhouses: 10:00 A.M.–4:00 P.M. daily.
- *Plants:* Labeled. Botanical and horticultural exhibits in Aboretum Center.
- *Physically handicapped:* Main greenhouse and most of the grounds, including Synoptic Garden, accessible to wheelchairs (the latter provided the ground is hard and dry). Coe Hall has ramps for easy access.
- *Parking:* Free, within the grounds.
- *Address:* Planting Fields Arboretum, P.O. Box 58, Oyster Bay, Long Island, N.Y. 11771. Tel. (516) 922-9200.
- *Location and directions:* In the community of Oyster Bay on Long Island's North Shore. Best way is by car. From New York City, take Long Island Expressway (Interstate 495) to exit 41N, then drive north on New York 106 to New York 25A. Turn left (west) at this intersection. After ½ mile, turn right onto Mill River Road. Arboretum directional signs begin here.
- *Gift shop:* Within Arboretum Center.
- *No snack bar or restaurant.* Soft-drink machine in restroom facility across from Arboretum Center.
- *No picnicking.*

Like the Morris Arboretum, Planting Fields was a garden attached to a house and to a family before it became an arboretum. Therein lies its special charm. The two families who successively owned the estate each put their own special stamp on the garden: the small formal Italian gardens date from the

Byrne era; the great sweeping lawns and the magnificent specimen trees were the Coes' additions.

Planting Fields is not just a spring attraction. Whatever the time of year, there is plenty to see, even if one ignores the greenhouses. The fact that the arboretum flyer, "What's in Bloom," is printed twelve months of the year testifies to the diversity of its trees and shrubs.

Horticulture and botany are taken seriously at this institution. While it is a garden to enjoy, it is also a place to learn. The Synoptic Garden is a living museum exhibiting some five hundred shrubs that grow well on Long Island. The rhododendron, azalea, holly, and dwarf conifer collections are attractively presented and educational. Small exhibits on botanical and horticultural topics are mounted in the Arboretum Center. It is not surprising that students from the local universities use this arboretum as an outdoor laboratory. The flyer, mentioned earlier, constitutes a thoughtful and considerate service to the visitor; it is a gesture of welcome. Clearly, the staff want you to share their enthusiasm for the world of plants.

At the entrance, pick up the map and the current copy of "What's in Bloom." Both will serve you well.

THE SYNOPTIC GARDEN: Begin at this garden, whose ramped entrance is opposite parking lot 1. (Flanking the gate are two dwarf white pines, *Pinus strobus* 'Nana.') The name comes from *synopsis*, which literally means "affording a general view of a whole."

The Synoptic Garden

And this is precisely what it does: it exhibits all those superior ornamental shrubs that grow well in the vicinity. Arranged alphabetically according to the initial letter of the genus, *Ilex*, or holly, is next to *Juniperus*, or juniper, for example, and *Philadelphus*, or mock orange, is next to *Pieris*, or andromeda. This arrangement does separate the members of a family unless they happen to be in the same genus, but this disadvantage is offset by the ease of finding individual plants; each lettered section is well signposted. Having been attracted by a picture in a nursery catalogue, the gardener can come here and appraise the real thing. And if it is not here, the reasons may be worth investigating.

Another advantage is that it facilitates communication between the professional staff and the visiting public. The writer of the monthly flyer is free to discuss any plant in this garden, confident that the reader can pinpoint it promptly. The Synoptic Garden typifies the serious purpose of the arboretum in disseminating knowledge about plants.

Obviously, in five acres not all the desirable species of a particular genus can be shown; some that are missing here will be found elsewhere in the arboretum.

Note that although this is a teaching garden, aesthetics have not been ignored. The positioning of the sections, often in cul-de-sacs, invites exploration, while the grassy paths and the attendant trees provide a variety of texture and color, making the whole "gardenesque." In spring and fall, flowering bulbs are additional embellishments. Not infrequently in botanical gardens we are exposed to things called "systematic beds," which are plants arranged in their families. The Synoptic Garden is a great improvement on these.

While you are in section C, look across the lawn towards Coe Hall. On the right is a magnificent specimen of the golden English elm, *Ulmus procera aurea*. A yellow mutant or sport of the English elm, it is the largest of its kind on Long Island. If you get close to it later, verify that its leaves, like those of all elms, are lopsided at their bases.

One rare tree to look for close to section W–Z is the yellowhorn, *Xanthoceras sorbifolium*, from China (see p. 160). Being a tree, it is technically part of the background.

Proceeding westward you next come to the Dwarf Conifer Garden. Conifers are woody, seed-bearing plants that tend to become large trees. Among them are some of the largest living things on earth—the giant sequoia, *Sequoiadendron giganteum* —and some of the oldest—the Great Basin bristlecone pine, *Pinus aristata*. For reasons of size the majority are unsuitable for the small garden, and yet, being evergreen, they are highly desirable trees, especially for winter effects. Consequently, gardeners have propagated a whole host of mutant dwarf varieties (cultivars). Here you can inspect 150 of them, all of suitable proportions for suburban backyards. They are well identified and include a broad range of genera from all over the world.

CONIFERS: *Except for the primitive ginkgo with its flat, fan-shaped leaves, all the gymnosperms (conifers and their allies) have leaves that are like needles or scales. Pines,* Pinus *spp., have long needles arranged in groups of two to five on short spurs. Bald cypress* (Taxodium *spp.),* Metasequoia glyptostro-boides, *fir (*Abies *spp.), spruce (*Picea *spp.), hemlock (*Tsuga *spp.), and yew (*Taxus *spp.) have moderately long needles ar-ranged singly, while true cedars (*Cedrus *spp.) and larch (*Larix *spp.) have short needles arranged in dense clusters. Arborvitae (*Thuja *spp.), false cypresses (*Chamaecyparis *spp.), and true cypresses (*Cupressus *spp.) have opposite pairs of scalelike leaves. Junipers (*Juniperus *spp.) have some leaves that are scalelike and some needlelike. It should be clear why deciduous trees belonging to the flowering-plant group (angiosperms) are called broadleafs.*

Conifers differ from the angiosperms in that they have no true flowers. Their sex organs are borne on conelike structures. The male cones, bearing pollen sacs, produce clouds of dust-like pollen, which is carried to the female cones by wind. Air spaces in the pollen grains make them buoyant. At the time of pollination the female structures or ovules are exposed on the scales of the female cones. Fertilization occurs when pollen settles on the ovules. Male and female cones are usually borne on the same tree. In contrast, angiosperms enclose their ovules within a structure called an ovary, which has a special receptive organ for the pollen called the stigma. The names of these two major groups of plants are derived from this basic difference: gymnosperm *means "naked seed";* angiosperm *means "seed within a vessel."*

This garden demonstrates convincingly that dwarf conifers can do wonders for a small garden. They have a timeless beauty that contrasts well with the changing broadleaf trees. In this garden small flowering bulbs add charm and interest in fall and spring.

Now continue westward to the holly collections. Because they are evergreen, hollies are also valuable trees for the winter landscape, while in summer their dark green foliage is a good foil to the paler colors of the deciduous plants. Here, in section G–K of the Synoptic Garden, we can inspect English and American species with their respective cultivars, a selection of the most desirable types hardy on Long Island.

HOLLIES: *The hollies are dioecious plants, meaning that male and female flowers are borne on different trees. If female trees are to bear berries, there must be male trees nearby to supply the pollen, which is carried by bees. Holly flowers are white and pleasantly scented. The only English species,* Ilex aquifolium, *is very similar to the American* I. opaca, *except that it has dark glossy leaves, while* I. opaca *has matte leaves. Both have beautiful red berries in the fall and winter. From time immemorial holly has been used for Christmas decorations, especially in England, whose native flora included only three woody evergreens: holly, box, and juniper. It is not surprising, therefore, that the old English carol "The Holly and the Ivy" includes the line: "Of all the trees in the greenwood the holly bears the crown."*

Many desirable cultivars and hybrids have been obtained from these two species, some with variegated foliage, some with yellow berries and some with strangely shaped leaves. (A sample is shown here.)

Ilex opaca *is not the only native American holly. Elsewhere in this book,* I. vomitoria, *the yaupon, and* I. cassine, *the dahoon holly, have been described (see pp. 86, 76). Other American hollies are deciduous, and some have black berries like the Japanese holly,* I. crenata.

THE CONIFER TRAIL: Farther westward, you come to the Conifer Trail, a collection of large pines, firs, and spruce, some dating back to the days of the original estate. New specimens and species are added from time to time. At the beginning of the trail are a number of species rhododendrons from Asia. These were obtained from Tacoma, Washington (as were many of the other newly acquired rhododendrons and conifers), the objective being to determine their degree of hardiness on Long Island. The state of Washington is ideal rhododendron country—at least near the coast. Because of the moderating effects of the surrounding sea, Long Island's winters are appreciably warmer than those of the rest of New York State. Many borderline plants that cannot be grown in nearby Westchester, for instance, flourish here. Retrace your steps and cross over the lawn in the direction of Coe Hall.

COE HALL GROUNDS: The hand of the Olmsted Brothers, the landscape designers hired by William Coe, can be seen here. The huge trees set down in the middle of expansive lawns, the rhododendron parks, the drives, and the conservatories were constructed after the style of an English country estate of the early nineteenth century, reflecting no doubt Coe's nostalgia for the land of his boyhood.

The huge copper beech, *Fagus sylvatica* 'Atropurpurea,' was one of a pair of mature trees moved from Mrs. Coe's home in 1915. The problems involved in transporting the trees from Massachusetts were monumental—a team of seventy-two horses was required to move them from a specially built dock on the Sound. Not surprisingly, one tree died in transit. (For more on 'Atropurpurea,' see p. 170.)

The copper beech

An equally huge weeping silver linden, *Tilia petiolaris*, used to grace the west lawn but was destroyed by a freak tornado in the summer of 1980. At the northeast corner of the house note a large cedar of Lebanon, *Cedrus libani*—a true cedar. The Bible-reading colonists thought that any conifer with sweet-smelling wood must be a cedar, hence the confusing use of the name cedar for species of juniper and arborvitae.

After exploring the lawn area, find the portico that brings you to the boxwood walk leading south into the formal gardens. These date from the Byrne era and are Italianate in design, with pool, teahouse, and small statuary. They have an air of neglect about them, and understandably so. Planting Fields' number one priority is caring for and adding to its marvelous collection of woody plants. From late spring a variety of annuals are bedded out in this section. If the lilacs are in bloom, walk west to see the display of species and cultivars.

AZALEA AND RHODODENDRON WALKS: Peak bloom for azaleas at the arboretum is mid-May. All the azaleas you see here are either evergreen oriental species or hybrids derived from them by crossing. Among the latter are the Kurumes developed in Japan, the Glenn Dale group from the United States Arboretum, and the Gable series bred by the late Joseph Gable of Pennsylvania. Undoubtedly the best of the oriental species is the royal azalea, *Rhododendron schlippenbachii*, a shell-pink deciduous form from China. Some shade for the azaleas is cast by dogwoods, *Cornus florida*, and Japanese maples, *Acer palmatum*. (For more on azaleas, see pp. 45, 146–7.)

Walking east, you come to South Rhododendron Park. Blooming time for these flowers on Long Island starts in mid-May and continues through June. (If they are not flowering, skip the two parks marked on the map and head for the Arboretum Center.)

William Coe had a special interest in rhododendrons and azaleas. His first consignment in 1916 came from Waterer's Nursery in England, which had been breeding hardy rhododendrons for the northeastern United States since the mid-nineteenth century. The hardy genes in the Waterer "ironclads," as they were called, came from two native American species, *Rhododendron maximum* and *Rh. catawbiense*. The improved flower color came from the genes of Himalayan species. From 1820 on, East Asia increasingly became a source of wonderful new species, many of which bloomed too early in the season for British and American

gardens. In the ironclads most of the best features of the Asian and American species were combined. In the 1930s Coe, like so many other wealthy horticulturists, bought some of C. O. Dexter's new and hardy hybrids, bred from Asiatic stock. Subsequently, Coe selected and named some noteworthy Dexter seedlings. 'Mrs. W. R. Coe' is perhaps the best of these and is seen here. (For more on the Dexter hybrids, see pp. 158–9.)

RHODODENDRONS: *The present popularity of rhododendrons can be attributed to the breeding of new cultivars, hardy in the Northeast and of a diversity of color to rival roses. This was achieved by combining the hardiness of American species from the Blue Ridge Mountains with hundreds of new types discovered in the Himalayas, Malaysia, and Indonesia since 1900 by intrepid plant explorers.*

Rhododendrons are evergreen shrubs confined to the Northern Hemisphere and found mainly in Asia; some are native to this country but only four to Europe. Some are dwarf alpine cushions; others grow to be huge trees, sixty feet high. Rhododendrons need not be the "muddy" purple so often seen in the suburbs; they can be snowy white, a scintillating pink, or a vibrant yellow.

Low maintenance is the aim of every modern gardener. Needing little attention besides a good mulch and an acid soil, rhododendrons (unlike roses) adapt beautifully to benign neglect.

Even when they are not in flower, their large shiny leaves lend beauty to the garden. This is especially true in winter, when they lord it over roses, which at that time look like so many dead sticks. On a winter's morning rhododendrons can indicate the temperature before you even leave your house. If it is below freezing, the leaves curl up and hang vertically. This is an adaptive feature. Desiccation by drying winds and bright sun can be dangerous when the ground is frozen. The tiny pores (stomates) through which moisture transpires are all concentrated on the lower surface of the leaf; curling encloses them within a cylindrical leaf chamber. Some rhododendrons have a woolly underside, which also protects the stomates from drying winds. According to one of its fans, the leaves of the exquisite Japanese Rh. yakusimanum have the feel of a horse's nose. (You will find this species at Planting Fields.)

These "rose trees," as their name means in Greek, have bee flowers, whose structure and color are designed to lure this type of insect. The contrasting colored blotch on the upright petal is thought to be a honey guide, pointing the way to the nectar deep in the petal tube. The blotch may vary from pale yellow to a deep purple. But beware: if you are a beekeeper, do not go in for rhododendrons or for azaleas (which also belong to the genus Rhododendron). Honey made from these flowers contains a deadly poison, acetylandromedol. Gorging rhododendron honey is now believed to have caused the sickness that struck Xenophon's starving army in 400 B.C. during its retreat through Turkey following defeat by the Persians. (Rhododendron flavum, the native Pontic azalea, was the culprit.) Not just the nectar but all parts of the rhododendron plant are poisonous, and this is also true of its near relatives the kalmias, or mountain laurels.

The present director has added many new hybrids and species, not just of rhododendrons, but of all kinds of woody ornamentals. He realizes that the arboretum's function is not just to maintain the status quo. To be viable it must keep up with new trends in modern horticulture. When money is tight there is always a tendency to retrench, particularly on the part of former estates—showplaces in their day—that have become public gardens. This has not happened at Planting Fields. Take the Synoptic Garden, for instance: a new idea, expensive and time-consuming to implement, but today a unique teaching tool that continues to prove its worth.

The weeping hemlock

ARBORETUM CENTER AND MAIN GREENHOUSE: At the Arboretum Center the visitor has an opportunity to buy an assortment of pamphlets and booklets and to view exhibits.

On a wintry day the main greenhouse can be an escape into the tropics for a brief spell. Apart from the seasonal displays—poinsettias and cyclamens at Christmas, lilies at Easter, and chrysanthemums in the fall—the greenhouse has permanent collections of orchids, cacti and succulents, economic plants—coffee, cocoa, citrus, banana, pineapple—and bromeliads and other tropical ornamentals. (For more on orchids, see pp. 9, 34; on ferns, pp. 227–8; on bromeliads, pp. 32–3; on cacti and succulents, pp. 228–9.)

Don't fail to visit the weeping hemlock, *Tsuga canadensis* 'Pendula,' on the south side of the greenhouse. It must be the largest of its kind on Long Island—not tall, but spreading like a veritable tent, its branches drooping to the ground. This is a beautiful tree for a large lawn and is placed to advantage here.

If you have energy left, a walk down the drive to the Carshalton Gates on Chicken Valley Road is recommended. These gates were handwrought in England in 1712 for Carshalton Park. In 1921 William Coe bought them after seeing an advertisement in an English magazine, *Country Life*. It was not without difficulty that he imported such a national treasure into the United States.

On your return you may wish to explore the new Carl F. Wedell Memorial Sanctuary; its entrance is on the right. Its main feature is a pool presided over by a statue of Saint Francis. Planted around it are trees and shrubs that have fruit attractive to birds. Beyond the sanctuary is the Edwin Costich Wildflower Garden. New trails have expanded this garden farther into the wooded area. In spring you can be sure to find many of your favorite wild flowers in this lovely natural setting.

Planting Fields, a horticultural gem in the middle of a densely populated area, has much to offer out-of-town visitors as well as local residents, not to mention students and schoolchildren.

Note: While in the vicinity, be sure to visit Old Westbury Gardens (see pp. 232–40).

MOHONK MOUNTAIN
HOUSE GARDENS

New Paltz, New York

UNIQUE FEATURES	• A picturesque Victorian garden in a rugged landscape setting.
	• A balanced combination of formal, old-fashioned gardens with self-guided nature trails in the Shawangunk Mountains.

HISTORY: The Mohonk Mountain House began in 1869 when two Quaker brothers, Albert K. Smiley and his twin, purchased the land and a broken-down tavern. The tavern developed into a hotel of 305 rooms, as popular today as it was in 1900. The garden was a more difficult proposition. Although the lake and rugged terrain made a wonderful backdrop, topsoil on this mountaintop was practically nonexistent. Mr. Albert, a "passionate" gardener, was undeterred; cartloads of soil were brought in by horses. Between 1888 and 1905 a "naturalistic" garden was created. Today it is little changed except for the tremendous increase in the variety of plants. Also, walking trails were developed so that hikers and nature lovers could explore the native flora of the Shawangunk Mountains.

The Smiley family continues to run this century-old resort, preserving and promoting Mr. Albert's enthusiasm for the natural world.

- *Admission:* Free to hotel guests. Entrance fee for day visitors.
- *Hours:* Open all year, 8:00 A.M. to sunset daily.
- *Plants:* Most are labeled, or identifiable using pamphlets available at hotel or gatehouse.
- *Physically handicapped:* Facilities not adapted for wheelchair visitors.
- *Parking:* For day guests, free at Mountain Rest Gatehouse;

parking fee if space available near hotel. For hotel guests, free near hotel.

- *Address:* Mohonk Mountain House, Mohonk Lake, New Paltz, N.Y. 12561. Tel. (914) 233-2244.
- *Location and directions:* 90 miles from New York City; 6 miles west of New Paltz, N.Y. By car: Leave New York State Thruway at exit 18. Turn west on New York 299 and go through New Paltz. Immediately after crossing bridge over Wallkill River, turn right at Mohonk sign. Bear left at next "Y" and follow Mountain Rest Road to Mohonk gate. Walk to Picnic Lodge Day Visitor Center (right turn off Garden Road, near greenhouse); or car service available for small fee. Hotel guests may drive straight to hotel. By bus: Trailways express bus service from Port Authority Terminal in New York to New Paltz (1¾ hours). By train: Penn Central to Poughkeepsie. With advance notice, Mohonk cars will meet buses and trains (fee).
- *Gift shop:* Pamphlets, self-guides to trails available at Mountain Rest Gatehouse or at hotel.
- *Snack bar:* At Picnic Lodge Day Visitor Center.
- *Restaurant:* Within the hotel; advance reservation required. Price of meal includes use of hotel, gardens, trails, and regular entertainment offered overnight guests.
- *Picnicking:* Picnic areas at Picnic Lodge, Skytop Tower.
- *Note:* Day visitors may visit award-winning gardens, greenhouse, and Barn Museum and use the many miles of hiking trails. They are not permitted in hotel or its immediate vicinity (with exception of those taking lunch or dinner—see above).

The gardens at Mohonk are a mixture of Victorian picturesque and naturalistic styles. The sweeping lawns, the splendid specimen trees, and the drifts of springtime daffodils constitute the naturalistic component, while the show gardens with their beds of brilliant flowers set in a landscape dotted with fanciful rustic gazebos are pure Victorian. Even the picturesque element owes much of its charm to the exploitation of the natural beauty of the setting, which is the very essence of naturalistic gardening. The distant crags, the random outcroppings, and the surrounding pine woods make a wonderful backdrop for the entire scene. That the essential beauty of the gardens lies not just in their floral display is apparent in early spring and fall: at these times the naturalistic garden is best appreciated.

Still, most visitors come to see the eye-catching riot of color that the show gardens become in late June, lasting to the first frost. They have been called "old-fashioned" because they grow many of the flowers that have vanished from our modern gardens. In an age of uniformity and mass production it is easier to produce thousands of annuals of one, two, or three kinds than a broad mixture. Thus the local garden center or nursery carries the same old things year after year—geraniums, petunias, impatiens, marigolds, and zinnias, with perhaps antirrhinums and ageratum for variety. Have you ever tried to find *Salpiglossis*, the treasure flower, or *Gazania*? If we want these beautiful exotics, they must be grown from seed.

At Mohonk, however, all summer flowers, common and uncommon, can be seen. One of its brochures says that it grows all the flowers pictured in seed catalogues, and this is true. Some of the more unusual noted in 1980 were star-of-the-veldt (*Dimorphotheca*), *Nemesia*, *Clarkia*, *Calendula*, *Matthiola*, *Convolvulus tricolor*, *Salpiglossis*, and *Gazania*. Not only are the old-fashioned scented flowers like mignonette, *Reseda odorata*, and heliotrope, *Heliotropium peruvianum*, grown here but also the new varieties. In 1980 the newest strain of *Nicotiana* was displayed. All are annuals, raised in the greenhouse and bedded out in June, as frost can be late in these mountains.

In keeping with Mohonk's old-fashioned air, the center bed is an example of the now discredited but once popular Victorian art of carpet-bedding. Colored leaves and flowers are planted in

The hotel and show gardens

designs or patterns like those on Persian carpets. The silvery leaves of *Senecio* contrast with the red leaves of begonia, which in turn contrast with the white flowers of *Alyssum*. To produce the carpet effect the plants must be low-growing and cushiony; only the centerpiece may be tall. Here the centerpiece is unexpectedly a solitary cycad—although these primitive conifers can be decorative when quite small.

---

*R*OBINSON AND JEKYLL: *In England at the turn of the century, William Robinson and Gertrude Jekyll led a campaign against the artificiality of carpet-bedding. They insisted that each species of plant had its own intrinsic beauty of form and texture which carpet-bedding denied, plants being used simply for their color, like paint. The English herbaceous border was the outcome of the Robinson-Jekyll influence. Such borders, inspired by the cottage gardens of English villages, depend upon carefully juxtaposed perennials that flower in sequence.*

Carpet-bedding is still practiced in some public gardens in Europe, laborious and time-consuming though it is. As an extreme example, floral clocks still tell time in some cities, Edinburgh being one.

At Mohonk only the central bed is treated in this fashion. The rest of the annuals are grown in rows so that each kind of plant can be examined—as well it might, since it is unlikely that many will be seen outside of a catalogue.

For a good photograph, climb the two-story gazebo, a rustic structure taken straight out of Andrew Downing's book—the well-known landscape architect who advised Mr. Albert. The various other gazebos perched whimsically on rocky outcrops are functional as well as picturesque, providing shady lookouts or resting points for hikers. Other picturesque embellishments are rustic arbors smothered in climbers such as trumpet vine, *Campsis radicans*, and wisteria, *Wisteria sinensis*.

Besides the annual beds, there are a herb garden, a rose garden, and a rock-wall garden, all of which are small. In the herb garden fragrance may be sampled by pinching the leaves. The rose garden is more quaint than beautiful—the rustic fence necessitated by the hungry winter deer is distracting. But it does display some old-time roses like the sweetbriar, *Rosa rubiginosa* (or *R. eglanteria*) which has not only fragrant flowers but fragrant foliage. It is good to see these old species roses, little grown

Garden retreats

nowadays because of their short flowering period and their sus-
ceptibility to disease. Mohonk has a considerable "gene bank" of
old-fashioned flowers, shrubs, and trees that are impossible to find
in today's nurseries. Nurturing these rare species is in effect
preserving their inheritance factors for possible use in future
breeding programs.

Planted on the lawn after the manner of an English park are
various specimen trees. The most remarkable is the weeping
beech, *Fagus sylvatica* 'Pendula,' planted in Albert Smiley's day,
which is on the left of the main drive as you walk north from
the show gardens. Nearby is another beech cultivar, the fernleaf

Spring with gazebo

beech, *F. sylvatica* 'Laciniata,' while on the far side of the show gardens is the copper beech, *F. sylvatica* 'Atropurpurea.' Near the cutting garden is the Japanese tree lilac, *Syringa amurensis japonica*, seldom seen, yet hardy as far north as Canada. Of the same genus as the common lilac, it produces white flowers in June. Near the small arbor is the sweet bay, *Magnolia virginiana*, apparently quite hardy in this harsh winter climate.

Out-of-bounds to day visitors but readily located by hotel guests is the Japanese umbrella pine, *Sciadopitys verticillata*. The fact that it is close to the hotel wall may explain why this beautiful conifer (not a pine, but related to them) is grown successfully here at Mohonk. Normally, it prefers warmer regions. Nearby on the porte-cochère is the rather unusual vine hydrangea, *Hydrangea petiolaris*, also native to Japan. In spring it produces umbels of sterile white flowers, which remain intact all summer long. Being deciduous, it comes to life in spring and is a good contrast to the unchanging aspect of ivy, *Hedera helix*. In summer the night-blooming cereus, *Hylocereus lemairei*, is spotlighted so that overnight guests may enjoy the beauty and fragrance of its nocturnal blooms (a precious but charming gesture that could be made only by hoteliers truly captivated by growing things).

For more on the show gardens and a map, purchase the booklet *The Mohonk Gardens*, by Ruth H. Smiley.

Two self-guided trails have been made for those who want to explore the native flora of these mountains. The Fern–Wildflower Trail, just west of the Stone Summer House, involves a minimum of walking; it can be seen in fifteen minutes or an hour, depending on your interest. The Bruin Path Nature Trail begins at the little wooden bridge at the northeast end of the garden. Winding through the natural area, it takes about an hour. (For each a handy guide is available at the gate or the hotel.)

On the Fern–Wildflower Trail all the ferns (about thirty species) are labeled; wild flowers are labeled only when blooming or if interesting in some other way. Collected here are practically all the fern species native to the Mohonk region. Among the wild flowers are some imports, such as the twinleaf, *Jeffersonia diphylla*, and the purple fringed orchis, *Habenaria psychodes*, as well as the Mohonk natives. An unexpected tree on this trail is the native umbrella magnolia, *M. tripetala*, not so hardy as the sweet bay; it is surprising to find it this far north.

Instead of labels, the Bruin Path Trail has numbered stations that refer to the numbered descriptions in the guide. More general than the other trail, its topics are rocks, animals, and general ecological features as well as plants.

If you prefer not to bother with information, but simply to hike in the woods and over the peaks, some seven thousand acres of Mohonk property are here to explore.

Throughout the year guests at the hotel have a chance to join free garden tours and nature walks conducted by experts. And for serious gardeners, Mohonk holds a "Garden Holiday" every August. Lectures, demonstrations, and walks are part of the program (write or telephone Mohonk House for further information).

Mohonk is attractive because it is so unusual. Dedicated amateurs have created the gardens and the trails. And lest we be superior about amateurs, let us recall that the great naturalist, Charles Darwin, was an amateur.

GREEN ANIMALS

Portsmouth, Rhode Island

| UNIQUE | · The finest collection of topiary shrubs—geometric |
| FEATURE | and animal forms—in the United States. |

HISTORY: This seven-acre estate was purchased in 1872 by Thomas E. Brayton, who was treasurer of the Union Cotton Manufacturing Company in Fall River, Massachusetts from 1879 to 1920. After his death in 1939 his daughter, Alice Brayton, took over the estate, giving it the name "Green Animals." Brayton's interest in topiary was sparked by a visit to a botanical garden in the Azores that featured this form of horticultural art. Almost all the present topiary at Green Animals was created after 1893 by Joseph Carreira, a native of the Azores and Thomas Brayton's superintendent. After Carreira's death in 1934 his son-in-law, George Mendonca, assumed the superintendentship. Miss Brayton, herself a horticulturist, encouraged the preservation and development of the gardens under Mr. Mendonca. When she died in 1972 she left Green Animals to the Preservation Society of Newport County. Because there is no endowment, the garden is dependent upon gate receipts and profits from the gift shop, which sells plants and produce from the estate.

· *Admission:* Entrance fee.
· *Hours:* Open May 1 through September 30. 10:00 A.M.–5:00 P.M. daily.
· *Plants:* Plant list available, identifying species in numbered beds.
· *Physically handicapped:* Garden is accessible to wheelchairs.
· *Address:* For information, write or call the Preservation Society of Newport County, 118 Mill Street, Newport, R.I. 02840. Tel. (401) 847-1000.
· *Location and directions:* 7 miles north of Newport, on Cory's Lane, off Rhode Island 114, Portsmouth; 3/10 miles south on

114 from junction with 24. By car: From Interstate 95 at Wyoming exit, take Rhode Island 138 east to Newport. At junction of R.I. 138 and R.I. 114, take 114; Cory's Lane is 7 miles north on the left. By train: Old Colony and Newport Railway line from Newport to Cory's Lane reopened in 1979 for tourists; for schedule write The Preservation Society of Newport County (see above) or call Newport County Railroad Foundation, (401) 849-7594.

- *Parking:* Free, within the grounds.
- *Gift and plant shop:* Sells home-grown fruits and vegetables.
- *No snack bar or restaurant.*
- *No picnicking.*
- *Note:* The Rhode Island Children's Toy Museum is within the main residence.

This most unusual garden can be explored in an hour or two depending upon your degree of interest. A visit to Green Animals is easily combined with a tour of the Newport mansions and is made even more enjoyable by riding the historic train to the garden. Pick up the brochure at the entrance. It includes a detailed map and a plant list related to the numbered beds.

The garden is formal in that the beds are geometrically arranged and edged with box, *Buxus sempervirens.* An unusual yellow variegated form, *B. sempervirens* 'Aureomarginata,' is seen here. Besides the decorative flower beds with their attendant

The plant zoo

topiary trees and shrubs, there is a fruit-and-vegetable garden, including a small herb garden.

"Old-fashioned" would be the adjective reserved for this garden; the parterre-like flower beds, exhibiting some old-time annuals, the topiary, itself a throwback to the seventeenth century, the rustic arbors, and the espaliered fruit trees are all evocative of past garden design. It brings to mind the small gardens of Williamsburg, yet it lacks their prim formality. The exuberant flowers that seem to overflow their beds are not in the Williamsburg tradition. At Green Animals the Dutch order and precision of the seventeenth century have been wedded to the Victorian mania for bedded-out plants.

Still, we are here not to dissect the garden design but to inspect curiosities of a bygone age: evergreens clipped into animal and geometric forms.

The formal parterre gardens in the southwest corner highlight a few of the topiary; each is given specimen status within its little hedge or parterre. On the western boundary is a row of geometric forms, while in the southwest corner of the flower garden is a veritable zoo of green animals. Among them the most realistic, and therefore the most remarkable, are the giraffe, the camel, the rabbit, and the elephant (before he lost his trunk to a clumsy tourist). Geometric topiary can be seen at Williamsburg, both animal and geometric forms are on display at Longwood, but there is nothing in the United States to rival the specimens before you for size, variety, and numbers. Highly labor-intensive

The green giraffe

Geometric forms

as it is, it is hardly surprising that topiary is a vanishing art. Ladders must be custom-designed to make it possible to trim the ears and noses of some of these beasts.

The traditional evergreen materials used in topiary, at least in England, were yew (*Taxus baccata*) and box—yew for large-scale work and box for smaller objects. (Note: we are already referring to plants as "material," just as if they were inanimate. Perhaps that is the source of our ambivalent attitude towards topiary: it denies the living plant the right to grow according to its nature.) Here in Rhode Island yew is too slow-growing—only fair-sized trees can be sculpted into topiary—while box at this latitude is not reliably hardy. The choice made was California privet, *Ligustrum ovalifolium*, a relatively rapid grower and evergreen except in the worst of winters. All the green animals here are made in privet, although some of the geometric figures, like the columns on the western border, are executed in juniper, *Juniperus* sp., some in false cypress, *Chamaecyparis* sp., and one (number 36 on the map) in box.

TOPIARY: *The art of shaping shrubs into animal and geometric forms by shearing and pruning seems to have originated in ancient Rome. Pliny the Younger (A.D. 62–110) describes his garden in Tuscany as "embellished with various figures and bounded with a box hedge, from which you descend by an easy slope, adorned with the representation of divers animals in box." Pliny had five hundred slaves and a toparius (Latin for gardener).*

The name hints at the importance of this horticultural art in Roman gardens.

Recent excavations at Fishbourne in Sussex have revealed the remains of elaborate Roman gardens in England. Did the Romans perhaps introduce topiary into Britain?

The first recorded description of topiary in England concerns Henry VIII's garden at Hampton Court in 1533. The topiary craze, however, did not hit England until the period 1660–1714. The enforced exile of Charles II and his court in France during Cromwell's Commonwealth afforded them the opportunity to observe French gardens, which were formal and Le Nôtrean in design. On their return to England in 1660, French gardening ideas were put into practice and subsequently reinforced by the Dutch horticultural ideas of William and Mary, who came to the throne in 1689.

It was during this period that the most famous topiary garden, Levens Hall in the Lake District, was created. Designed by a French pupil of Le Nôtre, it has persisted for three hundred years. The original topiary yews are now enormous.

During Queen Anne's reign (1702–1714) the formality of English gardens was attacked by famous writers like Joseph Addison and Alexander Pope. Topiary, being one aspect of this formalism, came in for much ridicule. The time was ripe for change. The eighteenth century saw the English garden transformed into a pseudo-landscape under the direction of efficiency expert "Capability" Brown. Only a few formal gardens miraculously escaped his axe, among them Hampton Court and Levens Hall. The latter was still regarded as an anachronism early in the nineteenth century; a gardening manual states: [Here] the topiary foible of our horticultural predecessors is still maintained in all its quaint antagonism to Nature."

Not until the late nineteenth century did topiary begin to make a comeback in English gardens. In this context, it is interesting that Thomas Brayton of Green Animals saw his first topiary, not in England, but in the Azores (fortunately beyond the range of "Capability" Brown's juggernaut).

Topiary continued to flourish throughout the eighteenth century in the colonies of the New World. Today it can be seen in the Dutch-English gardens of the Williamsburg Restoration (see p. 108).

Horse and rider in privet

You may have reservations about topiary, feeling that to clip trees "in the most awkward figures of men and animals, than in the most regular of their own"* is a form of horticultural blasphemy. Even so, you should visit this garden. You may succumb to its charm. And if you don't, your children will. Of all the gardens in this book, aside from amusement parks like Cypress Gardens in Florida, this "plant zoo" is the most appealing to youngsters. They enjoy its horticultural frivolity.

* Alexander Pope, *The Guardian* (1713).

GARDEN IN THE WOODS

❧

Framingham, Massachusetts

UNIQUE FEATURES	• The largest landscaped collection (fifteen acres) of native plants in the northeastern United States. • A botanical garden of native plants developed by two individuals with vision.

HISTORY: Will C. Curtis bought the land in 1930 with the intention of converting it into a naturalistic wild garden. He was joined in 1933 by Howard O. Stiles; together the two men developed and landscaped the garden and planted it with native plants from many habitats, both here and abroad. In the 1940s, Garden in the Woods achieved botanical-garden status. By 1965, however, Curtis and Stiles felt incapable of continuing the work alone. An intermediary arranged the transfer of the garden to the New England Wild Flower Society, which raised an endowment of $225,000 from individual contributions. Under the aegis of the society, Curtis became the garden's first director and Stiles its first curator. Today its forty-five acres are the headquarters of the society, with a staff of nine.

- *Admission:* Entrance fee.
- *Hours:* Open April 1 through November 1. Monday to Saturday 8:30 A.M.–4:30 P.M., including all holidays. Closed Sunday. Library and book/gift shop open all year.
- *Plants:* Labeled.
- *Physically handicapped:* Plans afoot to make all or parts of garden accessible by electric cart on certain days of the week. Call numbers below for information.
- *Address:* Garden in the Woods, Hemenway Road, Framingham, Mass. 01701. Tel. (617) 877-6574; (617) 237-4924 (Boston).
- *Location and directions:* Half-hour drive from downtown

Boston. By car: From north, south, or east, take Massachusetts 128 to U.S. 20; west on U.S. 20 to Raymond Road (second left after railroad tracks in South Sudbury); continue on Raymond Road to Hemenway Road. From west, take Massachusetts Turnpike to U.S. 9; east on U.S. 9 to Edgell Road exit; turn left at lights onto Edgell Road; from Edgell Road, turn right at lights onto Water Street, then left onto Hemenway Road. By bus: Take Ritchie Lines bus from Park Square in Boston to South Sudbury, then walk to garden along Raymond Road (1½ miles). Or take Gray Lines bus to Shopper's World or Edgell Road, then taxi to garden.
· *Parking:* Free.
· *Shops:* Book/gift shop; plant sales in season.
· *No snack bar or restaurant.*
· *No picnicking.*

As in the case of the North Carolina Botanical Garden, you must be appreciative of the wild flora to enjoy this garden. Its understated beauty is not for everyone. It is poles apart from gardens like Longwood. But if you delight in small growing things and believe in the analeptic* quality of nature, you can look forward to a treat.

For those who like to know exactly what they are seeing, this is perhaps the most satisfactory of wild flower gardens. Each plant is labeled; natives, plants indigenous to North America, are distinguished from exotics, plants belonging to another continent. Although you may prefer more showy plants, these are the species from which our cultivated plants have come, bred and selected over the years, even centuries, for greater size, color variety and intensity, and hardiness. For example, the beautiful *Lewisia cotyledon finchii*, blooming here in mid-June in the Western Rock Garden, is a highly prized garden alpine in England. Found wild in the Western mountains, it was named for Meriwether Lewis of Lewis and Clark fame.

Maintenance at the Garden in the Woods is of a high order, reflecting staff dedication, volunteer energy, and money. Having visited on a day prior to a plant sale, we can testify to the enthusiasm of the workers and the camaraderie between staff and volunteers.

---

* This word, which means "restorative," appears in David McCord's dedication plaque at Longwood. We needed *our* dictionary!

Will Curtis was a naturalistic landscape designer. He saw the possibilities of a terrain carved out by the glaciers ten thousand years ago. The eskers (ridges of sand or gravel left by the glacial streams), the huge rocks, and the kettleholes were exploited as habitats for plants with different requirements. And just as important, he used them to paint pictures pleasing to the eye. Progressing along the trail, we cannot quite see what is beyond. Each new habitat comes as a surprise, shielded from us by a ridge or a clump of shrubs. The Curtis Self-Guiding Trail is only about a mile; if you explore all trails you cover about three miles. Consequently, in a relatively compact space, a great deal is to be seen and explored.

In the visitor center pick up a map or, better still, the Curtis Self-Guiding Trail pamphlet, which includes a map. (The guide to the whole garden is more expensive and may provide more detail than you need.) Only those species not mentioned in the guide, or mentioned only in passing, will be described here.

The first part of the trail traverses the areas originally landscaped by Curtis and Stiles in the early 1930s. One major reason for the uncontrived, natural beauty of this garden is the length of time it has had to age, for the plants to spread, for the shrubs to grow up. Many native species, especially woodland types, are notoriously slow-growing because their period of photosynthetic activity each year is so short. When trees leaf out, light is drastically reduced on the forest floor. One can prove this by comparing readings taken with a light meter, one in early April, the other in mid-June, at the same woodland spot.

DECIDUOUS WOODLAND: The yellow lady's-slipper, *Cypripedium calceolus*, blooming here in May, requires a much less acid soil than the pink species, *C. acaule*, found on the Lady Slipper Path (see p. 272). The higher the concentration of hydrogen ions in the soil, the greater its acidity. The pH factor is the value used to measure acidity and its opposite, alkalinity. The pH scale ranges from 0 to 14, 7 being neutral. A reading below 7 means the soil tends towards acidity; above 7, towards alkalinity. (This is grossly oversimplified; those who wish to know more should consult a science text.) One problem with acid soils is that the bacteria of decay are absent so that dead vegetation accumulates (as in peat bogs). The valuable nutrients locked up in it are not available to roots. Obviously, in this preserve much attention has had to be paid to the pH of the different habitats to ensure success. For instance, the yellow lady's-slipper thrives at a pH of 6.5, while the pink likes a pH of 4.5.

The plantain lily, *Hosta*, and epimedium with its heart-shaped leaves grow in these woods. The fact that both are wild flowers of the Orient demonstrates that natives of one country often become the cultivated plants of another, with improvements achieved by methods mentioned earlier. Another exotic to be found here is *Rodgersia aesculifolia*, a native of China often seen in British gardens. Its huge leaves like those of the horse chestnut produce an unusual tropical effect. (*Aesculus* is the scientific name for horse chestnut, so *aesculifolia* means "horse-chestnut-like leaves.")

Two rare native plants are the goldenseal, *Hydrastis canadensis*, a member of the buttercup family, and bowman's-root, *Gillenia trifoliata*, a tall member of the rose family, whose roots were used by the Indians as an emetic. Both produce white flowers, in May and June respectively.

The gorgeous torch azalea, *Rhododendron kaempferi*, which like all members of the genus *Rhododendron* is acid-loving (pH 4 optimum), was discovered in Japan in 1898. It has been used as a parent in producing some spectacular hybrid azaleas, the Kurumes, the Gables, and the Exbury evergreens (see pp. 146–7). The native flame azalea, *Rh. calendulaceum*, has also been used in breeding programs.

SHADY ROCK GARDEN: In April the intriguing native Dutchman's-breeches, *Dicentra cucullaria*, as well as the charming little European wood anemone, *Anemone nemorosa*, will be seen here. An unfamiliar plant is the galax from the southern Appalachians, *Galax aphylla*, with evergreen leaves like *Shortia* and tall white inflorescences appearing in June.

THE POND: Most visitors tend to linger by this pond located in an ancient kettlehole, looking for frogs, turtles, and possibly a water snake. Pollinating insects are always around during the flowering season, which is long in this mini-habitat—April to September. September brings the blue globes of the closed or bottle gentian, *Gentiana andrewsii*. If you wonder about its pollination, watch and perhaps you will get your answer. Bumblebees dive into it head first, parting its reluctant petals and sucking

The Pond

up the nectar, meanwhile receiving pollen. It is an amusing sight
to see these insects literally standing on their heads, rumps in the
air. August and September also bring forth our only truly red
native flower—the cardinal flower, *Lobelia cardinalis*, pollinated
by hummingbirds. Bees are blind to pure red, but all nectar-
eating birds are attracted by it. Picked for its beauty, it is unfortunately becoming a rarity in the wild. One sees it only in
nature preserves. In summer the eight-to-nine-foot-high Turk's-
cap lily, *Lilium superbum*, arrests attention with its showy orange,
purple-spotted flowers, its six petals attractively recurved. This
is perhaps one of our most striking native herbs. Don't miss the

Variegated plants

delicate, finely divided leaves of the royal fern, *Osmunda regalis*, its young leaves in spring tinged with a rust color. Many more plants than we have space for await discovery on the pond's edge.

As you ascend the path from the pond, look for the collection of variegated plants. In nature variegation is not a favorable mutation because it reduces the food-making (photosynthetic) area of the leaf. But it is ornamental, so man has pampered mutants of this kind. Note the variegated Japanese Solomon's-seal, *Polygonatum* sp.

In June, Laurel Bend is a splendid sight. The native mountain laurel, *Kalmia latifolia*, is one of the most valued of ornamentals both here and in Europe. Its flowers have a unique pollination mechanism. When one of the ten stamens, lying in the ten petal pouches, is touched, all stamens spring towards the flower's center, depositing pollen on the insect's back. Look closely and you may see some flowers with tripped mechanisms, others still virginal.

THE BOG AREA: The most interesting plants here are the carnivorous or insect-eating plants (CP for short; see pp. 96–7 for more)—the sundew, *Drosera* spp., with leaves bearing sticky tentacles, and the pitcher plants, *Sarracenia* spp. Both of these grow on acid soils; the insects they digest supply the nitrogen these habitats lack. In early summer look around here for the showy lady's-slipper, *Cypripedium reginae*, its white flowers suffused with pink. Unfortunately, this is another endangered species, partly because its habitats are being destroyed.

The rocks around here have been fertilized with a mixture of manure and lampblack to encourage the growth of lichens (a new procedure to the author). Lichens are small flowerless, gray-green, amorphous plants. Rocks are their natural habitat. Presumably, the fertilizer helps to trap lichen spores, providing immediate nourishment after their germination.

PINE BARRENS HABITAT: This area in New Jersey has a unique flora, due to a unique kind of habitat—infertile sandy soils that may be either dry or wet (bogs). Three species are typical of the dry barrens: the turkey-beard mentioned in the guide; the pyxie moss, *Pyxidanthera barbulata*, very difficult to grow and rare in its distribution (pine barrens of southeastern Virginia, eastern North Carolina, and New Jersey); the sand myrtle, *Leiophyllum*

Turkey beard

buxifolium, not so exacting in its habitat requirements as pyxie moss and therefore having a wider distribution. Incidentally, pyxie moss is not a moss but a flowering plant.

WESTERN ROCK GARDEN: In mid-June the beautiful *Lewisia* mentioned earlier blooms here. Other natives of our West, for example, the sulfur-flowered eriogonum, *Eriogonum* sp., the Oregon grape, *Mahonia aquifolium*, and the gray rock spiraea, *Petrophytum* sp., from the mountains of Washington, are also found here.

In summer, take the side trip into the Sunny Meadow. Unlike woodland species, those of the meadows bloom from midsummer to fall, when insects are most abundant. In order to arrest plant succession, which naturally would convert this meadow into deciduous woodland over a period of time, mowing has to be done periodically to kill off shrub and tree seedlings.

LADY SLIPPER PATH: If the month is May, don't fail to take the path through the coniferous woodland to see the pink *Cypripedium acaule*. In passing, note the herbaceous evergreen spotted wintergreen, *Chimaphila maculata*, and another variegated herbaceous species, the rattlesnake plantain, *Goodyera pubescens*—not a plantain but an orchid, blooming in August. The clubmoss, *Lycopodium obscurum*, often mistaken for a tiny conifer, is a not uncommon inhabitant of rich woods like these. A fern relative, it reproduces by spores that float away from its upright "candles." It is, of course, like ferns, flowerless.

You will now have seen all the landscaped areas. The rest of the preserve has been left as natural woodland for teaching purposes. The commonest trees are white pine, *Pinus strobus* (five needles per bunch), larch, *Larix laricina* (a deciduous conifer), and various maple species, *Acer* spp.

In the gift shop you will find two pocket-size wild-flower guides written by Lawrence Newcomb, treasurer of the society. Both would be useful references to keep (see Bibliography, p. 301) as well as helpful companions here.

Probably the best months for a visit to the Garden in the Woods are April and May. The author, however, went in mid-June and found an abundance of bloom. Spring, of course, comes late this far north. June might be late for a trip to the North Carolina Botanical Garden—also devoted to the culture of native plants—but not for Framingham. September and October are delightful months; fall flowers compete with the incomparable foliage colors of the New England woods.

Note: The New England Wild Flower Society owns six other sanctuaries in three New England states. For details, obtain a brochure from the visitor center (also membership forms).

ISABELLA STEWART GARDNER MUSEUM

☙

Boston, Massachusetts

UNIQUE	· A small indoor garden in the courtyard of a
FEATURE	Venetian palace of the Renaissance era.

HISTORY: Around 1895 Isabella Stewart Gardner began collecting works of art for the museum she and her husband, John Lowell Gardner, planned to build. Her primary interest was the art and architecture of Renaissance Italy. Bernard Berenson, whom she had assisted in his European travels and who became the internationally famous art connoisseur, was the adviser for most of her major purchases after 1894. In 1898 John Gardner died. Realizing that at fifty-eight she was no longer young, Mrs. Gardner immediately began making plans for her museum to be built on the Fenway. Scouring Italy for columns, archways, and fountains, under her supervision she had these incorporated into the fabric of her "Venetian palazzo." Meantime, she continued to add to her collection of paintings and other art objects. In 1903 the museum was opened to the public. Mrs. Gardner continued to live on the fourth floor until her death in 1924. Her will provided for the maintenance of Fenway Court exactly as she had arranged it. The indoor court with hothouse flowers was an important element in Mrs. Gardner's design. This, too, has been maintained exactly as she would have wished.

· *Admission:* Suggested minimum entrance fee of $1.00.
· *Hours:* Open all year. Wednesday to Sunday 1:00 P.M.–5:30 P.M. Tuesday 1:00 P.M.–9:30 P.M. (1:00 P.M.–5:30 P.M. in July and August). Closed Mondays and all national holidays.
· *Tours:* Free tour every Thursday at 2:30 P.M.
· *Plants:* Not labeled.
· *Physically handicapped:* Outdoor garden and first floor easily

274

negotiable by wheelchairs, except for several single steps. Elevators to upper floors.
- *Parking:* On the street; easier on weekends because nearby colleges have no classes.
- *Address:* 280 Fenway, Boston, Mass. 02115. Tel. (617) 566-1401.
- *Location and directions:* On the Fenway, next to Simmons College. By car: From downtown Boston take Huntington Avenue; turn right on Louis Prang Street, which feeds into the Fenway. By trolley: From Park Street Station or Copley Square take Arbor Way or Brighton Circle car to Ruggles/Museum stop. Walk approximately north along Louis Prang Street till you reach the Fenway.
- *No gift shop.* Sales desk within museum for books, pamphlets, and slides.
- *Café:* Lunches and snacks; terrace open in outdoor garden in good weather.
- *No picnicking.*

To lend credibility to palazzo life in a harsh climate, some simulation of the balmy, luminous Venetian outdoors was needed. The four-storied courtyard with a glass roof (approximately 1,500 panels of glass) was Mrs. Gardner's inspired answer —floral color and fragrance would always be part of the environment. Dark and gloomy Mediterranean interiors are acceptable only because the exterior is brilliant with sun and color. The somber, ecclesiastical mood of the museum is both accentuated and dispelled by the contrasting light and airiness of the court. At certain seasons, cascades of orange nasturtiums, *Tropaeolum majus*, descending from the balconies unite the upper stories with the floral display below.

The court itself is a highly formal garden of classical statuary, evergreens, a fountain, and a changing collection of potted flowers, viewed against a background of vaulted Renaissance arches. The centerpiece is a mosaic that Mrs. Gardner purchased from an excavation near Rome. Surrounding it is a carpet of baby's-tears, *Helxine soleirolii*, a Corsican plant belonging to the nettle family, on which various statues and artifacts stand. Baby's-tears forms the ground cover for the entire garden, replaced by wood chips where the potted plants are set down. Although steps lead down into the courtyard and a path circumscribes the mosaic,

Courtyard, looking south

this area is out of bounds to the public. On the south wall between the two flights of a staircase is a fountain with a seventeenth-century Venetian pool in which grow *Spathiphyllum patinii*, an aroid that thrives in dim light (for more on aroids, see p. 27), and the umbrella plant, *Cyperus alternifolius*, related to the Egyptian papyrus from which the first paper was made. Growing around the relief of the Maenad and the two dolphins is the creeping fig, *Ficus pumila*. Two types of palm, *Chamaedorea elegans* and *Rhapsis* sp., embellish the far sides of the staircase.

During the summer pots of oleander, *Nerium oleander*, flank the three sets of steps leading into the court on the east, west, and

Courtyard, looking north

north. Native to the Mediterranean—it is depicted in Pompeian murals—oleander is now cultivated in the semitropics worldwide. Prized for its fragrant pink, red, and white flowers, it is a highly poisonous shrub of the milkweed family—so poisonous that meat barbecued on its twigs has proved fatal. (In recent years a murder was perpetrated in Florida by serving shish kebabs cooked in this manner.) Part of its value as an ornamental is its ability to withstand long dry periods. Its gray, leathery leaves transpire very slowly.

At the north end are two tree ferns, *Cyathea* 'Filices,' five to six feet in height. Behind them in the northeast and northwest corners are fig trees, *Ficus sycomorus.*

The potted flowers change regularly since the museum has an extensive greenhouse and a staff of horticulturists. In June (1980) the featured flowers were a beautiful hydrangea cultivar, *Hydrangea macrophylla* 'Blue Wave.' The inner fertile flowers, glistening with nectar, are surrounded by large blue sterile flowers. The reason for the longevity of many garden hydrangea blossoms is their sterility. Pollination provides the stimulus for petal-drop, but if pollination is impossible, petals persist indefinitely. Orchids —featured here year-round—also persist in a pristine condition for as long as a month because the flowers never get pollinated. Self-pollination is structurally impossible, and the particular insect pollinator to which they are adapted is not likely to be flying around the Gardner Museum. (For more on orchid pollination, see p. 9.)

The seasonal displays are worth special visits: poinsettias and cyclamen at Christmas, lilies and cinerarias at Easter, Indica azaleas, jasmine, freesias, and nasturtiums in the spring, and chrysanthemums and begonias in the fall.

Renaissance gardens, as we have said elsewhere, have three important elements: water, statuary (preferably classical), and evergreens. This tiny Renaissance garden has classical statuary in abundance, evergreens, and one self-effacing fountain (for a Renaissance fountain it is sadly deficient in water sounds and sights). Flowers, fragrant and flamboyant, are untraditional. No one, however, will quarrel with this unhistorical departure. In the depths of the Boston winter the flowers promise the return of spring. And at all times, they celebrate the dynamic beauty of living things in contrast to the static beauty of human art.

(If you are interested in the statuary, buy the guide from the sales desk. Most of it is authentic Egyptian, Greek, or Roman.)

In the warm months of the year the outdoor gardens are accessible through the Chinese loggia on the east side of the court. Entirely walled, the gardens are not remarkable in themselves. But in this museum setting they provide a contrast as well as a retreat in which to enjoy the air or perhaps a snack purchased at the adjacent café. And for comfort, many welcoming benches are conveniently placed.

On the far left (north) as you emerge from the loggia is a woodland rock garden with curved paths and some Japanese garden ornaments—a lantern and two water basins. It is not, however, a Japanese garden, although evergreen shrubs preponderate: dwarf pine (*Pinus* sp.), Japanese holly (*Ilex crenata*), *Leucothoe* sp., mountain laurel (*Kalmia latifolia*). The ground cover is English ivy, *Hedera helix*, and intermingled with it are various wild flowers—false Solomon's-seal (*Smilacina racemosa*), jack-in-the-pulpit (*Arisaema* sp.), Mayapple (*Podophyllum peltatum*), Spanish bluebell (*Endymion hispanicus*), and white violets (*Viola blanda*). Chinese crab apples, *Malus spectabilis*, here and in other parts of the garden, herald the spring with pink and white blossoms.

A statue in a niche embellished with ironclad rhododendrons (see pp. 249–50), English ivy, and lily-of-the-valley, *Convallaria majalis*, greets you as you emerge from the museum. Mrs. Gardner called this the Monk's Garden.

In 1977 a new garden to the south and at right angles to the Monk's Garden was created by Eleanor McPeck. More formal

The Monk's Garden

than the original garden, it has straight walks, grassy lawns, and a short avenue of katsura trees, *Cercidiphyllum japonicum* (see p. 184), leading to a statue of Diana, goddess of the hunt. Steps flanked by white petunias lead to this focal point, while four oriental star magnolias, *Magnolia stellata*, form the background and *Pachysandra terminalis* the ground cover. Terra-cotta urns planted with geraniums and petunias give color to this otherwise green-and-white garden. The south wall is covered with Boston ivy, *Parthenocissus tricuspidata*.

This minute outdoor garden constitutes a kind of *hortus inclusus* in the center of metropolitan Boston, though in ambience far from it. Horticulturally, it is not significant. But a successful garden need not be a showplace. If it gives pleasure and comfort to the soul and the body, it can be considered successful. And judging from the demeanor of its visitors, this it appears to do.

ARNOLD ARBORETUM

❧

Jamaica Plain, Massachusetts

UNIQUE FEATURE	· The largest collection in the United States of woody trees and shrubs from all over the North Temperate Zone, hardy in the Boston area.

HISTORY: The James Arnold bequest of 1869 gave Harvard the means to establish an arboretum, but it was not large enough to purchase land. Consequently, the arboretum had to be located in Jamaica Plain, not Cambridge, on land recently given to Harvard for a horticultural station. In 1872 Charles Sprague Sargent, a rich young man, Harvard-trained and interested in horticulture, was appointed professor of horticulture and curator of the new Arnold Arboretum. While the Jamaica Plain property was being prepared Sargent worked with Asa Gray, the famous Harvard botany professor, learning all he could about plants. In 1879 he moved to the Arnold Arboretum, devoting the next forty-eight years to its development.

Realizing that the Arnold bequest was woefully inadequate to restore the broken-down Bussey farmland, Sargent, together with Frederick Law Olmsted, devised a plan whereby the city of Boston would adopt the arboretum as one of its parks and provide maintenance service. Unpopular with both city and university, the scheme was reluctantly adopted thanks to Sargent's unflagging efforts. In 1882 Harvard deeded 125 acres to the city, which it then leased back to Harvard for one thousand years at the rate of one dollar per year, provided the public was admitted from sunrise to sunset. Meanwhile Olmsted, who was designing the Boston parks system, landscaped the arboretum.

Sargent's goal was to grow every tree and shrub that would survive the Boston winters. To this end he himself explored the West, Japan, and South America, and subsequently persuaded the English explorer Ernest H. "Chinese" Wilson to direct the

Arnold Arboretum's plant-hunting expeditions from 1904 to 1922.

Running this infant arboretum required more funds than the Arnold bequest supplied. The additional money came from Sargent's personal fortune and from the pockets of his wealthy friends. The library was almost entirely amassed with Sargent's money. And because of his administrative skills, these funds were wisely husbanded.

By the time he died in 1927, Sargent and the Arnold Arboretum were synonymous. Wilson, who expected to become the new director, was passed over in favor of Professor Oakes Ames. Wilson lacked Sargent's administrative acumen, and moreover, Professor Ames was a well-connected Bostonian who might be expected to attract money. Mention can be made only of the Case estates in Weston, deeded to the arboretum in the 1940s, and the Mercer Trust, which made possible the construction of the Dana Greenhouses in 1962.

The days of the rich Boston Brahmin being over, the arboretum today is actively seeking money from public bodies. Recently, it received a National Science Foundation grant to computerize the very precise records of its seven thousand types of trees and shrubs. Funds are currently being sought to enlarge and renovate the administration building and to build a visitor center and a parking lot.

- *Admission:* Free, as of 1980. This will change to a modest fee by 1981–82.
- *Hours:* Open all year, sunrise to sunset daily.
- *Tours:* For information on free tours and lectures, call (617) 524-1718.
- *Plants:* Labeled. Staff members available to give information on weekdays.
- *Physically handicapped:* As of 1980, admitted in cars by permit only. Permits issued at administration building for weekdays only, 9:00 A.M.–5:00 P.M. (Automobiles not admitted Saturdays, Sundays, and holidays.) Tractor-tram will be in operation by 1982; call for information.
- *Address:* The Arnold Arboretum, The Arborway, Jamaica Plain, Mass. 02130. Tel. (617) 524-1718.
- *Location and directions:* 4 miles southwest of downtown Boston in Jamaica Plain. By mass transit—MBTA from downtown Boston: Take Forest Hill subway (Orange Line) to Forest Hills elevated station. Forest Hills gate of Arnold Arboretum is about

2 blocks west. Or take Huntington surface car (Green Line) to the Monument in Jamaica Plain. Jamaica Plain gate of arboretum is 4 blocks west. By car: Take U.S. 1 towards Providence and New York. At traffic circle in Jamaica Plain, go south on Massachusetts 203 (Arborway). Jamaica Plain gate is approximately 200 yards from traffic circle.
- *Parking:* Free. Some spaces within Jamaica Plain gate; others on street. New parking lot planned.
- *No gift shop.* Guidebooks and postcards on sale in administration building, Jamaica Plain gate.
- *No snack bar, restaurant, or soft-drink machines.*
- *No picnicking.*

It may seem sacrilegious to say that the Arnold Arboretum is not, in the author's opinion, "America's greatest garden,"* if the definition of garden includes "man's comfort and pleasure." The arboretum is a marvelous living museum of north-temperate woody plants, and like that of most museums, its primary purpose is educational. Except for the spectacular mass displays of spring-flowering trees and shrubs and the typical New England fall colors, it is not a mecca for the average garden-club visitor. It is huge—265 acres; one cannot hope to see it all in one day. One's legs give out and one's interest wanes. But there is hope: an electric tram is to be installed in the near future.

Like any other museum, the Arnold is a place one "does" piece by piece: today the conifers, tomorrow the oaks, next week the maples. This suggests that its real value is to the neighborhood. The tourist may be lucky enough to arrive in early spring or fall. But if his visit is in midsummer, displays intended to inspire enthusiasm and send him scurrying back to his own garden to change this or that are conspicuously absent. Some displays, of course, are year-round in appeal—the conifers, for instance. And the "Calendar for Visitors" lists plants in bloom for almost every month —the map will help you locate them. It's not a sure thing, however; the author never did find the *Stewartias* (see p. 57) nor the *fortunei* rhododendrons. But the author takes the blame for these frustrations. Still, there is one big problem for the novice, no matter how well the map is executed: if, say, one cannot recognize hickories at a distance yet wishes to study them, one has to traipse up to every labeled tree in the vicinity. This may be the

* Quoted from the Arnold Arboretum brochure, 1980.

major problem with large arboreta: so much legwork and few or no people around to help. The gardeners do not necessarily know the answers (we tried them). The promised tram may help. Even though the student can learn only on foot, the tram ride may help to pinpoint the quarry.

A good feature is the frequency of benches. In comfort, you can restudy the map or admire Olmsted's effective landscaping while you reflect on the fact that this is the American shrine of exotic-plant introduction. For the plantsman there is a certain thrill in being at the historic center of American horticulture. The fruits—if that is the right word—of plant exploration in the Far East were first welcomed and grown here under the en-

Japanese snowbell

thusiastic care of Charles Sprague Sargent, whose name is remembered in the specific epithets of many ornamentals to be seen here, like the hardy early-flowering cherry *Prunus sargentii*.

If you wish to relive a little of this horticultural history, find Bussey Hill on the map. Using it as a landmark, make your way into the Chinese Path Area, also marked. Here are many of "Chinese" Wilson's introductions. The paperbark maple, *Acer griseum*, should be easy to find with its ruddy peeling bark. This is the actual sapling Wilson brought back from central China in 1902. Its seeds are sterile for the most part, making it a rather rare tree. Another of his finds was the dove tree, *Davidia involucrata*—not flowering here every year as it does farther south, but surviving (for its story, see p. 189). The hardy variety of the silk tree, *Albizia julibrissin rosea*, which Wilson found in Korea, arrived at the arboretum in 1918. Hardier than the species, *rosea* produces its spherical pink blossoms from mid-July to early September in the Boston area. Although its flowers are most un-pea-like, it belongs to the pea family, Leguminosae or Fabaceae. Several species of *Cotoneaster*, such as *C. divaricatus*, and apple, *Malus theifera* and *M. toringoides*, were also part of Wilson's haul. Incidentally, cuttings of these original Wilson introductions will be sent to the museum being built in his memory at his birthplace, Chipping Camden in Gloucestershire.

D ISCONTINUOUS DISTRIBUTION OF SPECIES: *Some explanation is in order for the high percentage of Asiatic and, to a lesser extent, American ornamentals in today's gardens. For this we need to consider the Ice Ages during the last 25 million years. With the advance of the ice the warm-temperate vegetation, which at that time covered most of the earth, was pushed inexorably southward. In Asia and America the flora went as far south as 30 degrees latitude and even farther, where it continued to flourish. With the eventual retreat of the ice, plants gradually spread northward, reinvading their old habitats. But in Europe, because of the east-west mountain chains of the Pyrenees and the Alps and ultimately because of the Mediterranean, the vegetation got trapped at approximately 45 degrees latitude. Most of the warm-temperate plants were exterminated by the cold, so that when the ice retreated there was little left of this flora to move north.*

This explains the relative paucity of species in the European flora, and also the fact that European gardens did not become the showplaces they are today until plant explorers brought back their glorious loot from China, Japan, the foothills of the Himalayas, and the southern states of North America. It also explains the discontinuous distribution of certain genera and families, more or less wiped out in Europe but flourishing in North America and the Orient, for example, rhododendrons, magnolias, and members of the tea family such as camellias.

The arboretum has an especially fine collection of cherries, *Prunus* spp. and varieties, crab apples, *Malus* spp., and hawthorns, *Crataegus* spp. Most of these rose family genera are clustered west of Bussey Street. It was recently discovered that many species in the *Crataegus* genus are parthenocarpic—literally, "having virgin fruits": they can produce viable seed without fertilization. The seeds of such a plant will produce exact replicas—clones—of itself because there has been no change in its genes. This is not unusual in the plant kingdom; the common dandelion, *Taraxacum officinale*, is also parthenocarpic. But it is a dangerous mutation within a species. Without the variability of offspring that sexual fusion brings, a major change in the environment could spell extinction in the wild. This quirk within the hawthorns is mentioned here because Sargent spent many years classifying the genus. Not knowing of its irregular sex life, he was led into many errors, which are now being corrected.

In early spring this area of the garden presents a wonderful display as all of these species and varieties blossom. Simultaneously, the magnolias around the administration building put on a show. Wilson's magnolia, *Magnolia wilsonii*, is not part of this collection, being too tender for Boston winters.

Sargent was not only interested in acquiring exotics; he also encouraged the use of native American species as garden ornamentals. As you explore this arboretum, study the labels; it will be apparent that many superb specimens are indigenous. Because Sargent was catholic in his tastes, this is a garden in which to study native woody plants as well as exotics—unlike the Morris Arboretum (see p. 180), where the scales are tipped towards the latter. Among the conifers, for instance, are many from the Pacific Northwest that were originally discovered by British explorers and ultimately reached the eastern states by way of England. The Douglas fir, *Pseudotsuga menziesii*, is a case in point.

If it is September, ask the whereabouts of the Franklin tree, *Franklinia alatamaha*, discovered in Georgia nearly two hundred

years ago and never found in the wild since. Named for Benjamin Franklin, it is a gorgeous flowering member of the tea family. All plants of this species now alive are descendants of the few trees found by John Bartram, the famous eighteenth-century American plant explorer. The mountain laurel, *Kalmia latifolia*, another cherished ornamental, was discovered by the English naturalist Mark Catesby in the early eighteenth century.

Native azaleas—the deciduous kind—are well represented here, with the exception of the tender Florida azalea, *Rhododendron austrinum*. Naturally, they bloom here later than they do farther south. In mid-June the flame azalea, *Rh. calendulaceum*, is at its most beautiful along the road leading from the administration building. The Japanese torch azalea, *Rh. kaempferi*, and the royal azalea, *Rh. schlippenbachii*, also from Asia, bloom somewhat earlier. The Ghent hybrids, of part-American ancestry, are at their peak in May. (The author found that though trees were meticulously labeled, shrubs often were not—no doubt a temporary lapse.)

The dwarf conifer collection beside the Dana Greenhouses is wide-ranging; every strange and weird cultivar is well identified —a useful service to the home gardener with a small plot. It is regrettable that the nearby bonsai collection has to be imprisoned in a square lath house, closed forever to the public. The exquisite, timeless beauty of these dwarfs is obscured by the separating horizontal bars. There must be some better way to secure their safety.

On your way out of the Jamaica Plain gate you will find the dawn redwood, *Metasequoia glyptostroboides*. This is a historic tree—a fossil that suddenly came alive. Like two other conifers, the larch and the bald cypress, it is deciduous, turning russet in the fall and shedding branchlets. This arboretum played a praiseworthy role in its fascinating story. In 1941 a fossil that had puzzled botanists for years (obviously a near relative of the two giant conifers of California, the redwood, *Sequoia sempervirens*, and the big tree, *Sequoiadendron gigantea*) was assigned to a new genus, *Metasequoia*, by the Japanese scientist then studying it. The very same year an extraordinary find was made in southwestern China in the province of Szechuan by a Japanese forester: several unknown conifers, all obviously of the same species. A Chinese scientist, Dr. Hu, eventually identified them in 1946 as living representatives of the "fossil" *Metasequoia*! He gave the species the formidable name of *M. glyptostroboides*. Because Dr. Hu had been a student of Dr. Elmer Merrill, then director of the Arnold Arboretum, he sent him specimens. Forthwith Merrill dispatched money to Dr. Hu to organize an expedition on behalf of the arboretum to bring back seeds and seedlings.

In 1948 Merrill received two pounds of seeds. Samples were sent with alacrity to nearly one hundred institutions in the United States and Europe, in keeping with the arboretum's policy of plant introduction. This was a wise move, since no one knew how long the seeds would remain viable or what conditions of soil and climate they required.

Meanwhile, Dr. Ralph W. Chaney of the palaeontology department at the University of California (Berkeley), having received seeds from Merrill, decided on a stunt trip to Szechuan (now Sichuan) to hunt the *Metasequoia*, accompanied by a newspaper reporter. Funding came from the "Save-the-Redwoods" League. On their return tremendous publicity centered around the "dawn redwood"—as Chaney called it—a plant thought to have been extinct for 20 million years. The newspaper articles implied that Chaney had found it and introduced it to the world.

Understandably upset, Merrill scathingly, though in private as befits a Bostonian gentleman, criticized Chaney's three-day publicity trip to "Metasequoialand" at a time (March) when the trees would bear neither leaves, flowers, nor cones. But this bit of scientific chicanery had one good result: Chaney's infectious enthusiasm for the tree helped the "Save-the-Redwoods" League.

The very name "dawn redwood" furthered the cause, even though the prefix "dawn" in palaeontology suggests an ancestral species and there is no evidence that *Metasequoia* is ancestral to *Sequoia*.

Meanwhile, Merrill's seeds had sprouted. Trees like the one before you are now thriving all over the world. Those at the Morris Arboretum (see p. 181) came from this source. The tallest tree, now well over ninety feet high, is at Williamsburg, Virginia. *Metasequoia*'s value lies in its ornamental nature rather than its timber. On an expanse of lawn its pyramidal shape and its color in spring and fall are especially pleasing.

Nearby is a large bald cypress, *Taxodium distichum*, a close relative of *Metasequoia* and surprisingly hardy in a region where temperatures can plunge to minus 30 degrees Fahrenheit. Compare the foliage of the two species. Though they are very similar, the needles and branchlets of *Metasequoia* are opposite to one another, whereas those of *Taxodium* alternate. Their cone scales are also arranged differently: the dawn redwood's in pairs, the bald cypress's spirally. (For more on the bald cypress, see pp. 71–2.)

After virtually ignoring the public for a century, the Arnold Arboretum is now awakening to the fact that without general public support, rather than bequests from a few rich individuals, its future would indeed be grim. To this end funding is being solicited from diverse sources, and by 1982 the arboretum will present a welcoming face to its public. Here for all to see and enjoy are the acquisitions from plant exploration extended over three centuries and several continents.

Dwarf conifer collection

Note: With the help of government funding, an interpretative guide to the Arnold Arboretum and its living collections is being developed (summer 1981). Inquire at the administration building.

MINI-TOURS

The gardens described in this book fall into regional clusters. Each cluster can become the subject of a garden mini-tour. Based on our experience, the following are suggestions for such tours, should you find yourself in any of the locales listed below. The current Rand McNally *Road Atlas* will be useful for those traveling by car.

FLORIDA

After seeing Vizcaya (pp. 15–21) and Fairchild Tropical Garden (pp. 3–14) proceed north on Interstate 95, taking Exit 40 to Palm Beach to the Four Arts Garden (pp. 22–7)—a trip of approximately 1½ hours. To reach Marie Selby Botanical Gardens (pp. 28–35) drive west to Fort Myers, first on U.S. 441, switching to Florida 80 at Belle Glade. At Fort Myers take U.S. 41 North to Sarasota (3¾ hours). To reach Cypress Gardens from Selby, take Florida 72 to Arcadia, then proceed north on U.S. 17 to Bartow. Here take Florida 60 to U.S. 27. Sixteen miles north is Florida 540, which takes you to Cypress Gardens (3 hours). Dundee, a couple of miles north on U.S. 27, is the nearest town with motels, although Cypress (pp. 36–41) has its own motel. This order can of course be reversed. Circular tours are also feasible, beginning and ending in Miami, Orlando, or Sarasota (all have airports).

CHARLESTON, SOUTH CAROLINA

If you plan to stay in Charleston during the peak season (mid-March through April), be sure to make advance hotel reservations. Magnolia Plantation and Gardens (pp. 52–60) are 10 miles south of Charleston on S.C. 61. Middleton Place (pp. 61–7) is 4 miles farther out, also on S.C. 61. Cypress Gardens (pp. 68–72) is 17 miles from Middleton (a ½-hour drive) and 24 miles from downtown Charleston.

Note: This mini-tour can be extended northward along the coast up U.S. 17 to Brookgreen Gardens (pp. 73–7), a 1½-hour drive. Continuing up U.S. 17 through Myrtle Beach and into North Carolina, you will reach Orton Plantation (pp. 78–83) in 2 hours, while the Tryon Palace Restoration at New Bern (pp. 84–92), still close to the coast, is 2 to 2½ hours north and east of Orton, continuing on U.S. 17.

BRANDYWINE VALLEY, DELAWARE/PENNSYLVANIA

Wilmington, Delaware, is the best place to stay for the three du Pont gardens. A car is essential; no public transportation goes to any of these gardens. (Wilmington itself can be reached by train or plane.) Winterthur (pp. 155–63) is 6 miles from Wilmington on Delaware 52. Longwood Gardens (pp. 164–77) is 12 miles away. From Winterthur continue north on Delaware 52; the Longwood entrance is on U.S. 1 near the Pennsylvania 52 (north) intersection. Nemours (pp. 149–54), the closest to Wilmington and only 20 minutes from Winterthur, is approached by way of U.S. 202 North out of Wilmington.

WASHINGTON, D.C.

Dumbarton Oaks (pp. 129–39) is situated in Georgetown, a short taxi or bus ride away from downtown Washington. The National Arboretum (pp. 140–8) is not nearly so accessible; a car is desirable, though not absolutely necessary. It is located at the other end of Washington from Dumbarton Oaks, being in the northeastern section. In azalea time (April–May) a car may be a liability within the grounds because of crowds. Gunston Hall (pp. 122–8) is 20 miles south of Washington in Lorton and close to Interstate 95.

Note: Williamsburg is about a 3-hour drive from Lorton. Advance reservations are needed in and around Williamsburg at all times of the year (pp. 105–21).

NEW YORK CITY AREA

For the five gardens in the New York area, Manhattan is the most central place to stay. The best method of getting to the New York

Botanical Garden in the Bronx (pp. 221–31) is by Conrail train from Grand Central Station—20 minutes to the Botanical Garden station (timetable available at Grand Central Station). For the Brooklyn Botanic Garden (pp. 206–20), take the Lexington Avenue IRT subway train from Grand Central Station, changing at Nevins Street station in Brooklyn. Get off at the Brooklyn Museum station. The Cloisters can be reached by bus from Madison Avenue midtown (pp. 198–205). The trip takes 1 hour. Or take the IND Eighth Avenue A train to 190th Street/Overlook Terrace.

All the gardens within the city can easily be reached by car, and parking is no problem. Driving directions can be found on the pages noted in the foregoing paragraph.

Plan to spend a day on the North Shore of Long Island seeing Planting Fields Arboretum (pp. 241–52) and Old Westbury Gardens (pp. 232–40). The drive from Manhattan takes about 1 hour. The two gardens are about a 15-minute drive apart. For both, take Queens Midtown Tunnel to the Long Island Expressway (Interstate 495). Exit at 39S for Old Westbury Gardens and at 41N for Planting Fields. Alternatively, the Long Island Railroad from Pennsylvania Station stops at Westbury, and taxis always meet the trains. Car travel, however, is recommended.

BOSTON AREA

For the three gardens in the area, Brookline is the obvious place to stay. The Isabella Stewart Gardner Museum (pp. 274–9) is a short taxi ride from Beacon Street, Brookline. The Arnold Arboretum (pp. 280–8) can be reached either by taxi or the MBTA. The Garden in the Woods, Framingham (pp. 266–73), is about a 30-to-40-minute drive west from Brookline along U.S. 9. For this a car is necessary.

From downtown Boston, follow the directions given on the pages noted in the foregoing paragraph. (For Garden in the Woods, take U.S. 20 out of Boston.)

Note: Green Animals (pp. 260–5) is about 1 hour's drive south of Boston. It can easily be included as a side trip in a north or south drive between Boston and New York City. A stopover of 1½ to 2 hours here would be sufficient.

GLOSSARY

allée: A long avenue bordered by trees.

angiosperm: (literally, "seed within a vessel") A plant whose seeds develop within a fruit. Often called a flowering plant, because the seeds come from special reproductive shoots called flowers. (Conifers also have seeds, but no flowers, and the ovules are exposed on the scales of a structure called a cone.) An angiosperm may be a tree, a shrub, or an herb: e.g., maple, rose, buttercup.

bract: A leaflike part closely associated with a flower or inflorescence. It is sometimes colored—e.g., red in poinsettia, white in dogwood— and may serve to attract insects.

conifer: See gymnosperm.

cotyledon: An embryonic leaf in the seed. It may store food, and it may come above ground during germination to serve as a leaf. The seed may contain one or two cotyledons.

cultivar: A variety that has arisen in cultivation either by deliberate manipulation, as in breeding, or accidentally, as a "sport" or mutation (q.v.).

dicotyledon (*dicot*): A member of a large group of flowering plants that have certain common characteristics: two cotyledons, leaves with net-veins, flower parts usually in fives.

family: A group of related genera (q.v.) whose members have fewer features in common than those of the smaller group, the genus. Still, the relationship is often clear: e.g., all palms belong in the family Arecaceae.

flowering plant: See angiosperm.

gene: A unit of the hereditary information (DNA or deoxyribonucleic acid) that controls the development of a particular characteristic.

genus (plural *genera*): A group of species having so many characteristics in common that it is easily identified, even by nonbotanists, e.g., roses, pines, goldenrods, oaks, maples. The genus is the taxonomic rank between the species and the family. Occasionally, a genus contains only one species: e.g., *Metasequoia*, the dawn redwood.

gymnosperm: (literally, "naked seed") A nonflowering seed plant, often called a conifer because its seeds develop on the scales of structures known as cones. Gymnosperms are usually evergreen trees: e.g., pine, fir, yew, bald cypress.

hortus inclusus (or *hortus conclusus*): A small walled garden, dating back to the Middle Ages.

hybrid: A new kind of plant produced by crossing two different species.

inflorescence: A group of flowers all arising on one main stalk.

monocotyledon (*monocot*): A member of a large group of flowering plants that have certain characteristics in common: one cotyledon, leaves with parallel veins, flower parts in threes.

mutation: A spontaneous change in a gene (q.v.). The mutant plant differs in one or more characteristics from the rest of the species. The copper beech arose as a mutant.

organic: Originally, this meant "derived from a living thing." Today an organic substance means one that consists usually of large molecules containing carbon atoms.

ovary: The female part of the flower that contains the ovules. After fertilization of the ovules, the ovary becomes the fruit.

ovule: The structure within the ovary that contains the egg. After fertilization, the ovule becomes a seed.

parterre: A patterned garden, comprising variously shaped beds outlined by clipped evergreens (usually box) and containing flowers, turf, or colored gravel. It is intended to be viewed from above. *Parterre de broderie* is a parterre so elaborate in design as to resemble embroidery.

pergola: An archway or walkway consisting of trelliswork over which vines are trained.

photosynthesis: The making of sugar and other organic compounds from carbon dioxide and water in the green parts of plants in the presence of light.

pleached allée: A walkway bounded by trees whose interlacing branches form its wall and roof.

pollen: Tiny grains, each of which contains two male nuclei (the plant's equivalent of sperm). During fertilization one male nucleus joins with the egg to form a seed.

pollination: The placing of pollen on the stigma (q.v.) of a flower, a necessary prelude to fertilization.

seed: A sexually derived reproductive body containing an embryo plant and a food store; produced only by flowering plants and conifers.

species: A particular kind of plant (or animal) whose members freely interbreed and which maintains its distinct characteristics over time (*sp.* is the abbreviation for one species; *spp.* indicates two or more species). It has a binomial scientific name, the first indicating the genus, the second, the specific epithet: e.g., *Magnolia grandiflora.*

spore: A reproductive body capable of growing into a new plant. Usually it is produced asexually and consists of only one cell. It is typical of ferns, mosses, liverworts, and fungi.

stamens: The male parts of the flower, which split when ripe to liberate the pollen.

stigma: The part of the female organ of the flower (the pistil) that receives the pollen.

stomates: Microscopic pores on the surface of leaves and green stems through which carbon dioxide enters and water vapor exits. They are capable of opening and closing.

style: The stalklike part that protrudes from the ovary and ends in the stigma (q.v.).

succession: The progressive change in plant communities exhibited by a disturbed patch of land until a stable community, called the climax, is attained. The plant composition of the climax depends mainly on rainfall: forest in areas where it is adequate; grassland or prairie where it is low.

taxonomy: The classification of plants and animals according to relationships of descent.

transpiration: The giving off of water vapor by the aerial parts of the plant, especially the leaves. Most of the vapor escapes through the stomates.

BIBLIOGRAPHY

Berrall, Julia S. *The Garden: An Illustrated History*. New York: Viking Press, 1978. There is also a paperback edition, published in 1978 by Penguin Books.

Coats, Peter. *Great Gardens of the Western World*. New York: J. P. Putnam's Sons, 1963.

Cowell, F. R. *The Garden As Fine Art*. Boston: Houghton Mifflin Co., 1978.

Galle, Fred C. *Azaleas*. A Southern Living Book. Birmingham, Alabama: Oxmoor House, 1974.

Gault, Miller S. *Color Dictionary of Shrubs*. New York: Crown Publishers, 1976.

Hay, Roy, and Synge, Patrick M. *The Color Dictionary of Flowers and Plants for Home and Garden*. New York: Crown Publishers, 1975.

Huxley, Anthony, ed. *Encyclopaedia of the Plant Kingdom*. New York: Chartwell Books, 1977.

Hyams, Edward. *A History of Gardens and Gardening*. New York: Praeger Publishers, 1971.

———, and MacQuitty, William. *Great Botanical Gardens of the World*. New York: Macmillan Co., 1969.

Johnson, Hugh. *The Principles of Gardening*. New York: Simon & Schuster, 1979.

———. *The International Book of Trees*. New York: Simon & Schuster, 1973.

King, Ronald. *The Quest for Paradise: A History of the World's Gardens*. New York: Mayflower Books, 1979.

Logan, Harry Britton. *A Traveler's Guide to North American Gardens*. New York: Charles Scribner's Sons, 1974.

Morton, Julia F. *Exotic Plants*. A Golden Nature Guide. New York: Western Publishing Co., 1971.

Newcomb, Lawrence. *Newcomb's Wildflower Guide: An Ingenious New Key System for Quick, Positive Field Identification of Wildflowers, Flowering Shrubs, and Vines of Northeastern and North Central North America*. Boston: Little, Brown & Co., 1977.

Perry, Frances, ed. *Simon & Schuster's Complete Guide to Plants and Flowers*. New York: Simon & Schuster, 1974.

Scott-James, Anne, and Lancaster, Osbert. *The Pleasure Garden*. Harmondsworth, Eng.: Penguin Books, 1979.

Thacker, Christopher. *The History of Gardens*. Berkeley: University of California Press, 1979.

Wyman, Donald. *Trees for American Gardens*. Rev. ed. New York: Macmillan Co., 1965.

———. *Shrubs and Vines for American Gardens*. Rev. ed. New York: Macmillan Co., 1965.

The Brooklyn Botanic Garden publishes a series of handbooks. A list is available on request. Send a postcard to The Brooklyn Botanic Garden, 1000 Washington Avenue, Brooklyn, New York 11225.

ABOUT THE AUTHOR

Doris M. Stone was educated at Oxford University.
Since coming to the United States she has been a
plant breeder at the Brooklyn Botanical Garden and
an education coordinator at the New York Botanical
Garden. She is the author of *Projects: Botany* and
has patented the magnolia hybrid *Magnolia
brooklynensis* 'Evamaria.'